Tandem Dances

Tandem Dances

Choreographing Immersive Performance

JULIA M. RITTER

OXFORD
UNIVERSITY PRESS

OXFORD
UNIVERSITY PRESS

Oxford University Press is a department of the University of Oxford. It furthers
the University's objective of excellence in research, scholarship, and education
by publishing worldwide. Oxford is a registered trade mark of Oxford University
Press in the UK and certain other countries.

Published in the United States of America by Oxford University Press
198 Madison Avenue, New York, NY 10016, United States of America.

Library of Congress Cataloging-in-Publication Data
Names: Ritter, Julia, author.
Title: Tandem dances : choreographing immersive performance / Julia M. Ritter.
Description: New York, NY, United States
of America : Oxford University Press, 2021. |
Series: Oxford studies in dance theory |
Includes bibliographical references and index.
Identifiers: LCCN 2020016653 (print) | LCCN 2020016654 (ebook) |
ISBN 9780190051303 (hardback) | ISBN 9780190051310 (paperback) |
ISBN 9780190051334 (epub)
Subjects: LCSH: Interactive art. | Choreography. | Art and dance. |
Future of StoryTelling Festival (2017 : Snug Harbor Cultural Center)
Classification: LCC N7433.915 .R58 2020 (print) |
LCC N7433.915 (ebook) | DDC 700.28—dc23
LC record available at https://lccn.loc.gov/2020016653
LC ebook record available at https://lccn.loc.gov/2020016654

1 3 5 7 9 8 6 4 2

Paperback printed by Marquis, Canada
Hardback printed by Bridgeport National Bindery, Inc., United States of America

Your very flesh shall be a great poem and have the richest fluency not only in its words but in the silent lines of its lips and face and between the lashes of your eyes and in every motion and joint of your body . . .

Walt Whitman, Leaves of Grass (1855)

Contents

Acknowledgments

Over the past seven years I have been asking questions about the relationship between choreography and what has come to be called immersive theater of anyone who would answer. I have sidled up next to fellow audience participants after performances, sent copious DMs through social media, hit the "Send Fan Mail" button in Tumblr dozens of times, cold-emailed artists and scholars, and dialed up international producers for off the record chats. I must have asked the right questions in the right ways and at the right times as I have been extremely fortunate that so many individuals have responded positively to my queries. Thus, my first thanks goes to everyone I have interviewed for this project who has generously shared their thoughts and knowledge, including numerous choreographers, artistic directors, performers, designers, playwrights, audience participants, scholars, stage managers, presenters, producers, journalists, bloggers, and members of fandoms. I am grateful to Fiona Templeton, who generously shared a DVD of her landmark 1988 production of *YOU-The City* as well as her perspectives on guiding audiences into and through performances. Thank you, Noah Nelson, for answering one of my cold-emails and talking to me about founding No Proscenium, and introducing me to Lauren Ludwig and Monica Miklas of Capital W. My appreciation to Teddy Bergman of Woodshed Collective and Jennifer Weber, choreographer, for speaking to me about the production of *KPOP*. Additional thanks to Gemma Brockis for sharing her thoughts on the early works of SHUNT (United Kingdom); to Erin Mee for insights into productions by This Is Not a Theatre Company; and to Aaron Vanek and Nina Runa Essendrop for taking the time to contextualize and illuminate Nordic Larp (live action role play). While I was not able to distinctly amplify the voice of each person with whom I've had the pleasure of speaking, every interview, email correspondence, and DM response has richly informed the writing of this book and for that I am very grateful.

Maxine Doyle of Punchdrunk has been especially beneficent in describing and clarifying her processes. Given her commitment to the craft of choreography, as well as her belief that "the artistry of the dancer is second to none," it is not surprising she went above and beyond to connect me with dancers working with Punchrunk in both the United States and China, as well as introducing me to Felix Barrett. My deep thanks to performers Conor Doyle, Tori Sparks, Paul Zivkovich, Tony Bordonaro, Tim Heck, Nicholas Bruder, Emily Terndrup, Ting Ting Tang, and Eric Jackson Bradley for sharing their insights. The generosity of those in the international *Sleep No More* fandom has been unparalleled: thank you for graciously sharing your experiences, artworks, and writings. In addition, I appreciate the help of members of Punchdrunk and Punchdrunk International based in both the United Kingdom and Shanghai, as well as Emursive staff, including Sarah Davies, JoJo Tyhurst, Maya Ophelia, Rosalind Coleman, Alistair Zhang, David Tocci, and Becki Heller. My sincere appreciation goes to Zach Morris, Tom Pearson, and Jennine Willett, co-artistic directors and founders of Third Rail Projects, for graciously providing information about their work. I am equally thankful to have been introduced to core members of Third Rail including Elizabeth Carena, Tara O'Con, Rebekah Morin, and Marissa Neilsen-Pincus and am grateful for our engaging conversations. Stephen O'Connell and Lucy Simic, along with Ciara Adams, Sabrina Reeves, and Richard Windeyer, who make up bluemouth inc., as well as guest artist Daniel Pettrow, welcomed me with open arms in 2014 as I tagged along with their run of *Dance Marathon* during the Magnetic North Festival in Nova Scotia. It was delightful to see this renowned collective take up residency in that community for two weeks and bring its citizens to a level of sweaty, ecstatic joy that spread far beyond the walls of the Olympic Hall Community Centre in central Halifax.

My appreciation continues for my dissertation committee, including Jordan Fuchs and the late Linda Caldwell, for embracing my ideas when I was not yet sure of them myself. Rosemary Candelario was instrumental in shaping my thinking as I worked through large sets of data and interdisciplinary concerns, and I value immensely her continued guidance. Penelope Hanstein inspired me to pursue my doctoral degree and her encouragement during the writing of this book is greatly appreciated. Norm Hirschy, my Oxford University Press editor, has steadfastly encouraged me since I approached him with my ideas about choreography and immersive performance at the 2015 Society of Dance History Scholars (SDHS) and Congress on Research in Dance (CORD) conference in Athens, Greece. Finally, my gratitude to the anonymous readers whose very generous feedback has been instrumental in sharpening the focus of this project.

The book has evolved through dialogue over time with many colleagues in the fields of dance, performance, dramaturgy, and theater criticism. I am grateful to Hervé Guay, editor of *Revue Tangence*, for encouraging my early investigations of dance and immersive performance. James Frieze and I had several illuminating conversations around the idea of extended audiencing, for which I am most thankful. A shout out to Gerald Beegan and Jacqueline Thaw, my colleagues in the Art & Design Department at Rutgers for guiding me toward resources that would assist in contextualizing design. My deep thanks to Cheryl LaFrance for helping me understand the metacognitive links between my choreographic and writing processes. I am indebted to Carol Martin and Richard Schechner, as well as Mariellen Sandford, of *TDR/The Drama Review* for enthusiastically supporting and constructively critiquing my work. I greatly appreciate the encouragement of colleagues Sherril Dodds, Aili Bresnahan, and Kate Elswit, as well as the opportunity to speak with both Janet H. Murray and Maxine Sheets-Johnson about their ground-breaking scholarship. Words are not sufficient for the gratitude I feel for the long-term support (ten years!) of fellow Texas Woman's University doctoral graduates Darrah Carr and Caroline Sutton Clark; their incisive feedback and ability to find the humor in everything makes me look forward to our weekly Write Club sessions. Lastly, there is nothing that compares to the kindness and brilliance of my colleague and friend Ayrin Ersöz, and her husband, Yavuz, both of whom have generously hosted me at their home in Turkey for writing retreats and who are always at the ready to dive into inspiring, passionate conversations.

My thanks to the faculty and staff of the Dance Department at Mason Gross School of the Arts, Rutgers University, where I serve as chair and artistic director; their conscientious commitment to the work we do to train the artist-scholar-educators of the future has allowed me to step away at critical moments to focus on writing. To family and friends whose company I haven't been able to enjoy as much as I would have liked while pursuing this project, I thank you for your love, support, and patience. Finally, a big TU to Jorge Luis Barrientos Sacari (Mr. B.), who never fails to offer an unexpected perspective, which gives rise to much laughter and appreciation.

Earlier versions of some sections of this book have appeared in different form in the following publications, and I thank the Presses for permission to reproduce them here:

"Fandom and Punchdrunk's *Sleep No More*: Audience Ethnography of Immersive Dance." In "Reclaiming the Real," edited by Carol Martin. Special issue, *TDR/The Drama Review*, 61:4 (Winter 2017): 59–77.

"The Body of the Beholder: Insider Dynamics Transform Dance Spectatorship in *Sleep No More*." In *Reframing Immersive Theatre: The Politics and Pragmatics of Participatory Performance*, edited by James Frieze, 43–62. London: Palgrave Macmillan, 2016.

"Danse en tandem: Étude du mouvement des spectateurs et des performeurs dans *Sleep No More* de Punchdrunk." In "Engagement du spectateur et théâtre contemporain," edited by Hervé Guay and Catherine Bouko. Special issue, *La Revue Tangence: Revue d'Études Littéraires*, no. 108 (Autumn 2015): 51–76.

Introduction

In October 2017, four internationally influential practitioners of immersive experiences gathered at the Snug Harbor Cultural Center on Staten Island in New York for a panel discussion on the creation of immersive productions. The panel, entitled "All the World Is a Stage," was part of the Future of Storytelling Festival 2017 (FoST FEST), advertised as "the world's leading immersive storytelling event."[1] During this discussion, each of the four panelists described examples of their work. Hector Harkness, Associate Director of Punchdrunk International, explained how the company created productions that "rip up the rules for the audience" so they can "go beyond the boundaries of closed environments."[2] Food technologist, experience designer, and multimedia artist Emilie Baltz described inviting audiences to step up to a microphone and use their tongues, teeth, and lips to play musical popsicles in an installation called *PopStars*. Jon Sands, founder of Poets in Unexpected Places, revealed how his strategic placement of poets on subway cars across New York City turned commutes into impromptu poetry slams for unsuspecting riders, some of whom joined in by improvising their own poetic works. Justin "JB" Bolognino, CEO (Chief Experience Officer) of META, an experience production company, described his commissioning of Jon Morris, artistic director of the Brooklyn-based Windmill Factory, to design a music-festival queue into an experiential artwork.[3] Entitled *Right Passage*, the work was a "room-scale sound and light performance installation" involving moving walls that guided festival participants efficiently into the concert venue (Windmill Factory 2017).[4] Through their detailed descriptions of how their productions organized the bodies of performers and spectators in space and time, the panelists hinted at the presence of choreography in their productions.

And yet, none of these practitioners' responses explicitly referenced dance or choreography as disciplines, practices, or methods for setting the conditions for participation. I was an audience member at this panel, and the omission of choreography from the discussion piqued my curiosity. During the Q&A, I addressed the panelists: "I heard you each describe in different

Tandem Dances. Julia M. Ritter, Oxford University Press (2021). © Oxford University Press.
DOI: 10.1093/oso/9780190051303.001.0001.

ways how you manage the movement of performers and audiences. Does dance play a role in your work, and if so, how?" My question was met with a prolonged, thoughtful silence. Finally, Baltz, who had studied and performed modern dance earlier in her career, broke the silence to note that choreographic concepts did inform the design of her projects. The panelists then quickly moved on to the next audience member's question.

Later on, I had an opportunity to speak to Harkness and Bolognino, who both affirmed the criticality of choreography in the immersive works they create.[5] What the FoST Fest anecdote left me with was a general impression of how dance tends to be occluded from the discourse surrounding immersive performance. If we consider choreography to be the organization of bodies in space and time—or, as dance scholar Susan Leigh Foster has stated, "a plan or orchestration of bodies in motion"—then *any* orchestration of *any* bodies in space and time, whether to be realized in dance or some other form of action, involves choreography (2009:98). With this definition in mind, my experience at FoST Fest raises a puzzling question. Why, in discussions about immersive performance, is dance referenced only obliquely or perfunctorily, if mentioned at all?[6] The FoST Fest anecdote points to a larger lack of acknowledgment, in the discourses attending to immersive works, of the central role played by choreography within immersive performance. Remedying this omission is essential if we are to understand the mechanisms by which these productions enable practitioners to shape the movements and actions of not just performers but also of audiences as participants.

Tandem Dances: Choreographing Immersive Performance proposes dance and choreography as frames through which to examine immersive theater. The idea of tandemness—suggesting motion that is achieved by two bodies working together and acting in conjunction with one another—is critical throughout the book. I argue that choreography is essential to the creation and reception of immersive productions, for two distinct yet entwined reasons. First, in the creation of these productions, choreography is deployed as a primary means of non-verbal and physical expression. As practitioners of immersive works devise and structure performance content intended to immerse audiences, dance is often prioritized over other communicative media due to its potential for kinesthetic dynamism, the different kinds of perception it invites, and the varieties of interpretive analyses it affords. Second, choreography is critical to immersive productions in that it serves as a crucial mechanism by which the spectator's role is transformed into that of an active, immersed participant within the production, namely, a subject of choreography enacting an improvisational score. In articulating these two applications of choreography, I suggest that it is fruitful to understand immersive productions as *tandem dances*, meaning they function as choreographic events requiring the bodies of both performers and spectators to enact parallel movement scores. *Tandem Dances* foregrounds the choreographic in order to examine its specific impact on the evolution of immersive theater, investigating choreography as a discursive problem that is fundamentally related to creative practice, to agendas of power and control, and to concomitant issues of freedom and agency. I adopt the idea of *tandemness* as a way to explore the relationships between various interdependent concepts and disciplines that are relevant to immersive productions, and to do so without defaulting to reductive binaries. One such binary is the culturally constructed division between dance and theater in Western societies. While acknowledging such binaries, the idea of tandemness enables us to untangle immersive productions' generative interplay between dance and theater, between choreography and dramaturgy, between freedom and control, between agency and embodiment, and between performers and spectators. In analyzing these generative interplays, and foregrounding the role of choreography in immersive productions, two challenges must be kept in mind: first, the longstanding separation of dance and theater, and second, the thorny questions of agency that are raised by the suggestion that spectators of immersive productions are being choreographed.

First, in seeking to uncover choreography's role in immersive productions, we must grapple with the ways that dance and theater have long been maintained as separate academic disciplines and continue to be disconnected in the research surrounding contemporary performance, including participatory forms such as immersive theater. To challenge this view, I draw on recent scholars who have taken up the work of bringing the discourses of these disciplines closer together. These include Nadine George-Graves and Kate Elswit, who possess significant backgrounds in each of these fields and self-describe their research and careers as straddling, not always comfortably, both disciplines. George-Graves, as editor of the *Oxford Handbook of Dance & Theatre* (2015), and Elswit, in her work *Theatre & Dance* (2018), advance compelling arguments for dissolving binary distinctions between the disciplines, citing how their confluence is engendering new forms and insights. Throughout this book, I return to George-Graves and Elswit's call to bridge the schism between dance and theater, specifically building on Elswit's use of the term *interdependency* to supplement my idea of tandemness when theorizing the role of dance in immersive works.

A second challenge in foregrounding choreography's role in immersive productions is the question of spectators' agency. Choreography is defined in this book as the designing and planning of movement in ways that are to be realized in dance as well as other forms of action. As such, the idea that choreography could be applied to spectators raises uncomfortable questions about the power and control that may be deployed in designing immersive experiences in ways that include audience participation. Even though choreography may yield ways of immersing (or appearing to immerse) audiences so they can perceive themselves as having agency and contributing in different ways to the event itself, the very notion of being choreographed connotes a lack of agency as an autonomous being in the world. As theater scholar Gareth White notes, "few things in the theatre [are] more despised than audience participation" (2013:1). We can surmise from such a statement that what audiences might despise are potential feelings of embarrassment or uncertainty about what will be asked of them during live performance contexts. This aversion to being compelled into the production is precisely a resistance to having one's agency revoked. White's remark, while not specific to immersive works, highlights the very real fears audiences have regarding the possibility of being manipulated during live, participatory performance situations, whether covertly or overtly. On the other hand, some audience members are surely *impelled* to participate because they desire and appreciate the effects of being controlled; for example, some people may have a penchant for escapism or fantasy, or an interest in role-playing situations where agency is relinquished. A certain ambiguity, then, must be recognized in immersive productions' use of choreography to structure spectators' participation. By recognizing the generative interplays within immersive productions—tensions between agency and control, between performer and spectator, between scriptedness and improvisation—we are able to understand choreography's nuanced role as a primary mechanism for shaping audience participation to effectively engender immersion as an affective outcome.

Locating Dance in Immersive Scholarship

To date, most of the literature on immersive performance comes from the discipline of theater. This scholarship defines what is distinct and exciting about immersive productions, establishes the foundations of a critical inquiry into the subject, and points to important precedents of the form. For example, scholars have identified parades and pageantry, circuses and carnivals, spontaneous and orchestrated "happenings" by 1960s artists, as well as promenade and site-specific performance as historical precedents of immersive performance.[7] However, the theater-based literature on immersive performance omits any rigorous engagement with the discipline of dance. Countering this omission, I argue that theater scholars' treatment of immersive performance as interdisciplinary, and their emphasis on how these productions' organizational design prioritizes the experiential embodiment and physical engagement of audiences, actually implies the centrality of choreography in immersive productions. Here, by situating choreography as central to these productions, I investigate the emergence of immersive theater through the frame of not only theater but also dance, and thereby address the latter's absence from the discourses surrounding immersive performance.

In her introduction to the anthology *Audience Participation: Essays on Inclusion in Performance* (2003), theater scholar and editor Susan Kattwinkel introduces the reader to productions that she describes as having been made by "artists who account for their audiences in every step of the creation and performance process" (x). While Kattwinkel herself does not use the word *immersive*—the term appears only once in the book in reference to technologies and online role-playing games, and not to live performance—her descriptions of the specific kinds of audience participation such productions might require can be readily understood in the context of immersive works:

> Either the performance is structured to include audience members, or the performance was created with the help of potential audience members, in concert with the artists, or greatly altered following audience response. Others of these performances were created with a very specific audience in mind and have no purpose for existence without the spiritual and vocal presence of that specific audience. (2003, x)[8]

Through Kattwinkel's emphasis on the ways in which artists conceptualize audiences in order to include them within performances, she laid the groundwork for other theater scholars to address questions of audience participation and immersion over the next decade.[9] Among the most prominent scholars to take up these questions are Gareth White (2013), Adam Alston (2016), James Frieze (2016), Rose Biggin (2017), and Josephine Machon (2009, 2013, 2016). A survey of these scholars' works reveals that they describe immersive theater as involving "embodiment" and "physical engagement," both of which are core concepts in choreography. Here, by reading these theater-based works from a dance perspective, I situate immersive works as tandem productions, materialized through a productive interaction between theater and dance.

Gareth White's work on immersive theater frames this genre in light of the larger discourse around audience participation, asserting that while all audiences are participatory in some respect—otherwise "performance would be nothing but action happening in the presence of other people" (2013:3)—the audience participation occurring in participatory performance, including works labeled as immersive, is unique. In *Audience Participation in Theatre: An Aesthetics of the Invitation*, White defines audience participation in these productions as "the participation of an audience or audience member *in the action* of a performance" (2013:3, emphasis added). White posits that through an audience member's "actions and experiences," that individual "becomes the artist's medium, and so the work's aesthetic material" (10).[10] In other words, spectators participate by actually becoming one of the materials that makes up the production. Like White, I am concerned with "identifying what it is that practitioners of audience participation work with," and for me, the aesthetic material includes the bodies of performers *and* audiences, as well as the dances realized through their bodies as they each enact choreography in tandem (14). If we accept that the aesthetic material White discusses can be the bodies of both performers and spectators, then we can understand his descriptions of the experiential nature of immersive as implying aspects and properties associated with dance and choreography.

Adam Alston, in his book *Beyond Immersive Theatre: Aesthetics, Politics and Productive Participation*, is, like White, concerned with how audiences are resourced to serve as aesthetic materials in productions, or as he puts it, are "expected to put their psychological and physiological capacities to work" during performances (2016:212). Alston's characterization of immersive theater draws on the neoliberal political philosopher Robert Nozick's notion of the "experience machine" (2), defined as "the pursuit of hedonism and subservience to a system that rewards subjects with desirable experiences at the

expense of independence" (2). While Nozick coined the term to refer to political structures, Alston applies the concept to immersive theater in order
to frame this type of production as a kind of proxy experience machine in
which spectators enter "enclosed and other-worldly spaces [that] . . . coalesce
around a central aim: to place the audience members in a thematically cohesive environment that *resources* their sensuous, imaginative and explor-
ative capabilities as productive" (2, emphasis added). Alston describes the
tendency of immersive productions to make demands upon audiences—
"demands to make more, do more, feel more, and to feel more intensely"—
as a form of "productive participation," and suggests that the expectation of
such participation is a "feature that recurs in neoliberalism's political and economic structures" (4). Alston's use of the term productive participation is
meant to critique immersive theater's aesthetic inclination toward "a romanticism, modification and enhancement of the audience's productivity" (4).
The resourcing of audiences as aesthetic materials in order that they might
productively pursue experiences affords what Alston has called the "objectification of experience as art" (7). In immersive theater, Alston claims, "audience attention is diverted from a more typical art object—be it a sculpture in
an installation or a performer on a stage—to the experiences that arise from
audience immersion and participation" (8). Building on Alston's claim, I assert that one primary mechanism through which the attention of audiences
is diverted toward their participation, such that their experiences can yield
immersion, is choreography. What Alston identifies as productive participation is, I argue, the resourcing of the spectator as a material of performance, that is, the spectator's transformation into a subject of choreography.
Through the spectator's choreographed labor, the "objectification of experience as art" that he speaks of can be ensured (7).

But how is the spectator engaged as an aesthetic material within the
production? James Frieze's answer to this question, in his introduction as
volume editor to *Reframing Immersive Theatre: The Politics and Pragmatics
of Participatory Performance*, is that the production hinges on the management of the spectator's attention. Frieze asserts that "the crux of participatory performance lies not in the object of our attention, what might normally
be called 'the content', but in the ways that our attention is managed, the
ways in which our engagement is co-opted *with and as* content" (2016:23,
emphasis original). Probing the implications of this management of spectator attention, Frieze questions the assumption that audiences have greater
agency in immersive productions than in traditional ones. For him, such

binary placements oversimplify immersive works as "positively valanced" with agency and traditional productions as "negatively valanced" with passivity, at least in participatory performance contexts (2). Frieze's explanation of why participatory, immersive works are valorized as agentive is that these works "offer the chance to do more than 'just' observe or study; they offer the chance to interact with, even to become, the object of attention" (1).[11] As Frieze notes, immersive theater "reflects an imperative to have (what used to be called) a '3D' experience, the sense of not just observing a spectacle but, literally and metaphorically, walking around it" (24). Here, Frieze reiterates White's idea of the spectator being "inside of the work," and echoes Alston's emphasis on the productive, entrepreneurial participation of audiences. And yet, the thrust of Frieze's argument is to suggest the ways in which spectators' experiences are shaped and managed by the creators and performers of the immersive production: "The entrepreneurial, embodied, empirical verification of the haptic-cinematic spectacle [of an immersive production] depends on the withholding of some secrets as much as on the revealing of others" (24). In other words, the productions depend to a certain extent upon spectators' *unwittingness*, their engagement with designed production elements that are invisible to them. I argue that one of those crucial elements, both operational and invisible in these productions, is choreography. Frieze thus indirectly reinforces my argument for how choreography is working to facilitate immersion. When situated as subjects of choreography, spectators become the object of their own attention; following Alston, their attention is diverted toward the "doing" of their own experiences and actions, through which they have opportunities to perceive immersion.

Choreography is also an invisible thread throughout Rose Biggin's *Immersive Theatre and Audience Experience: Space, Game and Story in the Work of Punchdrunk*, the first monographic study of the work of the UK-based company often cited as pioneers of immersive theater.[12] Biggin was embedded in the company as a research scholar for four years, with unprecedented access to choreographer and associate artistic director Maxine Doyle, and yet Biggin makes only one brief comment on Doyle's contribution to the production: "Doyle's distinctive choreography has appeared in many Punchdrunk shows and is a valuable part of the company's aesthetic" (17). Despite the brevity of this acknowledgment, Biggin's discussions of spectator experiences consistently refer to them, using terms that suggest the presence of choreography. For example, her descriptions of Punchdrunk's *The Drowned Man* (UK, 2013–2014) suggest spectators are impacted by the "energy of the choreography" (92), as well as by their individual navigation of the "wider layout of the space and the looping structure of the choreographed scenes" (91). In one passage that underscores my argument that both performers and spectators are choreographed, Biggin notes that "this layout is not influenced by an audience member's choice, although they have a certain amount of agency over where they go within that layout" (91). Stating, "the player/participant faces designed choices and procedures," Biggin goes on to describe how "the structure of the building implied a series of choices available regarding where an audience member might go" (92). Later, she explains that "an audience member's story, when considered as a linear journey with its own events and structure, is formed in the meeting place between their decisions (what door to go through, etc.) and the production's own choreography, direction and layout" (171). My notion of the tandemness of immersive productions is implied in this explanation by Biggin, in that she suggests audiences engage in journeys of their own within the context of the production's choreography. Based on these and other similar passages in Biggin's work, I suggest that even though she does not explicitly acknowledge or discuss the central role of choreography, she is, intentionally or not, implying its operational and affective impact in Punchdrunk's productions.

Finally, another theater scholar whose recent treatment of immersive performance implies the central, though under-discussed, role of choreography in these productions is Josephine Machon, who focuses her investigations on the sensorium of the spectator's body. In her 2009 book *(Syn)aesthetics: Redefining Visceral Performance*, Machon theorizes immersive theater as "quintessentially (syn)aesthetic," a term she uses to refer to how the form "encompasses both a fused sensory perceptual experience and a fused and sensate approach to artistic practice and analysis" (14). Building upon neurocognitive research on synesthesia, a condition understood as the production of a sense in one part of the body, such as hearing, that is experienced as a sensorial impression in another, such as color, Machon proposes her theory of "(syn)aesthetics" to analyze performance styles such as immersive theater as "an experiential audience event via the recreation of visceral experience" (1). In other words, Machon offers (syn)aesthetics as a means for understanding the ways practitioners emphasize the body's sensorial, affective, and cognitive capacities during the design and production of such events. For Machon, (syn)aesthetics explains how immersion affords audience participants "fused corporeal and cerebral experiences" during works that enable "shifts between sensual and intellectual, the somatic . . . and the semantic (the 'mental reading' of signs)" (4). Machon is distinct among immersive theater scholars in that she discusses choreography explicitly, particularly when describing the "very clearly choreographed" washing she received as a participant in the one-to-one performance of Adrian Howells's *The Pleasure of Being: Washing, Feeding, Holding* (2016:37).[13] However, Machon does not thoroughly investigate choreography's utility as a mechanism of audience participation, or as a means by which immersion manifests as an affect. Over the course of this book, I make explicit connections between dance and kinesthesia, broadly understood as the sensing of movement or "the first-person experiences of movement" as per dance philosopher Maxine Sheets-Johnstone, and what I believe to be the specialized role of choreography in the creation, presentation, and enactment of immersive performance ([1966] 2015:xvi). I return to Machon's ideas of (syn)aesthetics in Chapter 2, when exploring how kinesthesia impacts the ways audiences are *participating choreographically*.

Overall, the theater-based scholarship on immersive productions to date implies the presence of choreography in these works, but it stops short of fully explicating its role in these productions. White characterizes audiences as one of the "aesthetic materials" that makes up a participatory performance, which I understand as occurring through practitioners' resourcing of them as subjects of choreography. Alston builds on this view of audiences as aesthetic materials to frame immersive theater as an "experience machine" requiring the productive participation of audiences. His argument supports my claim that spectator enactment of choreography is what makes possible the objectification of experience as art. Frieze asserts that the means by which spectators participate in these productions is through the management of their attention, which raises questions about their agency; I argue that we can understand spectators' agency or lack thereof in terms of choreography's operational capacity to manage bodies. Finally, I note Biggin's repeated references to choreography in her explication of Punchdrunk's work, arguing that these references suggest an opportunity to investigate more fully the creative contributions of choreographer Maxine Doyle and other immersive company choreographers in order to better understand how these productions are informed by dance. Similarly, Machon's descriptions of the sensory aspects of choreography in several immersive productions provide a basis for these investigations. None of the theater-based immersive scholarship discussed in this section overtly denies that dance exists outside of academic theater discourse, including in immersive productions. What needs to be recognized, I argue, is that dance is actually critical to the functioning of these interdisciplinary works. As such, we need to surface and understand the central role of choreography in immersive productions. The notion of immersion is not without precedents and foundations within the world of dance scholarship, which has made scattered references to the term over the past several decades.

Locating Immersive in Dance Scholarship

Recognizing the under-theorization of dance's role in immersive theatre, we turn now to an exploration of how the concept of immersion has been present in dance practices and scholarship, if not named as such, over the past several decades.[14] Indeed, strategies now perceived as immersive— strategies that acknowledge and account for the audience as active participants during performance—have been integral to the experiments of both theater and dance artists since the mid-twentieth century, and it can be argued, long before that. Although the canon of dance scholarship contains few direct references to the concept of "immersion" as it is being examined in this book, we can find traces of intentional audience engagement as far back as the earliest recorded formal choreography. Chapter 1 will trace the lineage of the Western conceptualization of choreography as it related to audience engagement from the early days of the Renaissance. Here, though, a brief survey of dance scholarship suggests the emergence of immersion as a concept within dance as beginning with postmodernist dance artists in the 1960s and '70s and continuing through the increased use of immersive tactics in site-specific dance productions from the 1990s to the present. Most recently, dance scholars have begun to advocate for dance-based analysis of immersive theater, using dance as a counterpoint when discussing the connection of immersive works to cultural and socio-political structures rooted in Western forms of theater, a project that intersects with my interest in tandemizing the discourses.

One of the few uses of the term "immersive" in dance scholarship, and perhaps the first, occurs in Susan Leigh Foster's 1986 book *Reading Dancing: Bodies and Subjects in Contemporary American Dance*, specifically in her description of American artists who emerged from the Judson Church–era of dance experimentation in the 1960s and '70s. Foster's overall aim in this foundational work of dance scholarship is to elucidate choreographic methods and propose new ways to critically analyze dance-making and dance-viewing. In her discussion of the experimental dance emerging from the artists associated with the Judson Church, such as Meredith Monk, Foster uses the term "immersive" to describe the effects created by the fluid interactions of choreographer, dancer, and viewer. For example, describing the improvisational and interdisciplinary compositional strategies of Monk, Foster asserts that audiences of Monk's works "become involved in the choreography itself, helping determine the response they make, so that they become *immersed* along with the choreography and dancers in a playful yet critical interpretive practice" (227, emphasis added). Foster goes on to articulate the ways in which Monk's work "do not qualify as dance, that they occur, instead, at the interstices of existing mediums" (225).[15] Here, I suggest, Foster identifies the lexical gap around these productions; no term yet existed for naming for these works. It is this gap that has seemingly been filled in the twenty-first century by the contemporary use of *immersive*. I engage with Foster's analyses of Monk to suggest her as one example among several artists undertaking such experimentation in the twentieth century, and to make the larger assertion of dance's place in the history of these types of productions. Foster's writings illustrate how Monk's productions could have been understood at that time, as well as now, as engendering immersive experience. In this way, they can be situated among other works in the dance canon as precedents for current immersive productions. According to Foster, Monk's choices of how and where to stage her choreography in "parking lots, churches, or lofts" allowed her as a choreographer to "frame the audience as part of the action so that they see themselves as a defined group participating in an event" (223). Elsewhere in the book, I return to the work of postmodernist dance artists to discuss how practices that were developed during the postmodern period now operate in immersive productions.

A second precedent for immersive productions that we find in dance scholarship is the use of immersive tactics in site-specific performances. While site-specificity was present conceptually in Foster's writing in 1986, it is not named as such, and thus I look to more recent literature in contextualizing site-specific works in relation to immersive performance. The term *immersive* does not appear in *Site Dance: Choreographers and the Lure of Alternative Spaces* (2009), an anthology edited by Melanie Kloetzel and Carolyn Pavlik, although several chapters include explicit descriptions of practices that mirror today's immersive tactics and align with current attempts to define the genre.[16] Concepts such as interactivity and involvement, alongside the practical challenges of repositioning and moving spectators, as well as audience responses, are pervasive throughout the interviews and essays that comprise the book. For example, Los Angeles–based choreographer Heidi Druckler recounts to Pavlik how the presence of the audience, specifically their interactivity with her as well as the dancers during rehearsals, ultimately shaped her first site-specific project, entitled *Laundromatinee* (1988). Druckler secured permission to use an operational laundromat as the site for the production and held rehearsals during daily working hours, drawing the attention of individuals who watched while waiting for their laundry. Some of these onlookers offered unsolicited feedback while others returned to attend the performances.[17] In another work, *Most Wanted* (1997), set in a Los Angeles prison, Druckler explains that audiences "became characters in the work" when they were loaded into a sheriff's van, fingerprinted, and divided into groups to travel to different locations to watch dancers perform in prison cells (Druckler interview with Pavlik 2009:87).[18] These creative strategies deployed by Druckler in the late 1990s will be familiar to today's practitioners and spectators of immersive works. Indeed, through Druckler's performances, as well as the work of such artists as Eiko Otake, Stephen Koplowitz, and others who account for audiences in site-specific choreography, we can locate current tactics of immersive creation within these historical precedents of immersive dance practices.

One final puzzle piece that we can draw from dance scholarship to build a context for the use of choreography in immersive productions is the work of Royona Mitra, a scholar of dance and theater whose article "Decolonizing Immersion" proposes a broadening of the socio-political and disciplinary frameworks used to understand immersive productions. Mitra refers to the concept of *rasa*, a Sanskrit aesthetic theory of reception, to propose that immersion be considered as any work which "transpires interstitially between any audience, any artist and any art that is primarily premised on gestural dimensions of communication, and regardless of interactivity" (2016:89). My aim fundamentally differs from Mitra's in that I am investigating works that specifically focus on choreography as a mechanism *through which* spectators enact participation through physical movements as part of the performance event. Where I find Mitra's arguments productive for the present project, though, are her calls to expand the socio-cultural and disciplinary frameworks for understanding the term immersive, and the voices involved in the conversation, by asking who defines it—a question I examine further later in this chapter when discussing the ethical-political issues of

participation, agency, and authorship. In acknowledging Mitra's call to de-
colonize immersive theater, I suggest that the lack of diversity she perceives
stems in part from its emphasis on storytelling that has thus far prioritized
literary narratives from the Western European canon that tend to represent
and prioritize white male experiences.

Dance scholarship offers us several precedents and foundations for investigating dance's role in immersive performance. The few examples cited
here suggest how choreographers have long understood and grappled with
issues and contingencies that now concern practitioners of immersive theater but that have thus far been marginalized within the larger discourses
surrounding the form. Further investigation of the work of postmodernist
dance artists, as well as the experiments of subsequent generations of artists
with site-specific productions, would no doubt reveal innumerable instances
of choreographers prioritizing and foregrounding the audience experience
when conceptualizing their works. In recognizing the overlapping ways
dance and theater have been concerned with and address involvement of the
audience, I focus on identifying the tandemness of concepts and practices
distinct to immersive performance.

New (and Newer) Dramaturgies

Exploring tandemness as the generative interplay between theater and dance
opens up possibilities for expanding our understanding of how practices utilized within the creative processes of both disciplines, such as dramaturgy,
are operating within immersive performance. Historically, dramaturgy has
been understood as the theory and practice of dramatic composition within
the context of the theater. The dramaturg's role encompasses researching
various aspects of content and context, serving as a sort of proxy spectator
during the development process, and assisting artists from the inception
through the creation of a production that audiences will (hopefully) find
compelling. Conventional conceptions of dramaturgy can construe the
spectator as a static recipient of a work, and as such, the dramaturg's role as
a proxy for the spectator is often considered complete once the content of
a production has been sufficiently contextualized, that is, the realm of the
play has been established. In immersive productions, however, we can see
that this approach to dramaturgy can no longer be sufficient. With the spectator now constituting a component of the production, the dramaturgical

thinking surrounding their inclusion must be much more comprehensive. If immersive practitioners intentionally resource spectators as physically responsive subjects—as "materials," following White and Alston—*within* a performance, then the dramaturgy of such a production must account for them as mobile and agentive. Only by innovative approaches to dramaturgy can the spectator be situated as a subject who participates in the action with the potential of being immersed.

Alternative approaches to conventional dramaturgy first emerged in the 1990s, as dramaturgs began to increasingly emphasize process and collaboration. The phrase "new dramaturgy" was coined by Flemish dramaturg Marianne Van Kerkhoven in 1994 to refer to an emergent, iterative dramaturgy in which performances were created through open-ended and collaborative processes, shaped by an awareness of the audience as diverse, multiple, and eager consumers of new cultural experiences (18). Van Kerkhoven, who worked with Belgian choreographer Anne Teresa de Keersmaeker in the 1980s, declared that this new dramaturgy was "looking for a new relationship with its audience," a statement that proved prescient over the next two decades as practitioners increasingly focused on dramaturgical processes that connect spectators to productions at differing levels of participation (22). Van Kerkhoven's notion has since become pluralized, with the term "new dramaturgies" now deployed to reference the continual surfacing of experimental dramaturgical practices.[19]

In the realm of dance, dramaturgs have been working with choreographers since the 1980s, with two notable early dramaturg–choreographer partnerships being Raimund Hoghe and Pina Bausch at Tanztheatre Wupperthal in Germany, and later, Heidi Gilpin and William Forsythe at Ballet Frankfurt. However, only within the past fifteen years has dance dramaturgy become recognized as a distinct discipline. Gilpin is credited as the first to delineate dance dramaturgy as a discipline, in her identification of "the dramaturgy of movement in performance" (2015:10).[20] Today, the ontology and function of dramaturgy in dance remains less defined than in theater; the relationship between dramaturgical and choreographic practices continue to be debated, and questions remain regarding the distribution of labor within dance dramaturgy.[21] On one hand, Van Kerkhoven claimed in 1994 that "there is no *essential* difference between theatre and dance dramaturgy," citing that even though each form is composed historically of different materials, they maintain the same concerns of "mastering of structures; the achievement of a global view; the gaining of insight into how to deal with the material, whatever its origin may be" (146, em-phasis original). On the other hand, dance dramaturgs, such as Gilpin and Katherine Profeta, present contemporary movement performance as more dramaturgically complex than performances that prioritize text. This is be-cause movement performances are inherently multidisciplinary, drawing on dance, music, theater, visual arts, film, and other forms. Gilpin and Profeta argue that this multidisciplinarity, and in some cases, interdisciplinarity, requires its practitioners to engage in broader consideration of the particular ways in which different audiences make meaning of productions. As audi-ence members receive such densely crafted movement-based performances, they must interpret diverse performance languages and codes. For instance, Gilpin claims that audiences of movement performances "are not equally well versed" in the "many differing vocabularies (text, image, movement, sound) and disciplinary perspectives—none of which play a hierarchical central role" within the productions (1997:85). If Gilpin's assertion is true, at least in regard to some audience members, then the dramaturgical process for such productions requires consideration of the ways in which audiences may engage in a kind of code-switching between artistic disciplines.[22] This code-switching would be, then, the synthesis of aesthetic information with which they are less familiar with the knowledge they bring to the performances in order to make meaning from the totality of the event.

The concept of the spectator as a central concern in the dramaturgical process is a focus of the scholarship of both Gilpin and Profeta. Gilpin sug-gests that in movement-based productions, more is expected of spectators, as these productions involve levels of information that are layered, over-lapping, and transmitted through many disciplinary modes. Because of these layers of complexity, Gilpin maintains that the audience's ability to interpret these varied disciplinary languages is a key dramaturgical con-cern. Following Gilpin, yet focusing on the work of the dramaturg specifi-cally, Profeta declares that "anyone participating in dramaturgical thinking cannot *not* think about audience and still be engaged in the task of con-structing a performance" (2015:100).[23] While taking this stance, Profeta is also highly attuned to the ineffability of the spectator's experience of the per-formance. On one hand, she suggests that "it is certainly possible, and often quite useful, to defer or transmute this type of [audience-centric] thinking" (100). Profeta cautions that positioning a dramaturg as an "advocate" for the audience is problematic since "one cannot advocate for an unknown, irre-ducibly diverse, impromptu future collective" (88). But on the other hand,

Profeta also acknowledges that to abandon the notion of dramaturg as advocate "risks ignoring the sheer amount of time I nevertheless spend trying to conjure the perceptions and thoughts of imaginary spectators" (15). Both Gilpin and Profeta emphasize the essentiality of the spectator to dramaturgical thinking, while also expressing the numerous complications that arise when accounting for and accommodating them. Building upon Gilpin and Profeta, I propose that a newer form of new dramaturgical thinking has emerged in immersive performance, one that is primarily concerned with how to resource spectators as aesthetic materials (to cite White and Alston) when creating and implementing productions. In Chapter 3, I return to these analyses of new dramaturgies when proposing *elicitive dramaturgy* as a way of conceiving of and composing the spectator as a subject of choreography. As I show, this *new,* new dramaturgy has been developed as a way of conceptualizing and designing audience participation in immersive performance.

Agency, Audience Participation, and Authorship

The promise of "immersion into a world" is commonly used to advertise immersive productions. Notably, however, among the hundreds of immersive theater promotional materials I have reviewed, I have never seen a promise that spectators would be "choreographed into a world." The choice to emphasize immersion rather than choreography in marketing immersive productions makes a certain intuitive sense. Whereas the language of immersion may evoke an expectation of a pleasurable experience, an invocation of choreography might raise a suspicion that attending the production will involve being manipulated, coerced, or simply made to work too hard. This trend in marketing messaging suggests that, for many audiences of participatory performance, the prospect of being immersed is vastly more appealing than the prospect of being choreographed. The term "immersion," as used in this context, suggests the sublime, while the possibility of being choreographed may sound contrived, even oppressive. Beneath audiences' concern about being choreographed might exist a deeper aversion to surrendering one's agency, or even acknowledging delimitations on that agency. In a neoliberal age of entrepreneurial initiative and individual productivity, such a relinquishment of agency could read more as a deterrent than an enticing invitation.

And yet, for all the resistance to acknowledging choreography's prevalence in many situations, it is, as cultural theorist and philosopher Erin Manning has stated, "happen[ing] everywhere, all the time" (2012:91). By this, Manning is suggesting that we choreograph the social, cultural, and economic interactions of our lives and are also choreographed by them. More precisely, we are inevitably choreographed by the behavioral norms shaping the societies we inhabit; we are choreographed whenever we acquiesce to prescribed standards of conduct, whether that means waiting patiently in a check-out line at a store or stepping to the left side of an escalator so we can climb up past those riding on the escalator's right side. As Manning notes, referencing choreographer William Forsythe's assertion that "you don't need a choreographer to dance" (Forsythe quoted in Forsythe and Sigmund 2001), all that is needed for dancing to occur is "a choreographic proposition" (2012:97). That choreographic proposition can take such mundane forms as someone holding a door open for you or a restaurant displaying a no smoking sign. Indeed, in almost every circumstance of our lives, we encounter choreographic propositions that guide our actions. Even when attending traditional theater productions where we enact what White has called "conventionally constructed signals" such as sitting in our assigned seats, applauding, or laughing, we are embedded in choreographic structures that organize our bodies (2013:129).

Characterizing the structuring power of choreography, performance studies scholar André Lepecki asserts that choreography can be understood as an apparatus of capture, that is, it "captures" the bodies of dancers, orienting and defining their movements over the course of the dance. Lepecki's use of the term "apparatus of capture" in relation to choreography draws upon the work of philosophers Gilles Deleuze and Pierre-Félix Guattari, who were expanding on philosopher Michel Foucault's conceptualization of apparatus as any structure that exercises power in societies. By framing choreography as an apparatus of capture, Lepecki distinguishes it as the precise mechanism through which a dancer enacts the exact movements as prescribed by a choreographer. Lepecki, explaining this concept in a joint essay with theater scholar Ric Allsopp, states, "[c]horeography was invented in order to structure a system of command to which bodies have to subject themselves (freely, as Althusser would say!) into the system's wills and whims" (2008:3). Following Foucault, Allsopp and Lepecki understand bodies as "docile," or compliant, particularly when subjected to regulatory powers, and choreography as commanding (3). The proposal of choreography as an apparatus of capture, useful as it is for understanding how dancers' bodies are captured by the structures composed by choreographers, is perhaps even more compelling as an explanation of how choreography works in immersive productions. Specifically, in immersive performance, choreography can be understood as capturing the bodies of not only dancers but also spectators.'

This capture is not absolute or guaranteed, however. Allsopp and Lepecki identify a means for spectators captured by choreography to "slip out" of the apparatus of capture: namely, *improvisation*, defined as speaking and acting in a manner that is not planned or scripted within a production. Choreographers have long used improvisation as a tool to invent movement and support the creation of choreography; improvisation is also used as a form of performance itself. Today, it is generally accepted that choreography and improvisation are distinct modes of performance and that they can also coexist within a single work of performance. In previous writings, I have identified how spectators' movements and speech are organized by instructional movement scores provided by practitioners.[24] Such scores have long been utilized within the discipline of dance as a means by which choreographers and dancers generate movement for performance. In immersive performance, instructional scores are encountered by audiences and function as the mechanism for their participation within the production.[25] I have argued that the scores performed by the audience constitute choreography in immersive performance when developing my idea of tandem dances, building upon Foster's assertion that that choreography can "interpreted as a score or a set of principles that guide spontaneous invention" (2011:3). But implicit within the use of scores, given that they are improvisational to begin with, is the possibility of deviating from them through improvisation. This recognition of improvisational deviation from (or "slipping out" of) the pre-assigned instructional, choreographic structure of a score provides a frame for understanding how dance shapes audiences' participation in immersive productions without fully controlling that participation. Audiences' slippage from out of the instructional score may be either intentional or unintentional, a distinction I take up in Chapter 3.

As I have suggested, the nature and extent of spectator agency within immersive productions remains an open question. Previous scholarship on audience participation and authorship, particularly with regard to the body as a site of agency, helps us consider the ways in which audiences simultaneously have and do not have agency through dance within immersive productions. The body itself presents a paradox, as articulated by philosopher Drew Leder in *The Absent Body*, in that one's body is the "most abiding and inescapable presence" in one's life and yet "is rarely the thematic object of experience" (1990:1). In other words, while the body is inescapably the means through which we experience the world, it is not typically the center of our attention, and is often even ignored. Dance is a way to overcome this paradox, as pointed out by George-Graves, referencing Leder. The practice of dance brings the body into acute focus, prioritizing embodied experience while bringing sensations to the center of one's attention (2015:6). The body thus becomes both a site and a facilitator of the perception of agency. In immersive performance, spectators experience the production first and foremost as kinesthetic activity; through enactment of instructional, improvisational movement scores, practitioners are affording spectators access to intensified levels of kinesthesia, as understood by Sheets-Johnstone as "the first-person experiences of movement" (2015:xvi). This intensified embodiment is then inextricable from perceptions of *agency*, following interdisciplinary scholar Carrie Noland's theorizing of agency through kinesthesia. Agency is defined by Noland as "the power to alter those acquired behaviors and beliefs for purposes that may be reactive (resistant) or collaborative (innovative) in kind" (2009:9). Kinesthetic sensations, she claims, are a "particular kind of affect belonging to both to the body that precedes our subjectivity (narrowly construed) and the contingent, cumulative subjectivity our body allows us to build over time" (4). Kinesthesia affords us opportunities to "experiment with practices we have learned" and, following this, "knowledge obtained through kinesthesia is *constitutive* of—not tangential to—the process of individuation" (4, emphasis original). In other words, spectators' embodied, physicalized participation in choreographic structures, which affords them access to intensified levels of kinesthesia, can contribute to perceptions of agency and authorship—both of which, I argue, are critical to the efficacy of these productions as immersive experiences. Immersion depends upon perceiving the self as agentive, and it is immersion that serves to facilitate that perception of agency.

If spectators are or perceive themselves to be agentive within immersive productions, what implications does this have for authorship? What does it mean for practitioners to design structures for spectators to act and speak within, and in what sense are those spectators then co-authoring the production? These questions relate to broader debates about authorship in the twenty-first century, which has been constantly redefined over the past century. Since the mid-twentieth century, authorial control over the performative experience has been questioned by major artists across the disciplines of visual arts, theater, and dance, including Antonin Artaud, Bertolt Brecht, Andy Warhol, Yoko Ono, Marina Abramović, Merce Cunningham, and Yvonne Rainer, as well as many other postmodernist dance artists. In dance, authorship has long been understood in terms of co-authorship, meaning the works arise from collaborations and interactions among choreographers and dancers. The creative process of choreography resources dancers as innovators and generators of material, and in the moment of the performance, the dancer's interpretation of the choreography may be considered another mode of co-authorship. In immersive works, we may consider how spectators, too, are contributing as co-generators of choreography and co-authors of the experience of the production. Immersive performance as an emergent cultural product is designed to both invite and require the participation and contributions of the audience. Importantly, this co-authorship may not be conscious or intentional for the audience member. We must resist generalizing audience experience by suggesting that all spectators perceive themselves as dancing per se, or by assuming that everyone experiences immersion in the same way or at all, or perceives themselves as generating or performing content. Nevertheless, in practice, spectators *can* be choreographed even without their perceiving their participation as dance or dancing, and even without realizing that they are contributors to the performance. Dances, as Foster notes, "evince or articulate a choreography" (2011:3). Dance is a *realization* of choreography. While spectators will always have their own individual perceptions of their experience, it is through their enactment, that is, performance, of choreographic structures designed to guide their participation that they, alongside the performers, realize choreography as tandem dances. This participation can occur at an almost instinctual level, reflecting the kind of responsiveness we have to the kinds of choreographic propositions that occur throughout our daily lives, as mentioned earlier.

This discussion of audience participation and agency in immersive productions has raised a number of questions. Is immersion a relinquishment or an exercise of spectator agency? What role does the spectator's body play in facilitating or delimiting immersion, or both? What is the relationship between the designed elements of the production (including what is known as a *track*, the choreography that is crafted by practitioners and executed by a dancer or dancers) and the actual movements and speech of spectators who are "captured"—or not—by these improvisational scores? To get at these questions of agency in spectator participation, the concept I find most fruitful is that of *improvisation*, specifically, although not exclusively, that of movement. Improvisation, both dance and speech-based, is at the heart of spectators' potential to be agentive within choreographic structures. Dance improvisation as a concept and practice has not yet been theorized comprehensively in the discourses surrounding immersive performance, but the dance scholarship dealing with improvisation is instructive when considering the agency of the audiences participating in these productions.

Dance philosopher Maxine Sheets-Johnstone asserts that "movement is at the root of our sense of agency" and is "the generative source of our notions of space and time" (1999:xv). A former dancer and choreographer, Sheets-Johnstone draws upon paleoanthropology, evolutionary biology, phenomenology, psychology, and neuroscience in her interdisciplinary scholarship that argues for movement as a foundational means by which humans become attuned to, act within, and build knowledge about the world. Sheets-Johnstone's research on dance via philosophy of the mind led her, in 1981, to introduce the concept of *thinking in movement* as a way of understanding movement *as* thought. In other words, to move, including to dance, *is* to think. She argues that, "To think is first of all to be caught up in a dynamic flow; thinking is itself, by its very nature, kinetic. What is distinctive about thinking in movement is not that the flow of thought is kinetic, but that the thought itself is [kinetic]" (486). *Thinking in movement* is not an enactment of premeditated thoughts; rather, *thinking* and *doing* function as inextricable processes within movement, particularly within improvisation (xv). Indeed, Sheets-Johnstone identifies dance improvisation as a "paradigm" of thinking in movement precisely because of the "nonseparation" of thinking and doing; she asserts that the dancer is neither "thinking by means of movement" nor are "her/his thoughts being transcribed into movement"; rather, that "movement constitutes the thoughts themselves" (486 and 492).[26] This nonseparation of thinking and doing suggests thinking in movement is an interdependent, conjunctive process of asserting agency; following this, then, it is possible that an internal tandemness is occurring as audience participants perform improvisational scores, which, when realized, constitute one part of the overall tandem dance of the production.

However unplanned, fleeting, or ephemeral these moments of thinking in movement and realizing scores as dances may be, they are nonetheless examples of creative agency and authorship within immersive performance. Sheets-Johnstone notes, "dance improvisation is commonly described as an unrehearsed and spontaneous form of dance," yet such a description fails to encompass the fact that within dance improvisation, "the process of creating is not the means of realizing *a* dance; it is *the* dance itself. A dance improvisation is the incarnation of creativity as process" (1999:485). Sheets-Johnstone reminds us that during a dance improvisation, the "future is thus open. Where [the improvisation] will go at any moment, what will happen next, no one knows; until the precise moment at which it ends, its integrity as an artwork is uncharted" (485). Returning to Alston, we can see that through dance improvisation, audiences are resourced to realize scores as tandem dances; yet while these scores are choreographed, there always exists within them the possibility of agency, since agency is inherent within improvisation's ontology. Thus, while the choreographed labor of the audience, as improvisers, may be the "objectification of experience as art," the possibility of improvisation—which is present in any choreographic work— serves as a seductive draw: it is both the unknown and the means by which the audience might exert agency as aesthetic contributors to the experience (Alston 2013:7). Sheets-Johnstone both underscores my argument for immersive performance as a kind of tandem dance and suggests the potential for agentive, creative coauthorial contributions by audience participants when she states, "the world that I and other dancers are together exploring is inseparable from the world we are together creating" (2009:32). Here we can see agency as the entanglement of motivation, desire, aesthetic values, and creative action; when elided, these aspects help to explain the seductive nature of immersive performance for audiences who perceive it as a form that offers certain kinds of experiences and outcomes. Sheets-Johnstone's work on *thinking in movement* underlies my own suggestion of the potential for audience participants to make creative coauthorial contributions, driven by the seductiveness of agency as a creative act. Indeed, Sheets-Johnstone could very well be speaking of audience participants in immersive performance when she states that "the dancer has agreed to follow the rules, as it were, [...] rules that might very well generally be summed up under the rubric: dance the dance as it comes into being at this particular moment at this particular place" (1981:399).

Differentiating between improvisation and choreography within immersive performance can be challenging; both can be evidenced in a production, as interdependent as well as mutually exclusive processes. To this point, Sheets-Johnstone makes clear that the thinking in movement of which she speaks is "the process of creating the dance," that is, realizing the choreography, and is, thus, "different from thinking in movement as part of the process of choreographing a dance" (1981:402). Further distinction is necessary, however, between how thinking in movement as a process of realizing a dance manifests itself compared to how the processes of conceiving and designing choreography play out. The concept of *choreographic thinking*, associated with the work of choreographers William Forsythe and Susan Rethorst, is helpful in explicating the latter, and will be discussed in Chapter 1. The work of Sheets-Johnstone, as well as that of Noland's interdisciplinary research on the connections among kinesthesia, embodiment, and agency, helps us understand how the embodiment engendered through the performance of improvisational scores might translate into spectator perceptions of agency, including the ability to "trespass" the fourth wall that typically separates the worlds inhabited by performers and by audiences. Indeed, I argue it is the perception of agency that affords spectators the sense of asserting and including themselves in worlds typically understood as off-limits, and that this self-assertion is necessary in order to engender a sense of autonomy that can facilitate immersion as an affective outcome.

In short, choreography within immersive productions might be understood as establishing a different kind of fourth wall, one that effectively designates the roles and responsibilities between performers and spectators, situating both within conditions that prescribe and manage behavior. It is through analyses of agency and embodiment that the paradoxical operation of choreography in immersive performance is revealed. While spectators are afforded opportunities to trespass into these worlds through choreography, choreography also serves to effectively delimit and constrain spectator agency. Building on the generally accepted notion that choreography and improvisation can occur within the same production, my research demonstrates how improvisational structures are embedded within choreography itself. Key to my research, however, is the question of how practitioners incorporate improvisational scores as a design element through which audiences generate movement that contributes to the overall choreography of immersive performance. Yet another generative interplay within immersive productions, this tandemness between choreography and improvisation is a thread throughout the book.

Methodology

With the goal of understanding choreography's role in immersive performance, productions of works labeled and publicized as immersive by their creators constitute the primary sources of my research. Through participant observation of productions, especially my direct, first-person experiences, I engage in context-sensitive, close choreographic readings and careful theorization of immersive works from my perspective as a dance practitioner and scholar. My knowledge of dance composition and choreographic devices informs my analyses as I consider how these methods, among others, are deployed to impact the choices of spectators. Thick descriptions of performances I have experienced, as well as the voices of practitioners, performers, and spectators feature prominently in conjunction with analyses of theoretical literatures from multiple disciplines and qualitative interview-based research toward theory-building.

Yet my curiosity of how people were or were not talking about dance and choreography led me to seek out multiple kinds of sites to both listen and engage in conversation, including symposia, festivals, and summits dedicated to immersive entertainment and design. I draw upon dance, theater, and performance studies, as well as aesthetic theory, film studies, affect studies, embodied cognition, phenomenology, popular culture, and fandom studies to contextualize my experiences of research and to situate dance within the extant research on immersive performance. Integration of theoretical scholarship with qualitative data enables me to critically combine resources so as to analyze how these knowledge sources reinforce and augment the perspectives of those involved with immersive performance. Lastly, in light of the under-theorization of dance in relation to immersive performance, I propose my own concepts and neologisms to establish new ways of engaging with the form.

The book's specific geographic focus is the United States, the United Kingdom, and Canada, and analyses of over fifteen immersive productions shapes the research presented here.[27] While all of the productions I have experienced inform my arguments for how choreography contributes to performance, specific productions feature prominently, for several reasons. First, the UK-based Punchdrunk's long-running production of *Sleep No More* (London 2003, New York 2011–present, and Shanghai 2016–present) is foregrounded in my research due to its long-term, pivotal, international impact on the emergence on immersive performance. *Sleep No More* is often

cited by those working in the realm of immersive entertainment as a production that brought the concept of immersive theater into the consciousness of mainstream Western society.[28] In addition, the production's emphasis
on dance and choreography as a communicative mechanism, in conjunction with its sustained longevity, has made it a rich source of continued research. *Then She Fell* (New York 2012–present), by the Brooklyn-based Third
Rail Projects, is another long-running production, having surpassed 4,000
performances in 2019; it is frequently referenced in the discourses in the
field as influential, yet it has not yet been the subject of significant scholarly
attention. Lastly, *Dance Marathon* (2009–2015), by bluemouth inc. performance collective (Canada), is included as an example of an immersive production that has toured widely, with over fifty international performances.
This makes *Dance Marathon* unique within the canon of immersive works
established thus far. Most productions are site-specific, in that the architectural structures adapted through design to specifically serve a production
are often bound to certain locations, making touring or presenting in multiple locations both difficult and expensive. My experiences of the works of
critically acclaimed, yet lesser-known artists and companies have been critical to my research even though their productions are not addressed specifically here. These include Capital W in Los Angeles, founded by Lauren
Ludwig and Monica Miklas; the New York–based Woodshed Collective
(particularly *KPOP*, a collaborative production created by Korean dram-
atist Jason Kim); and *Say Something Bunny!*, by Japanese-Canadian artist
Alison S. M. Kobayashi.[29] My aim in researching immersive performance
has been to write only about productions I have personally experienced; live
performances that I was unable to experience, such as the early work of Fiona
Templeton, were analyzed via video, her texts documenting her work, and
photographs.

Theater scholar Helen Freshwater has asserted that "almost no one in theatre studies seems to be interested in exploring what actual audience members
make of a performance" (2009:29). Immersive practitioner and scholar
David Shearing made a similar statement about immersive productions,
that "immersive experience is often discussed without ever considering what
experiences are actually like for audiences or participants" (2018:291). While
these claims may be true, I submit that the neglect of audience perspectives
may be due in part to the fact that scholars from both theater and dance
lack access to frameworks for comprehensive audience research. Those interested in gathering data on spectators, especially their perspectives, are

stymied by the time and expense of conducting independent audience research. Both dance and theater would benefit from pursuing opportunities to conduct comprehensive qualitative and quantitative research on audience participation. In this regard, the work of Dee Reynolds and Matthew Reason, notably the *Watching Dance Project* (2008–2011), as well as the research of Kirsty Sedgman and the recent establishment of the International Network for Audience Research in the Performing Arts (iNARPA), are promising developments for the fields of dance, theater, and performance studies. Admittedly, much of my data disproportionately reflects the perspectives of self-described fans of the genre who actively seek out these types of experiences, as well as individuals who had one-off experiences of immersive performance that they particularly enjoyed. Individuals with no interest in immersive experiences, or those who have had experiences they perceive as negative, are much less likely to volunteer to offer their perspectives. It is my belief, nevertheless, that any study of immersive or participatory performance should attempt the inclusion of audience perspectives. Therefore, this book features a range of spectator perspectives drawn from my interviews and from social media, albeit reflecting evidence that is by nature anecdotal.

Chapter Overviews

This book elucidates choreography's role in and contributions to immersive performance, with each chapter incorporating theories of audience participation, dramaturgy, and authorship, as well as examples from multiple productions created over the past decade. First, to contextualize choreography's current status as integral to, yet invisibilized within, immersive performance, Chapter 1 illuminates thematic concerns of choreography in Western dance history, specifically the intentionality with which it is created, the portability of its concepts outside of the realm of formal dance, and its resulting ubiquity across domains in the twenty-first century. First used by European aristocrats in the sixteenth and seventeenth centuries as a practice for reinforcing structures of ritual and power when assigning societal roles, *choreography* as a term emerged alongside the professionalization of dance in the eighteenth and nineteenth centuries. In the mid-twentieth century, choreography became a tacitly borrowed resource for creators of physical theatre. Then, in the twenty-first century, choreography came to be seen as an expanded practice, having surged beyond the bounds of dance to the point that, I argue, it can be used to organize the behavior of spectators such that they perceive themselves to be immersed. In Chapter 2, I show that although choreography has been overlooked in discussions of immersive performance, it has, in fact, long been invisibly operating as a design strategy for immersing spectators in these productions. Drawing upon insights from directors of immersive productions, I examine how the compositional tools of dance are being adapted and combined with ideas from other disciplines to create choreographic structures for both dancers and spectators. The chapter also considers the rise of participatory culture and its influence on the emergence of immersive performance while foregrounding kinesthesia and kinesthetic empathy as key elements contributing to the facilitation of immersion as an affect.

Chapters 3, 4, and 5 are the heart of the book's theory-building. Chapter 3 proposes *elicitive dramaturgy* as a novel form of dramaturgical thinking that has emerged to account for the spectator as a mobile entity with agency. This dance-driven theory and practice of composing immersive performance affords spectators agency while simultaneously managing their contributions through carefully designed choreographic parameters. In Chapter 4, my focus on choreography becomes the point of entry to a deeper understanding of how spectators experience immersion. Drawing on theories of kinesthetic empathy and research on embodied cognition, I elaborate on my previously published work on *insider dynamics* to build a theory of embodied affective engagement as occurring in four distinct phases: complicity, porosity, contagion, and inclusion. I argue that insider dynamics occur as spectators access their kinesthesia, and that these dynamics function to guide the decision-making of audiences as participants in performances. It is because of insider dynamics, I propose, that immersion can extend beyond the boundaries of performances through communities known as fandoms. After encountering highly sensory, nonverbal, and choreographic performances, fans reflect upon their experiences of participatory engagement and transform those experiences into creative responses such as fan fiction and art. I identify *extended audiencing* as a recursive process within fandom, one that is perpetuated through behavioral responses of fans who repeat-attend, create art inspired by the production, and share their creations within the public sphere of the internet.

Chapter 5 introduces the idea of *actuating* to argue that once spectators are actuated, they can shift into *states of being coauthorial*, or *coauthorality*.

I suggest that choreographic structures compound spectators' perceptions of co-authorship for two reasons: spectators' direct physical engagement in improvisational scores and the interpretive flexibility of dance itself. In immersive productions, dance provides opportunities for audiences to conceive of their participation as generating and coauthoring content that contributes to the production. Finally, Chapter 6 looks forward, speculating on potential contributions of dance to the changing landscape of immersive performance, as strategies used to create participatory performance and experiential entertainment are increasingly adopted within commercial business sectors. The book concludes with a defense of dance as a broad field of study, and a call to properly acknowledge its contributions to the development of new cultural forms, including the innovation of immersive performance.

I acknowledge, paraphrasing George-Graves, that the work of dance and theater scholars has in common the idea of corporeality (2015:5). Indeed, in asserting the centrality of choreography in immersive performance, I make no claims that dance somehow has a monopoly on movement and the body; I recognize, as does theater scholar Collette Conroy, that just like dance, "theatre is fundamentally concerned with the human body" (2010:8). At the same time, I contend that the constant themes of embodiment and physical engagement within immersive discourses *without explicit discussion of choreography* can reinforce and perpetuate the kinds of valorized notions of immersive performance that Frieze, Alston, and White, among others, have pressed against. For example, Frieze offers a list of how he perceives immersive and interactive performances have been valorized and "heralded" in terms of their "spiritual effects," including "combatting the disconnectedness of the digital age, refreshing the senses, restoring communal and individual agency, and saving the theatre from stultifying traditions by bringing it to new audiences and new spaces" (2016:11). Without analyses of how choreography is operating in immersive performance, the discourses around immersive performance are at best incomplete, and at worst, promulgate the fallacy that audiences are somehow liberated from structures that organize and manage behaviors, such as the practices that occur in other theater-watching situations—which, as stated previously—are already choreographic.

When considering the schism between dance and theater, the points of contention seem to coalesce around the marginalization of dance, specifically the notion that it occupies a "subaltern" status in relation other arts disciplines, as argued by Lepecki.[30] The marginalization of dance is a gendered phenomenon evident in both higher education and performing arts industries, reflecting deeply layered and complex institutional misogynies. Young girls constitute the largest percentage of students in private dance studios and programs in public schools, a trend that persists as women enter higher education. While many arts subjects, including theater, are increasingly at risk of being eliminated from higher education curricula, dance occupies a place of particular precarity. Dance's gendering as a feminine activity leads to its denigration as a lesser pursuit; it has often been situated in physical education or theater programs as an ancillary subdiscipline.[31] Already underrepresented within institutions of higher education, departments and programs of dance in the United Kingdom and the United States are increasingly, in this century, being phased out due to misconceptions about dance as an unprofitable career. The realities faced by dance and dance artists is partly what spurs me to attend specifically to the role of choreography in immersive works, whereby I forthrightly and unabashedly advocate for dance as a discipline and call for recognition of the contributions of choreographers, many of whom are female. Women choreographers often labor unacknowledged in realms of live performance, immersive performance included, where male directors have been largely predominant. And, in the case of immersive performance specifically, male directors are disproportionately credited with advancing the form. In short, my situating choreography as central in immersive performance is not to suggest that dance is the only means by which we can better understand how such productions work; rather, it is to recover dance from the subaltern role that it has long played in interdisciplinary discourses surrounding contemporary performance. That subaltern role is explored in the next chapter, where the groundwork is laid for drawing choreography into conversations around immersive performance and recognizing its critical role among the several constituent elements of this emergent art form.

1

Tracing Choreography

Keep your head and body erect and appear self-possessed. Spit and blow your nose sparingly, or if needs must turn your head away and use a fair white handkerchief. Converse affably in a low, modest voice, your hands at your sides, neither hanging limp nor moving nervously.

***

West of House

You are standing in an open field west of a white house, with a boarded front door. There is a small mailbox here.

> Go North

North of House
You are facing the north side of a white house. There is no door here, and all the windows are boarded up. To the north a narrow path winds through the trees.

> East

Behind House
You are behind the white house. In one corner of the house there is a small window which is slightly ajar.

> Open the window.

With great effort, you open the window far enough to allow entry.

> Go in

Kitchen
You are in the kitchen of the white house. A table seems to have been used recently in the preparation of food.

The above passages are from a sixteenth-century French dance manual and a twentieth-century American computer game. Both are instances of choreographic instructions: written directives designed to serve as mechanisms for organizing behavior and structuring human experiences of embodiment.

Tandem Dances. Julia M. Ritter, Oxford University Press (2021). © Oxford University Press.
DOI: 10.1093/oso/9780190051303.001.0001.

In the first excerpt, from a 1589 treatise entitled *Orchésographie*, a French cleric and dancing master named Jehan Tabourot delivers instructions to a young man on how to behave within aristocratic society. In the second excerpt, from the computer game *Zork*, a set of instructions encoded by the game designer provides clues to the player as they choose how to make their way through an unfamiliar territory. Each of these passages represents a conversational exchange in which a "master" instructs a less-informed protégé or initiate in how to enter and navigate an unfamiliar world, whether real or imagined, by engaging in intentional movements and behaviors that are appropriate within that world. The texts communicating these masters' instructions, as well as the instructions themselves, are instances of *choreography*: communicative artifacts that are meant to organize and prescribe specific movements and actions by individuals other than the author of the words. These two passages from four hundred years and a continent apart only begin to hint at the vast range of settings in which choreography has functioned over the past several centuries as an effective technology for managing bodies in space and time.

The first text excerpted in the opening of this chapter, *Orchésographie*, was published posthumously under the author's anagrammatic pseudonym, Thoinot Arbeau, with a title drawn from the Latin *orchesography*, meaning the theory of dancing.[1] The treatise was written as a "dialogue between the elderly Thoinot Arbeau and an imaginary pupil" (Evans in Preface to Arbeau 1948:6).[2] *Orchésographie* begins as this pupil, a young man named Capriol, arrives on Arbeau's doorstep with aspirations of social mobility. Capriol is keen to gain entry to the ballrooms favored by the nobles of sixteenth-century France in order to advance his social standing, yet proper etiquette in these environs requires mastery of dancing. Lacking such skills, Capriol beseeches Arbeau to share his knowledge, and *Orchésographie* proceeds as tutorial, with the master instructing his pupil in the steps and behavioral protocols of a dozen recreational dances. Arbeau maps out the dances on the page (Figure 1.1) while simultaneously expounding on the virtues of dancing for well-being and social advancement.[3] Here, the master/tutor is one who knows of the physical decorum required in privileged society; choreography is not only the subject matter of his knowledge but also a means for him to communicate this knowledge to his less experienced pupil. The exchanges between the master and student, as in many pedagogical contexts, simulate the protocols and customs the student will later encounter within the social realms he is learning how to enter, which in this case is the aristocratic court

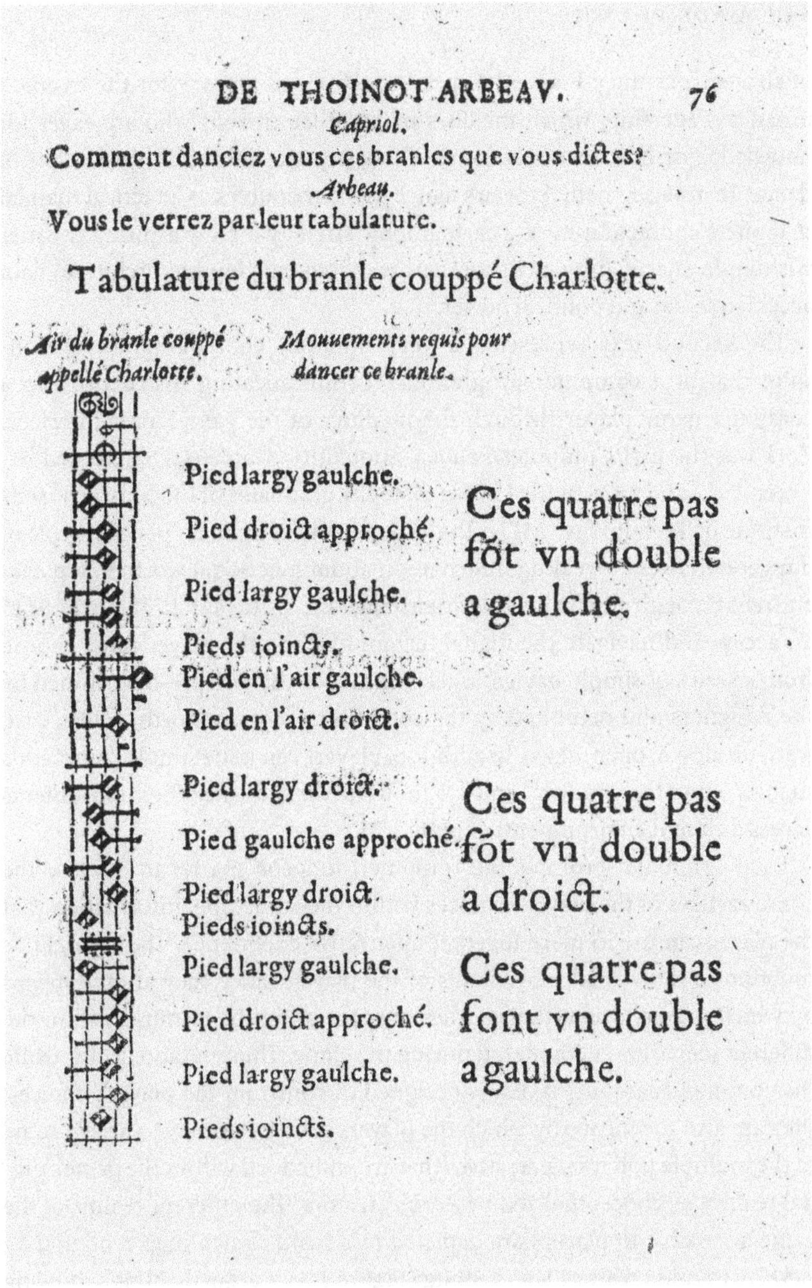

Capriol.

Comment danciez vous ces branles que vous diĉtes?

Arbeau.

Vous le verrez par leur tabulature.

Tabulature du branle couppé Charlotte.

Air du branle couppé appellé Charlotte.   *Mouuements requis pour dancer ce branle.*

Pied largy gaulche.

Pied droiĉt approché.

Pied largy gaulche.

Ces quatre pas fõt vn double a gaulche.

Pieds ioinĉts.

Pied en l'air gaulche.

Pied en l'air droiĉt.

Pied largy droiĉt.

Pied gaulche approché.

Pied largy droiĉt.

Pieds ioinĉts.

Ces quatre pas fõt vn double a droiĉt.

Pied largy gaulche.

Pied droiĉt approché.

Pied largy gaulche.

Ces quatre pas font vn double a gaulche.

Pieds ioinĉts.

Figure 1.1 Page from Arbeau's *Orchésographie*, with an example of conversational text between master and student, followed by image of Arbeau's notation of a simple Renaissance dance called a mixed branle, titled *Charlotte*. Thoinot Arbeau, *Orchésographie. Et traicte en forme de dialogve, par lequvel tovtes personnes pevvent facilment apprendre & practiquer l'honneste exercise des dances* (Imprimé par Iehan des Prevz, Lengre, monographic, 1589), image, Library of Congress, Music Division, https://www.loc.gov/55003658/.

of sixteenth-century France.[4] Capriol functions as a proxy for the treatise's broader readership, which includes many other citizens who are eager for knowledge of how to negotiate royal society via the skillful execution of dance. In a sense, then, Arbeau's dance manual doubles as a tactical manual that offers choreography as a cartographic strategy for any aspiring courtier wishing to successfully navigate their way into existing hierarchies to gain access to social and political power.[5]

The second text represents a very different choreographic relationship: that of a computer programmer communicating instructions to a computer game player through the medium of the game's user interface. *Zork* was the first Computer Fantasy Simulation Game (CFS), created between 1977 and 1979 in the United States by graduates of the Massachusetts Institute of Technology (MIT). In the game, the computer "plays the role of dungeon master," revealing information about a fictional world to a player entirely through descriptive, written language (Murray [1997] 2017:91).[6] To access and navigate the digital terrain of *Zork*, the player must choose from a series of simple navigational commands that are pre-determined by the designers and delimited by the computer program: north, south, east, west, up, down, open, close. In addition, players can issue simple commands such as "open the window" and "go in" to further advance their movements across different environments (Figure 1.2).

Each command prompts the computer/dungeon master to disclose the consequences of the player's choices within the landscape, information that the player can use to piece together a narrative experience. The commands function as the virtual movements of the players since they are the means by which players orient their bodies in space and time to move within the different scenarios encountered during the game. Thus, paradoxically, while the commands are intentionally designed to constrain the player's choices, they are also the means by which the players exercise agency to access some of the multiple potential narratives that are embedded within the game's digital realms, as conceptualized by *Zork*'s creators. The different realms of the game accessible to players are depicted in a hand-drawn map rendered by *Zork* artist and creator Dave Lebling (Figure 1.3). I argue Lebling's drawing is evidence of what theater scholar Rachel Fensham, in commenting on the research of Foster, identifies as a "cartographic imagination," that surfaces as "a means for managing embodied knowledge" (2014:101). Through the game's structure of command and response, *Zork* offers a form of dialogic

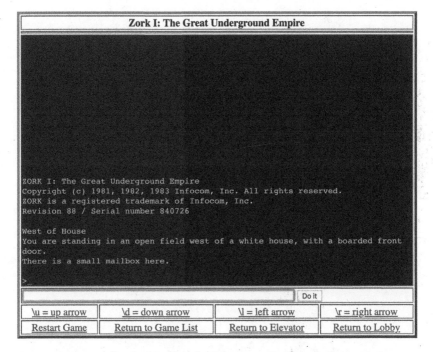

```
                    Zork I: The Great Underground Empire




ZORK I: The Great Underground Empire
Copyright (c) 1981, 1982, 1983 Infocom, Inc. All rights reserved.
ZORK is a registered trademark of Infocom, Inc.
Revision 88 / Serial number 840726

West of House
You are standing in an open field west of a white house, with a boarded front
door.
There is a small mailbox here.

>_
                                                   Do it
```

\u = up arrow	\d = down arrow	\l = left arrow	\r = right arrow
Restart Game	Return to Game List	Return to Elevator	Return to Lobby

Figure 1.2 Screenshot image of *Zork I: The Great Underground Empire* game during online play, August 2019. *Zork I* copyright © 1981, 1982, 1983 by Infocom, Inc., and copyright © 2000 by Activision, Inc. Screenshot image by the author captured from iFiction website, courtesy of Dave Walton, webmaster, www.iFiction.org.

communication, albeit with imperative undertones, in which the player chooses from among available commands, and the computer program responds to each choice by telling the player the impact of that choice.[7] Over the course of the game, the player's imagined experience of embodiment within the virtual world is incrementally informed and gradually understood through command and response.[8]

While the two examples that open this chapter may originate in different contexts and apply choreography toward different goals—*Orchésographie* toward the creation of a new persona, and *Zork* toward the creation of an adventurous virtual experience—both applications of choreography are designed to facilitate the individual's entry to a new world. Both Arbeau and the designers of *Zork* deploy written instructions to guide their audiences'

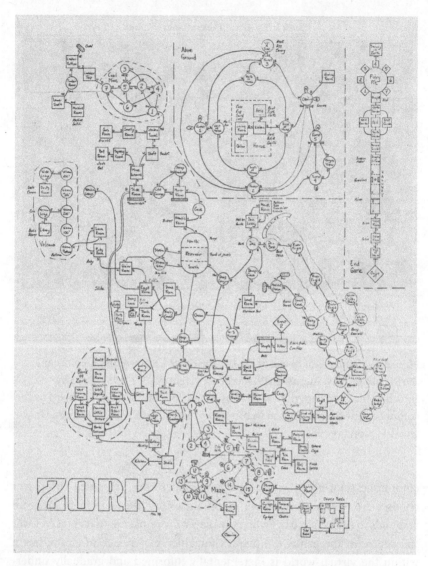

Figure 1.3 Artist and *Zork* creator Dave Lebling created this hand-drawn map of the game's "Great Underground Empire" in the late 1970s. Artist: Dave Lebling. Photographer: Rick Thornquist. Image courtesy of Dave Lebling.

behavior and embodiment, whether manifested in reality or projected into virtual contexts, by identifying movement and action as strategies that individuals can use to access unfamiliar realms.[9] The sixteenth-century court and the virtual realm of *Zork* are both places that demand permission for entry, or at least demand that entrants display certain kinds of behaviors and exercise specific skills of negotiation and navigation.

Although the term *choreography* had yet to be coined during the European Renaissance, the practice of choreography is nonetheless embedded within manuals such as those written by Arbeau, wherein three-dimensional movement is translated into instructional language and notational drawings. By the mid-twentieth century, the planning and design of embodied experiences began to be evidenced in the emergence of computer culture, particularly within video game design and digital storytelling; participants in these contexts experience choreography either entirely through their imagination or through an animated avatar, such as Super Mario (Figure 1.4), the hero of the popular Nintendo platform game *Super Mario Bros.*[10] Both passages in the opening of this chapter, from *Orchésographie* and *Zork*, represent contexts in which a master envisions an imagined participant as a mobile, physical subject, and places that participant at the center of a choreographic process. Within this process, a range of bodily based, physicalized directives are conceptualized and presented to individuals as a means for their participation within a new world, whether real or virtual. And indeed, both *Orchésographie* and *Zork* demonstrate the effectiveness of choreography as a tool for imposing the choreographer's intention and artistic vision upon individuals. Choreographic influence can occur whether or not the individuals being choreographed deliberately accept the opportunity to participate

Figure 1.4 Screenshot by the author of Nintendo Co., Ltd. video game company website page listing some of the physical skills of Mario, the eponymous avatar of Nintendo's *Super Mario Bros.* game franchise as follows: "Run-Dash-Jump." August 2019.

in the choreography; in some cases, individuals may even engage unknowingly in a process of being choreographed.

My expansive definition of choreography as a ubiquitous yet invisible technique for structuring embodiment naturally raises the question of what choreography is doing in the present day. Where and how might this practice be operating in the twenty-first century? Particularly fruitful sites of analysis are the new forms of participatory entertainment that emerged worldwide in the past two decades.[11] In these participatory productions, especially within the live performances that have been grouped under the label of "immersive theater," how might choreography be operating? The often-stated intention of immersive productions is to go beyond merely presenting performances for observers and rather to physically immerse spectators within experiential performance contexts. If we go looking for choreography in these new forms, what might we discover? How does the immersion of spectators occur within these productions, and what role might choreography play in that immersion? Can choreography in fact be understood as a means by which immersive practitioners intentionally influence spectators' perceptions such that immersion manifests as an affective outcome of their participation?

In using the term *immersive productions*, I am referring to works that aim to situate audiences as central within theatrical worlds specifically curated and designed to accommodate physical as well as cognitive and emotional participation. Two examples, among countless international options, are the productions *Sleep No More* (2011, hereafter *SNM*) and *Say Something Bunny!* (2018, hereafter *SSB*). The former is a New York City production of the UK-based Punchdrunk company, considered pioneers of immersive theater, in which hundreds of audience members are welcomed as guests to a building designed as a hotel. Audiences, cast as guests, must physically move throughout the hotel while adhering to the behavioral guidelines explained upon their entry, following around the performers whose choreographed movements reveal multiple storylines. By contrast, *SSB*, a "one-woman" production by Alison S. M. Kobayashi, invites a small group of spectators into a tiny apartment where they are seated strategically around a circular table, cast as extended family members.[12] Once seated, audiences are guided by Kobayashi to reconstruct the actions and arguments of a family dinner that ultimately culminates in a pivotal event. In *SNM*, Punchdrunk's choreography operates on multiple levels, as the setting itself, a labyrinth-like hotel, has been choreographed to compel the spectators-as-guests to move through space in order to discover the choreographed performances of the dancers.

The architectural and human choreography work together to provide audiences with experiences from which they can construct meaning. In *SSB*, on the other hand, Kobayashi's choreography tightly structures the participation of those seated at the table so that each member of this intimate gathering is involved in specific actions that contribute to the development of a linear narrative. Considered side by side, these two very different immersive productions help to illustrate how different applications of choreography, including its application to spectators, can be implemented toward a goal such as immersion. Choreography does, indeed, appear to be functioning in immersive theater, providing a means for both guiding and constraining specific embodied actions. In this way, choreography continues its long history within Western theatrical traditions as an effective technology for organizing embodiment.

The aim of this chapter is to contextualize, historicize, and theorize choreography as a strategy for engaging audience participation within immersive theater, or more broadly, immersive performance, which as a descriptor holds both dance and theater *in tandem*. In order to do so, however, we must understand how, in immersive productions, dance serves a dual, or dyadic, function. On one side of that dyad, a dance can be what some immersive practitioners refer to as a *track*. It can be choreographed and performed by cast members (paid professional performers) to communicate the content of the production to audiences and immerse them in its storyworld, as designed for their participation.[13] This "track" occurs often, but not exclusively, through the physicalization of narrative through choreography, which is crafted to express elements of the story through both representational and abstracted methods. The other side of the dance dyad relates to what I argue is a choreographic *score*, akin to a musical score. Through this score, the audiences themselves can be choreographed, such that they might experience immersion, among other affective outcomes, through their physical participation and their interactions with performers and other audience participants during performances. The choreographic scores that facilitate spectators' immersion are offered to them through performers' speech and actions, as well as through the spatial design itself, that together guide spectators' experiences within the production.

Crucially, the two sides of the choreographic dyad—the "track" of content enacted by performers and the "score" structures that guide audiences—are contiguous. While each choreographic framework is designed as a distinct structure, the two components are also linked in their common purpose: to serve as forms of content as well as critical processes through which the immersion of audiences is intended to occur. Audience participation is intentionally facilitated toward the goal of immersing audience members in the production, first by offering them opportunities to observe movement performed by professionals, and second, by setting the conditions for choreography to be the means by which audiences physically involve themselves in the action of the production. The duality of the choreographic structure is, I argue, our basis for understanding the performance of an immersive production as a sort of *tandem dance* between performers and audiences. In this chapter and the rest of the book, I investigate both sides of this dyadic relationship, addressing the former, the *track* (choreography as content enacted by paid performers) in order to explore in detail the latter, the *score* (choreography as structure for audience participation). In this way, we come to understand how immersive productions situate audiences as subjects of choreography.

My work of historicizing and theorizing dance in immersive performance is guided by two critical and interrelated characteristics of choreography, its intentionality and its portability. These characteristics help explain how, in the twenty-first century, choreography has become so ubiquitous as to be invisible to those whose lives it structures. To say that choreography is characterized by *intentionality* is to recognize that it exists to express the intention of its designer—be that a choreographer, director, or other practitioner—and that it can be applied anywhere that bodies' movements are consciously structured. The examples of Arbeau, *Zork*, Punchdrunk, and Kobayashi illustrate choreography's versatility as an effective technology. Simply put, choreography can occur anywhere that human bodies exist and someone has intentions as to how they should move. The *portability* of choreography, in turn, helps to explain how choreography has come to exist virtually everywhere. Choreography works by transferring the intentions of the choreographer onto the body of whoever is being choreographed, and this transfer can occur in so many different kinds of settings and contexts that the process often goes unnoticed, rendering the choreography itself invisible.

Recognizing the intentionality and portability of choreography, and particularly how these features have contributed to choreography's ubiquity and invisibility, is critical to an examination of how audiences of immersive performance are choreographed. The intricacies and implications of how choreography unfolds in immersive productions will be teased out in due time in the chapters that follow. For the rest of this chapter, I trace the use of choreography as a term and practice across the complex landscape of contemporary Western performance and cultural practices. This background serves to underscore my claims for how and why choreography has come to function as a central component of immersive performance, particularly as a means for organizing the participation of audiences—even if this function of choreography has previously gone unrecognized.

Intentionality

A common definition of choreography is "the art or practice of designing choreographic sequences."[14] The verb *design* is generally understood as involving the intent of the designer, who plans the design with a specific purpose or goal in mind. Choreography can thus be seen as an intentional exercise in realizing artistic and aesthetic purposes, with its intentionality referring to its purposefulness as a means for organizing behavior and structuring human experiences of embodiment.[15] The term *intentionality*, as I deploy it here, is not to be conflated with the phenomenological concept of intentionality, nor with choreographic intent as it has been considered within the discourse of dance studies as a means by which artists aim to have audiences experience certain emotions or feelings by observing the actions of dancers.[16] Rather, when I refer to intention and intentionality, I am specifically attending to what I understand to be the deliberate design choices of immersive practitioners, that is, whatever goals they are trying to accomplish when they design their productions. While I acknowledge Sedgman's warning not to "conflate intention with audience reception," meaning audience participation may not necessarily be democratic or empowering, even if that is what practitioners desire (cautions also expressed by Alston and Harvie), in the pages that follow, I explore the workings of immersive practitioners' choreographic intentionality and particularly the *perception* of agency within choreography. I argue that choreographic intentionality can be understood as a desire to shift spectators from traditional roles as observers into subjects of choreography (2018:291).[17] As subjects, their motion instantiates scores designed by practitioners, and yet spectators can *perceive* themselves as making things happen in the production specifically through their presence, agency, and actions. It is the *perception* of agency within choreography, by audiences, practitioners, or both, that is key to the discussion here.

As a starting point for understanding choreographic intentionality in Western theatrical dance, we can look to the European court dance of Arbeau (recognizing that the Renaissance was informed by ancient Greek practices), and notice how the choreographer serves as the designer of intent and the dancers serve to enact and instantiate that intention through the dance. Here we can intuit why it was desirable to keep hidden the choreographic mechanisms at play: because aesthetic motivations aside, in the early modern court, the social and political roles that choreography sought to reinforce were meant to be mistaken for reality itself. This dynamic is not so unlike what we see in twenty-first-century immersive productions, where the pressing need to hide the mechanics of a production, especially its choreography, stems from the complex relationship between free will and control that enables audience participation. These dynamics must be delicately navigated in order to facilitate the choreographed spectator's immersion within a new, perhaps unfamiliar world. The spectators within a work of immersive performance may generally acquiesce (or at least, not refuse) to engage in the production, but their movements and behaviors occur at least partly in accordance with the intentions of the choreographer, director, or designer of the production, and are contained within the production itself.

The operation of intentionality is, indeed, precisely how art in any form is made. In Graham McFee's analytical dance philosophy, a work of art that is constituted of dance can be understood, in the abstract sense, as a *dancework*, which can be materialized many times over on various occasions, albeit with variations in such details as casts, audiences, and stagings, in *performables* (2011:3). Like any artworks, danceworks are "intentional [. . .] embodying the intelligence (or the intention) of their creators" (267). Following McFee, I assert that many immersive performance events could be categorized as performables, including those discussed in this book; this classification helps us get at an understanding of the creator's role in and responsibility for the intentionality of the choreographic work, and to gain clarity about the role of audience as performer, that is, one who instantiates choreography. McFee avers that the failure to recognize intentional movement as part of a dancework is to "misperceive[e]" that work (16), and indeed, I argue that it is the misperception of movement in immersive performance that has contributed to the under-theorization of choreography in these works to date.

What is complicated about intentionality within immersive productions, of course, is that the intentions of audience participants also become involved, becoming entangled with the intentions of the designer(s) of the production as the production unfolds. While we may not know what precisely audiences intend through their performances, we can still make some sense of their work, specifically the sense in which their labor is a response to or enactment of choreography that was intentionally designed (by practitioners and performers) to structure their (the audience participants') movements.[18] If, as suggested previously, we accept audience participants as instantiating the scores provided by choreographers, then there may be a sense in which we can also accept them as co-authors of the performance. In that case, in what sense are their contributions differentiated from the part of the production for which the creators themselves are responsible? The answer to this question hinges on our understanding of what is happening to the spectator's body during the process of immersion: specifically, what sort of transformation is occurring, and what the spectator is being transformed into.

Transfiguration

The application of intention transforms the *material* of moving bodies into the *art* of dance. To understand how, we can look to philosopher Arthur C. Danto's views on visual arts, which influenced McFee's views on dance. In *The Transfiguration of the Commonplace: A Philosophy of Art*, Danto theorizes that "banal objects become transfigured into works of art" (1981:v) through a process of transfiguration.[19] According to Danto, objects like Marcel Duchamp's urinal (*Fountain*, New York City, 1917) and Andy Warhol's Brillo Boxes (*Brillo Soap Pad Box*, New York City, 1964) came to be accepted within the artistic canon because they had been transfigured from ordinary objects into artworks merely through "intention and context" (vii). For Danto, "really *no* material differences need distinguish the artwork from the real thing" (vii). Similarly, in the realm of dance, McFee asserts that dance is transfigured movement; even a movement as ordinary as sweeping the floor can be transfigured into art when it is contextualized as dance (2011:16). Just as McFee and Danto understand art as the transfiguration of "mere real things," I argue that in immersive performance, the art of the production—including the objectification of experience as art, following Alston—is created through the transfiguration of the embodied spectators (Danto 1981:104).[20] As I understand it, the audience participants in immersive performance become part of the choreographic intentionality when they, as spectators, are situated as subjects of choreography. This notion of audience participants as the materials of immersive performance has also been put forth by Gareth White and other scholars. Spectators' actions and motions must be recognized as artistically intentional because, even though they may seem ordinary, they are intentionally elicited as part of the immersive production, at least to the extent that audiences are often mobile rather than seated. When spectator actions are transfigured into the artistic work, they become the crux of the audience's inclusion as participants in the art of the production.

The transformation of human spectators into materials of the production (i.e., immersed participants) requires careful planning by immersive practitioners. Just like Duchamp had to conceptualize, plan for, and implement his urinal to exhibit as *Fountain*, so too do immersive practitioners when involving the moving and acting presence of the audience. What I am ascribing as the intention of immersive practitioners—to transform spectators into subjects of choreography—is precisely the transfiguration of spectators from the commonplace into art, or at least into performers whose enactment (instantiation, following McFee) of the improvisational scores constitutes the artistic experience. In such situations, spectators can be understood as functioning somewhat like "ready-mades," or found objects repurposed into works of art, following Duchamp. Dance scholar Mark Franko has made a similar connection:

> Pedestrian movement has conceptual links to the readymade—it is not mass produced but produced [. . .] by the masses—and has radical implication for dance making. Pedestrian movement acknowledges that dancing comes from the streets, from the way that ordinary people move there. [. . .] [F]ound movement reveals *the person in the dancer* rather than the dancer in the person. What pedestrian movement tells us is that bodies in ordinary motion are dance readymades. (2000:214, emphasis original)

Given the cultural zeitgeist in which immersive performance developed, which will be detailed later in this chapter, immersive practitioners are intending to offer the opportunity for spectators to shift from a banal existence, that is, experiences of traditional presentations of performance, to an extraordinary one by elevating them into art. As such, I believe that immersive practitioners conceptualize and choreograph for the potentiality of audience participants contributing content that is, within limits, original. Whether audiences themselves consider their involvement to be dancing, they are, nonetheless, subjects of choreography. And this subjectification occurs in a larger twenty-first-century context of the world at large, not just the art-world, opening up for the inclusion of audiences in participatory and creatively agentive ways.

Objects-in-Motion

If choreography is the means by which the artist (choreographer, director, or designer) transfigures ordinary materials—the moving bodies of the choreographed—into art, then what do we make of the fact that these materials are sentient? What is the spectator's affective experience of being choreographed? To dance is to *become* the dance, according to dance philosopher Maxine Sheets-Johnston, who writes that "the dance comes alive precisely as the dancers are *implicitly* aware of themselves and the form, such that the form moves through them" (1966:3, emphasis original). Critically, Sheets-Johnstone characterizes dancers as being "*immersed* in what they are creating" (3, emphasis added), implying that dance *qua* dance is by its very nature an immersive experience, whatever the circumstance. In her article "On Movement and Objects in Motion: The Phenomenology of the Visible in Dance" (1979), Sheets-Johnstone sets forth a distinction between "objects in motion," which *do* movement, and "objects-in-motion," which *become* movement. In dance, Sheets-Johnstone explains, dancers become the latter as they are transfigured, precisely through their bodily motion, from commonplace objects (so to speak) into extraordinary ones.

Sheets-Johnstone's assertion of the oneness between the dancer and the dance, which has been promulgated throughout the literature on dance studies, poses intriguing possibilities for how we might understand the affective experience of spectators in immersive productions, who are, I am arguing, subjects of choreography.[21] Applying her concept of object-in-motion to immersive performance, we can sense how a spectator's participation in the choreography contributes to their perceptual manifestation of the immersive world. According to Sheets-Johnstone, objects-in-motion "create their own space-time and in effect create a world peculiar to their own immediate presence" (40). In addition, such an object has "the generative power to bring certain things to pass; in its power to initiate motion, it commands a power of *doingness* by which [it] can *make something happen*" (41, emphasis added). The performance is not merely occurring in the storyworld—the dramaturgically, scenographically designed context and circumstances of the production as designed by the creators—but in fact, is being *made to happen* by the audience members who create a space-time experience as they move through the production. It is only by intentionally surrendering to the movement—engaging in the "doingness" of the choreography through instantiation of the score—that these spectators can hope to become a presence, make things happen, and experience perceptions of agentive impact.[22] The possibility of exercising agency through physical movement rather than passive embodiment is precisely what fuels the desire for participatory engagement that we see in individuals who seek immersive experiences in the twenty-first century. As Sheets-Johnstone puts it, "To be an object-in-motion is to fulfill a kinetic destiny, and to fulfill a kinetic destiny is to bring a qualitative world to life" (43). The intentionality of choreography in immersive performance, it turns out, may not be only that of the choreographer: the spectator, too, may dance with the possibility of agentively transforming movement into art. This potential to choreograph the spectator is made possible by a second feature of choreography: the readiness with which it can be transported to new realms and situations.

Portability

Choreography's effectiveness as a technology for transferring intentions from one person's body to another's renders this technology *portable*: it can be brought into any number of different contexts where bodies move deliberately. The discipline of dance does not have a monopoly on choreography any more than it has a monopoly on movement. Rather, choreography is a versatile practice that has been and can be adopted, adapted, and applied by different individuals across multiple contexts, ranging from the aesthetic to the utilitarian. By examining the history and lineage of choreography, we can shed light on how immersive practitioners are able to adapt choreographic techniques for transferring bodily intentionality. In asserting choreography's adaptability to a wide range of contexts, I am not dismissing the role that dance has played in establishing choreography as a technology; instead I am expanding the conversation to include the ways in which choreography functions broadly—a discussion that, in fact, draws attention back to the concepts from dance that underpin choreography. My analysis here intersects with dance scholar Kate Elswit's notion of the interdependency between theater and dance, which she deploys to analyze how the two disciplines share the concepts of theatricality and embodiment, among other concepts. Drawing upon Elswit's framing, I consider how choreography has operated as an important nexus of the interdependency between theater and dance forms as they have expanded to influence other forms of artistic creation, and I show how this operation of choreography sets the stage for the emergence of immersive performance.

Because there is no singular, linear progression of choreography's evolution as either a term or a practice toward its incorporation as a fundamental component of immersive performance, I focus here on tracing how, as it has developed over the centuries as a modality of public participation, its application has reinforced and perpetuated notions of control and power via European ideologies of socialization. Specifically, I examine dance and choreography using lenses informed by and focused on the histories of European and Anglo-American societies because this geographic and cultural focal point allows me to trace the specific origins of the term *chorégraphie* all the way from its introduction at the start of the eighteenth century in France to its contemporary usage as the Anglicized term *choreography* that refers to a range of intentional practices of organizing, directing, and controlling human behavior, particularly movement. Across a range of fields, I historicize and contextualize choreography from its early modern origins, through its presence in modernist, avant-garde, and postmodern dance, before considering two specific lineages in the twentieth century: physical theater and digital storytelling. The former has roots in the avant-garde and postmodern movements, while the latter emerged mid-century through advances in computer programming. I argue that both incorporate choreographic thinking in ways that have profoundly impacted the development of immersive design.

Early Modern Origins

Choreography, as we understand it within the Western theatrical dance discourse tradition, emerged in the early modern period as a practice and discipline for organizing systems of behavior in space and time by rewriting social relationships among constituencies.[23] Choreography's socio-political agenda of establishing new subjectivities and relationships between those who dance and those who watch is precisely what first distinguished the concept of choreography from dance itself. The sixteenth- and seventeenth-century European Renaissance of Thoinot Arbeau, alluded to in the opening to this chapter, is a natural place to begin tracing the portability of choreography. It is here that (portable) dance manuals like Arbeau's first served to make accessible the activity of learning choreographed dances, contributing to choreography's emerging role as a mode of control toward the engendering of specific kinds of socialization. Although the term *choreography* would not emerge until the eighteenth century, the concept was already operational among European aristocracy in the sixteenth century who used dance to reinforce structures of ritual and power when assigning societal roles. The dancing manuals written by Arbeau and others illuminate how choreography first emerged as a mode of socialization, as these texts explained and prescribed choreography such that the social roles it assigned would appear inevitable and natural.

When titling his dancing manual, Arbeau chose the term *orchésographie*, meaning "theory of dancing," which has as its root the Latin terms *orchesis*, the "art of dancing," and *orchesthai*, "to dance." Not until 1700, over a century later, would the term *chorégraphie* be introduced, as Raoul Auger Feuillet began recording dances via dance notation as per Figure 1.5 (Foster 2009:100).[24] Yet, evidence suggests that as early as the fifth century B.C., choreography was practiced by the ancient Greek figure of *khoregus*, who prepared and led groups of performers in song, dance, and text staged for audiences during ritual competitions (Cohen 1974:1). The term *khoros* referred to the group (chorus) as well as the dance performed. *Khoregus* would later become the root word for choreographer. Given this etymology, Feuillet's term *chorégraphie* literally means "dance-writing," emerging from a Latinized form of Greek *khoreia* (indicating chorus, or more specifically a circular dance accompanied by a singing chorus) and *graphein* (to write, as in writing down text, e.g., notating a dance).

Treatises by Arbeau, and those written later by Feuillet and others, reflect these dancing masters' concerted efforts to increase the general public's participatory engagement with dance.[25] Whereas the nobility had no need of treatises since they could afford to employ the dancing masters directly, the general populace benefited greatly from the availability of such texts. Written instructions were the educational means for those who wished to participate in culture by learning to dance. Dance manuals and treatises can thus be understood as presaging the instructional scores used by artists throughout the twentieth century, and now by immersive practitioners in the twenty-first. Dance scholar Margaret McGowan notes that the dance manuals of this period conspicuously lack any discussion of the pleasures to be found

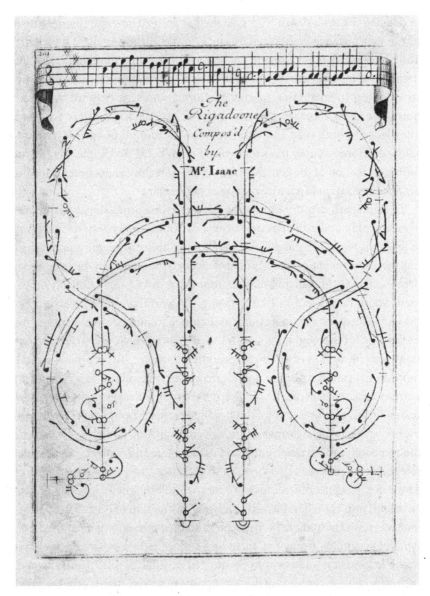

Figure 1.5 Image of Feuillet's notation for a dance titled *The Rigadoon*. Raoul-Auger Feuiller, *Orchesography; or, The art of dancing by characters and demonstrative figures Wherein the whole art is explain'd; with compleat tables of all steps us'd in dancing, and rules from the motions of the arms &c. Whereby any person who understands dancing may of himself learn all manner of dances* [Printed for, & sold by Ino. Walsh . . ., London, monographic, 1715], image, Library of Congress, Music Division, https//:www.loc.gov/item/22022367.

in dancing; instead, dance is "proclaimed as an instrument of management in the first instance, and a step towards power in the second" (2008:18).[26] The term *choreography* came to encompass the distinct development of the notation of movement, organized in such a way that one person could instruct others to take action specifically through the written word. As Foster notes, the term *choreography* was adopted by dancing masters who had knowledge to both read and write notation; as more intricate notation developed, choreographic treatises evolved from being accessible documents for the education of the general public to being technical documents for the professionalization of a narrow group of performers.

In eighteenth-century Europe, as dance became professionalized, choreography came under the purview of experts. Dancing masters, once serving as teachers, took on expanded roles as choreographers, designing and directing the movements of professional dancers. Choreography became more complicated as the dancing masters innovated increasingly difficult movement vocabularies and intricate staging. A definitive split opened up between performers and spectators, and choreography became a means for professionals (choreographers) to transfer their aesthetic and artistic intentions onto the bodies of other professionals (dancers). The move toward the professionalization of dance and choreography was about more than just putting dancers on stage; it was also reflective of a deeper political and economic shift, as power and wealth began to transfer from the aristocracy to the bourgeoisie.[27] The former dancers of court, mostly nobility, now became the audience of the theater venue, and as the venue and context shift, distinct roles begin to emerge for performer and audience. The professionalization of dance in the eighteenth-century Western world brought an infusion of new meanings into choreography as it took on the function of organizing performances viewed by audiences. These new modes of presentation required new types of spectating behaviors, including a more sedentary disposition, that is, the impetus for audiences to be situated in seats, be silent, and applaud, with each behavior enacted at the appropriate moment. Artists of subsequent generations would go on to problematize the split between performers and spectators in numerous ways, experimenting to create art that established different kinds of relationships with audiences.

Modernism

With the introduction of modern dance in the late nineteenth century, choreographic intentions shifted again, and artists continued to explore dance's purposiveness into the twentieth century. With each new artistic movement, artists were reconsidering issues of authorship and their relationship with the audience. Foster claims that the term *choreographer*, having fallen out of use in the eighteenth and nineteenth centuries, resurfaced in the late 1920s and early 1930s "with a new urgency and immediacy [...] in response to the radical approaches to dance-making associated with the burgeoning genre known as modern dance" (2016).[28] The authorial position of the choreographer, which had been established in the previous century as dance was professionalized, solidified further in the twentieth with the development of modern dance. This form emerged in the early twentieth century through the choreographic inventions of American pioneers such as Loïe Fuller and Isadora Duncan, as well as the experiments of German dance artists who predated the avant-garde Futurists and Dadaists. Fuller incorporated technology such as incandescent lights and voluminous fabric to create abstract imagery through dance, a departure from previous emphasis on narrative representation (Merwin 1998:79). Isadora Duncan's choreographic experiments also broke with traditional forms and techniques of expression, such as European ballet, by having dancers go barefoot and perform in gardens and other sites beyond proscenium theaters where they could come into closer proximity to audiences. Both Fuller and Duncan explored choreographic structures through which audiences could find new ways to connect to dance cognitively, aesthetically, spiritually, and kinesthetically. By developing new vocabularies, aesthetic visions, and presentation formats, these women brought about the emergence of new visions of choreography through which audiences in the United States and abroad were challenged to understand and spectate dance differently.

First-Wave Avant-Gardes

Another, concurrent precedent for immersive performance was the choreographic experimentation conducted in Europe by early-twentieth-century avant-garde artists working in music, theater, and visual arts, who newly explored ways to evoke and organize the movement of spectators in response to performances.[29] In the early 1900s, the Futurists and the Dadaists created—or, one could argue, choreographed—events around political and absurdist content that were intended to provoke audiences cognitively and physically. British art historian and critic Claire Bishop suggests these events took shape via two distinctly avant-garde approaches to audience participation: "an authored tradition that seeks to provoke participants" and "a de-authored lineage that aims to embrace collective creativity" (2006:11).[30] Describing them as either "disruptive and interventionist" or "constructive and ameliorative," Bishop asserts that these approaches continue to influence the practices and aesthetics of artists making participatory works to this day. The Futurists and Dadaists could never be sure of the types of responses they would receive from audiences; chaotic and violent responses were welcomed, even sought. The early events of the Zurich-based Dadaists are one such example, staged at the Cabaret Voltaire by German poet Hugo Ball. In a 1916 performance of *Flucht aus der Zeit* (Flight out of Time), Ball wore a cardboard costume he had created to resemble the cloak of an archbishop and chanted a nonsensical sound poem intended to question the sanctity of religious language. Another Dadaist who witnessed the performance, Tristan Tzara, described the audience as working themselves into a frenzy and tearing at Ball's costume (Young 1981:20). After such performances, audience discomfort with the perceived nonsense or blasphemy sent them out into the streets in varying states of unrest (Groys 2008:25). What audience members actually did next was of little concern to the Dadaists; the point was to activate audiences and move them beyond what the Dadaists perceived to be bourgeois complacency and passivity.

The European first wave of avant-garde reached its nadir in the "theater of cruelty" created by French playwright and drama theorist Antonin Artaud in the early 1930s. This philosophy and practice of theater, manifested in writings and live performance events, was based on Artaud's belief that "our sensibility has reached the point where we surely need theatre that wakes us up heart and nerves" (2014:33).[31] An initial inspiration for Artaud's work was a group of Balinese dancers he witnessed performing at the Paris Colonial Exposition in 1931.[32] Artaud later wrote of "the feeling of a new bodily language no longer based on words but on signs which emerges through the maze of gestures, postures" (Artaud quoted by Savarese and Fowler 2001:51). According to dance scholar Ana Sánchez-Colberg, this search for "language beyond words" led to Artaud's theater "being one of the phenomenal body, not only because the body is the center of the *mise-en-scène*" but because it placed the body outside the confines of language and prioritized a "metaphysics of the theatre via an immersion in the physical" (1996:43). Combining movement with lighting and sound, Artaud commenced with choreographing productions imbued with dark imagery and featuring fantastic sets, with the intention of disorientating audiences and evoking dream-like atmospheres and trance states in which various physical responses and reactions would be possible.

Second-Wave Avant-Gardes

The second wave of avant-garde artists, in America in the 1960s and 1970s, continued to experiment with strategies for eliciting specific audience responses and further expanded conceptions of art via participatory and interactive propositions for spectatorial engagement. Curator and art historian Sabine Breitwieser suggests that it was the visual artists of the 1920s who "started to choreograph their artworks like actors in a theater play space" (2016). Yet as the decades passed visual artists became increasingly interested in architectural space and the implications of time, shifting their intentions towards positioning "the organization of the art object in space and its encounter with the viewer [as] a major factor in their work" (2016). Pointing to the influential work of Allan Kaprow, particularly his *18 Happenings in 6 Parts* (New York City, 1959), Breitwieser suggests that events such as these "gave the impression of a broadening of rigid single-discipline art forms, accompanied by a departure from established art institutions" (2016). Kaprow's happenings, such as one where audiences were invited to climb around on and move large mountains of used tires, included the audience in what I consider to be choreographed, structured improvisations that prioritized participatory and interactive task-oriented assignments.[33] Indeed, Kaprow's stance was that in such productions where audiences participate willingly, they "become a real and necessary part of the work. It cannot exist without them" (2003:64). Similar participation is seen works by Yoko Ono, whose *Cut Piece* (Kyoto, 1964, and New York City, 1965) involved presenting her body to the audience as an object to be manipulated. She knelt on an empty stage wearing a suit jacket and skirt, with a pair of scissors in front of her, and instructed the audience members to come up to her and snip away bits and pieces of her clothing to take home with them, leaving her naked flesh exposed, and herself vulnerable to their agency and action.

Another strand of second-wave avant-garde work is that of theater director, scholar, and critic Richard Schechner, who in the late 1960s coined the term *environmental theater* for a genre in which he combined deconstructions of known dramatic texts with aspects of happenings, such as eliminating spatial divisions between audiences and performers and opening up possibilities for their interactions with one another and for audiences' participation in the action of the play.[34] Schechner's production of *Dionysus in 69* (*D69*), presented in New York City in 1968 deconstructs the classic Greek play *The Bacchae* by Euripides through an environment designed to allow both performers and audiences to participate. Following *D69*, Schechner proposed three rules for audience participation. First, the audience is in a living space and a living situation; things may happen to and with them as well as "in front of" them. Second, when a performer invites participation, they must be prepared to accept and deal with the spectators' reactions. Third, participation should not be gratuitous; for Schechner, "participation is only legitimate if it influences the tone and possibly the outcome of the performance" (2000:77–78). Some scholars have specifically cited environmental theater, in both concept and practice, as a precursor of immersive theater.[35]

New forms of choreographic, participatory, and interactive practices continued to emerge in American dance throughout the 1960 and 1970s. On the east coast, these innovations were largely inspired by the work that composer John Cage had done with aleatoric music in the 1950s and beyond. Cage's experimental sound compositions often incorporated chance elements, known as *chance operations*, that introduced indeterminate and random choice into creative processes, such as tossing a coin to determine the instrumentation, duration, and sequence of a composition.[36] Cage's artistic partnership with choreographer Merce Cunningham led to the incorporation of chance operations within the latter's choreographic methods; sound and movement may have no predetermined connection, and sequences could be determined by throwing dice. In pursuing aleatory techniques, Cunningham and Cage turned away from narrative and psychological themes, as found in the work of Martha Graham and other modernists of the previous generation, and these compositions opened up the possibility for audiences to more freely interpret what they encountered during performances.

On the west coast, dancer and choreographer Anna Halprin began innovating experimentation in dance in the 1930s. She founded the San Francisco Dancers' Workshop in 1955 and, for over fifty years, proceeded to create ground-breaking performances involving audience participation in both urban and rural landscapes. Halprin's *Parades and Changes*, which premiered in 1965, comprises multiple instructional scores that involve audiences participating in everyday tasks (Figure 1.6). One of the scores includes dressing and undressing, with audiences having the possibility to trade clothes with performers.[37] In her 1976 *City Dance*, dancers and members of the community moved along the city streets, stopping at specific points to engage in movement scores that had been publicized in local newspapers in advance of the performance. Among Halprin's students were Meredith Monk, Trisha Brown, Yvonne Rainer, and Simone Forti, who themselves became the next wave of dance artists, known as the postmodern generation.

An accompanist for Cunningham's classes, Robert Ellis Dunn, founded a series of workshops at Judson Church in New York City, where he encouraged students to subvert existing principles of dance composition by applying chance operations, as Cunningham had. Dunn's classes enabled new pedagogical and artistic frameworks that encouraged many artists, including Monk, Brown, and Rainer, as well as Steve Paxton, to question the choreographic processes of earlier dance artists and innovate their own creative practices.[38] For example, Brown began staging site-specific performances on SoHo's rooftops, while Monk was the first artist to create a work within the rotunda of the Guggenheim Museum in New York City (*Juice*, 1969). The events and happenings that emerged from Dunn's experimental workshops at Judson Church would irrevocably change conceptions of dance in the United States and influenced the work of dance artists throughout Canada, the United Kingdom, and beyond.

Postmodern Dance

The Judson Dance Theater artists' rigorous exploration and innovative application of choreography in different contexts suggested that choreography as a portable technology could be conceptualized and utilized differently even within the discipline of dance itself. The 1970s yielded a rich array of choreographic exploration, with the postmodern dance artists in North America, Europe, and other international locales pushing choreography in more conceptual directions and developing approaches through which they could further question their own creative practices as well as their relationships with audiences. Many postmodern dance artists, interested in expanding access to and participation in the choreographic process, afforded dancers

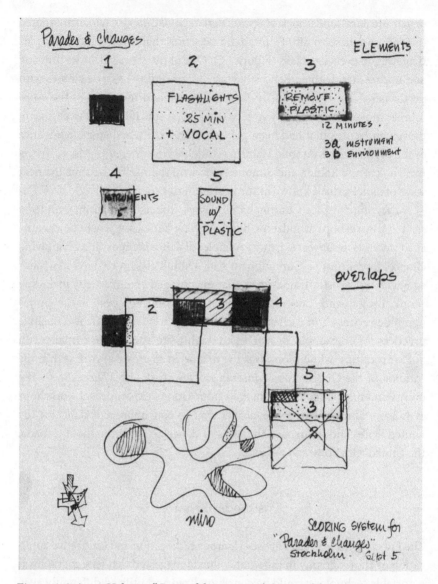

Figure 1.6 Anna Halprin, "Copy of dance score 'Elements' from Halprin's 'Parades and Changes,' Scoring System for Stockholm," *Anna Halprin Digital Archive*, accessed August 14, 2019, https://annahalprindigitalarchive.omeka. net/items/show/216. Anna Halprin Papers, The Elyse Eng Dance Collection, Museum of Performance + Design.

with opportunities to contribute to the creative process (rather than merely learning existing repertory) through the use of scores that allowed certain elements to be determined in the moment of performance. Following the axiom that "any body/anybody can dance," postmodern choreographers worked with artists from different disciplines as well as with nonprofessionals. While their artistic visions as individuals differed, their collective mission was to expand notions of beauty and equality, and to yield control and authorship, in hopes of achieving performances that were participatory and interactive. The postmodern generation of dance artists brought the audience into closer proximity by experimenting with, and sometimes stripping away, theatrical conventions. They performed in lofts and gallery spaces, not just proscenium stages; they wore their personal clothing in addition to designing elaborate costumes; and they worked with nonprofessionals as well as professionals through predetermined choreography as well as open-ended, improvisational scores devised to allow a wide range of individuals to participate. The postmodern choreographers' experimental strategies would expand possibilities for what dance could be, how it could be presented, and who could participate.

Postmodern dance is characterized by three practices that, to different degrees and extents, have gone on to serve the work of current twenty-first-century artists who utilize dance to create immersive performance. First, by shifting from formalized techniques to the incorporation of *pedestrian movement and practices of daily life*, postmodern dance artists investigated new movement vocabularies that could be easily understood by audiences, both in practice and interpretation, particularly if audience members, or pre-selected nonprofessional dancers, were enlisted as performers. In certain immersive productions, artistic directors incorporate pedestrian movement and practices of daily life as modes through which audiences participate in or gain access to performances. Second, postmodern choreographers' explorations of *probability*, as popularized by Cunningham and Cage's experimentation with chance operations, encouraged investigation of choreographic practices beyond formalist compositional skills. These investigations involved the development of experimental devices, including instructional, improvisational scores for dance.[39] Today, probability and chance operate in many immersive productions, in that performance events are designed to allow for a range of audience choices, which, in turn, affect how audiences experience the performance. Third, dance in immersive performance prioritizes *site specificity, site sensitivity* (including designed scenography), or both, to create possibilities for both artists and spectators to experience spaces of performance differently via broadly conceptualized ideas of proxemics and notions of intimacy. These features would all find new expression in the immersive productions that emerged at the end of the twentieth century and into the twenty-first.

Physical Theater

Acknowledging that *physical theater* is a contested term with a complicated history, scholars in both dance and theater cite the establishment of physical theater as a distinct genre in the 1980s in Europe, North America, and Australia.[40] As theater scholar Maiya Murphy notes, the term encompasses a wide range of forms, including "visually based theater, dance theater, mime, circus, movement theater, [and] commedia dell'arte," as well as the pedagogies of theater artists whose experiments gave shape to the genre (2015:126). As Sánchez-Colberg has noted, physical theater, by its very name, "denotes a hybrid character and is testimony to its double legacy in both avant-garde theatre and dance" (1996:41).[41] Theater scholars Simon Murray, John Keefe, and others emphasize that all theater is physical, noting that "the 'physical' in physical theatre is redundant excess, since all theatrical activity is embodied activity" (4). It is from this understanding of the *physical in theater*, including that which is found in *physical theater*, that I argue for the criticality of choreographic analysis and the theorizing of the choreographic within the discourses of live performance, specifically including immersive productions. Two key points about physical theater are critical for our purposes here: that the form is the most recent antecedent within the lineage of live performance avant-garde innovations from which immersive performance emerged, and that, as Elswit has shown, its emergence was tacitly premised on the borrowing of concepts and techniques from dance—a usage that was enabled by the portability of choreographic practices and by theater's long-privileged position in the performing arts.[42]

The origins of physical theater are identified by Murray and Keefe in their book *Physical Theatres: A Critical Introduction* (2007) as being rooted in a two-thousand-year-old Western theatrical tradition that includes mime, dance tradition, and avant-garde tradition (53). They assert that the "avant-garde is always with us" as "the rhythm and impulse of creative rejection," a notion furthered by Murphy in her analyses of the connections between postmodern dance and physical theater (64). Echoing their link to the avant-garde, Murphy states that physical theater and postmodern dance both "sought not a superficial change of style, but a much deeper change within the process of creating art itself—the demand for the performer to be endowed with a greater creative agency than traditional forms of Western theater and dance had allowed" (132). Murphy notes how the creators of physical theater and postmodern dance, whether choreographers or directors, enhance the agency of the performer by establishing "authorizing principles" that "validate" the power of the performer and afford them the "ability to act on the environment" (132). In both forms, performers can assert three levels of agency: "performing their role in the piece, creating their portion of the piece, and creating the piece's overall aesthetic structure" (132). While both postmodern dance and physical theater aimed to develop the agency of the performer, immersive practitioners would take this one step further and develop the agency of the spectator.

Importantly, by the 1980s, physical theater was recognized, according to Sánchez-Colberg, "as a distinct strategy of theatrical production which—as *tanztheater* had done in the 1970s—existed in the intersection of theatre and dance" (49). By connecting *tanztheater* and physical theater, Sánchez-Colberg alludes to the work of influential German choreographer Pina Bausch, whose career spanned from the 1970s through the 2000s, and points to the importance of choreography as an experimental technology of these burgeoning forms. Bausch's evening-length productions integrated choreography and theater in ways that troubled the boundaries between reality and artifice, contributing to the evolution of *dance theater* (*tanztheater*) as a distinct mode of performance that prioritized experimentation with theatricality via choreographic means in ways that preceded physical theater.[43] Bausch's choreographic approaches, involving sound, dance, and speech, have undoubtedly influenced immersive practitioners, although fulsome discussion of her influential oeuvre is beyond the scope of this project.[44]

Choreographic Thinking

Throughout this chapter, I have alluded obliquely to the concept of *choreographic thinking*. A precise definition is offered by the philosopher Erin Manning: "the activation, in the moving, of a movement of thought" (2012:103). In other words, to think choreographically is to translate ideas into embodied movements. Manning formulated this definition in close response to the work of American choreographer William Forsythe, who did much to develop the concept. For Forsythe, the choreographic object, the artifact in which choreography is encoded for transmission, can be thought of as a *score*, analogous to a musician's score, that is "by nature open to a full palette of phenomenological instigations because it acknowledges the body as wholly designed to persistently read every signal from its environment" (2011:91).[45] Forsythe's work, which is reflective of a long lineage of avant-garde experimental practice, has since the 1990s involved the creation of projects that involve audience participation in exploring what dance and choreography can do in the world.

One project, *White Bouncy Castle* (1997, London) created in collaboration with choreographer Dana Caspersen and composer Joel Ryan, premiered as the "world's largest bouncy castle," entirely filling The Roundhouse, a building 160 feet in diameter.[46] Filled with sound composed by Ryan and open to the public, *White Bouncy Castle* (Figure 1.7) offered to anyone who

Figure 1.7 William Forsythe, *White Bouncy Castle*, 1997. Created by Dana Caspersen, William Forsythe, and Joel Ryan. Photograph by Julian Gabriel Richter. © William Forsythe.

Figure 1.8 William Forsythe, *The Fact of Matter*, 2009. Installation view,
William Forsythe: The Fact of Matter, Museum für Moderne Kunst Frankfurt am
Main, Germany, 2015. Photo: Dominik Mentzos. © William Forsythe.

wished to enter the chance to "share the passion and recapture the instinc-
tive joy and the fearlessness with one's body that children possess" (Spier
2011:141). In this way, *White Bouncy Castle* served as a choreographic object, designed to elicit the physical engagement and exploration of audience
participants so that they, as well as Forsythe and Caspersen, could consider
the "fundamental and conceptual issues about the body in space, and about
engendering and composing movement" (141). Between October 2018 and
February 2019, the Institute of Contemporary Art in Boston brought together the first comprehensive exhibition of Forsythe's *Choreographic Objects*
(Figures 1.8–1.10) with the intention of "extending Forsythe's choreographic
explorations beyond the stage to public spaces and the layperson" and for the
purpose of "inviting visitors to move through the sculptures, creating their
own individual choreographies" (*ICA Magazine* 2018:7). Forsythe's oeuvre,
including such participatory projects and the ways in which they reflect conceptual ideas related to choreographic thinking and choreographic objects,
need to be considered a critical part of the discourses surrounding both audience participation and immersive performance.

Figure 1.9 William Forsythe, *City of Abstracts*, 2000. Photo: Dominik Mentzos. © William Forsythe.

Figure 1.10 William Forsythe, *The Differential Room*, 2018, installation view, ICA, Boston, 2019. Photo © Liza Voll.

The notions of choreographic thinking and choreographic objects resonates with Sheets-Johnstone's concept of thinking in movement, discussed previously, and with that of *choreographic mind* proposed by American choreographer Susan Rethorst. The term refers to a mind that has "a kind of spatial emotional map of a situation, the emotional psycholog-ical reading of place, and of people in relation to that place and each other" (2015:14). Rethorst asserts that the choreographic mind is "a heightening and specifying of the body's mind" (57), by which she means the latter is "physical functioning . . . [m]ore than knowing about physical things, it is knowing and learning, and feeling things via physicality—thinking physi-cally, perceiving physically" (56). Remarking on what she perceives as the widespread devaluing of the body's intelligence, she states, "there is a keen inclination to trust what can be put into words and known through language, and, on the other hand, to patronize what is known by physical means" and asserts instead "what we do and know through physicality is broader and more comprehensive than for what we credit it" (36). Furthermore, Rethorst argues the choreographic mind affords embodied, somatic thinking that enables individuals to move in ways that precede the "cognitive, analytical, linguistic faculty that normally goes by the name of thought" (37). While commonly associated with dance, the choreographic mind can be accessed and made operable by anyone, in any context, who is intent on "applying the same modes of perception that are both inclination and tool" (14).

The potential of the choreographic mind, as described by Rethorst, sug-gests that it encompasses both *thinking in movement* during dance improvi-sation, as per Sheets-Johnstone, and *choreographic thinking* toward the design of dance for the stage and/or participatory experiences, as per Forsythe. When considering how these three concepts contribute to immersive per-formance, it is helpful to give thought to a question put forth by Forsythe, in that he asks, "what else, besides the body, could physical thinking look like?" (91). Physical thinking, following the theorizing of these three art-ists, clearly manifests itself in multiple ways in myriad contexts, yet impor-tantly for this project, is evidenced within digital storytelling, an art form combining computer-based digital tools and technologies with narrative. As an important precursor of immersive performance, contributing both to its emergence as a form and influencing the design of productions, analysis of digital storytelling provides insight into choreography's impact on the form.

Digital Storytelling

In the digital revolution of the 1950s through the 1970s, which brought rapid developments in computer programming, choreographic concepts and practices were carried into the realm of digital storytelling. Programmers engaged in choreographic thinking, wittingly or not, as they designed worlds that could elicit player participation. The developments in the digital realm would later make their way back to the physical, as immersive practitioners would draw inspiration from digital storytelling's use of choreographic concepts and practices to design immersive productions that elicited audience participation.[47] The work of digital media scholar Janet H. Murray, author of *Hamlet on the Holodeck: The Future of Narrative in Cyberspace* ([1997] 2017), helps us historicize and contextualize the portability of choreography into the digital realm. Murray accurately predicted that the computer would offer us "special possibilities for storytelling that are continuous with older traditions but promise new expressive power," as well as the development of new audiences who would seek out and demand innovative participatory forms of culture ([1997] 2017 edition:113).

In characterizing the new digital environments, Murray outlines four principal properties: procedural authorship; participatory design; spatial navigation; and encyclopedic extent (113). The procedural authorship and participatory nature of the design "make up most of what we mean by the vaguely used word *interactive*" (87, emphasis original). As Murray states, "procedural authorship means [. . .] writing the rules for the interactor's involvement, that is, the conditions under which things will happen in response to the participant's actions" (187). Central to her model of interactivity is "scripting the computer and scripting the interactor so that their behaviors mesh, creating the experience of agency" (interview with author 2019). The other two properties of digital environments, their spatially navigable nature and their encyclopedic extent, "help to make digital creations seem as explorable and extensive as the actual world, making up much of what we mean when we say that cyberspace is *immersive*" ([1997] 2017 edition: 88, emphasis original).[48] Murray explains that "interactivity and immersion reinforce one another" because "when we are immersed in a consistent environment, we are motivated to initiate actions that lead to the feeling of agency, which in turn deepens our sense of immersion" (114).[49]

Importantly, Murray specifically likens procedural design—the intentional design of users' movements within the environment—to choreography. The details of this connection will be taken up in Chapter 3; here I simply want to point out that Murray's theorizing of "electronic composition," to use her term, includes a kind of thinking that is reflective of choreographic intentionality (188). For instance, Murray states that "in the computer game the interactor is the dancer and the game designer is the choreographer" (178). When asked about her use of these terms, Murray clarified, "I was looking for the language for the construction of space procedurally by writing rules and so of course, that is what a choreographer does" (interview with author 2019). Murray cites *Zork*, the game referenced at the start of the chapter, as an early exemplar of such strategies, arguing that the programmers demonstrated that "the first step in making an enticing narrative world is to script the interactor" ([1997] 2017 edition: 96). What made *Zork* distinct, according to Murray, was "the sophisticated computational thinking the programmers brought to shaping the range of possible interactions" between the user and the environment (96).

Murray's reflections on *Zork* raise an intriguing question: what is the relationship between computational thinking and choreographic thinking? In what ways did choreographic thinking advance the development of digital culture, beginning as it did as Murray suggests in the 1970s with games like *Zork*, and in what ways did it continue to impact electronic design/composition? As computer scientists morphed into storytellers in the 1970s, as Murray proposes they did, it is important to consider how these individuals employed not only literary and gaming conventions, but also choreographic conventions and principles.[50] Clearly, immersive performance presents us with an example of the interdependency that Elswit has called upon us to consider between theater and dance. At the same time, how might choreographic thinking be recognized as fundamental to and operative within other disciplines, contributing to the manifestation of other new forms, including digital storytelling? And might this importing of choreography to digital storytelling also present yet another instance of choreography's invisibilization? It would seem that the designers were engaged in choreographic thinking, particularly when we consider Murray's statements such as "the first step in making an enticing narrative world is to script the interactor" (96), and even more specifically, as mentioned previously, her analogy that situates the interactor as the dancer and the game designer as the choreographer. I argue that such comments do not simply reflect Murray applying the concepts of dance/dancer and choreography/choreographer as metaphors; rather, the procedural environments she discusses and the computational thinking that makes them possible are predicated on choreographic thinking. Indeed, such statements support my assertion that the design of these environments is intentional and possible as a result of choreography's portability as a technology.

Murray is unique among scholars writing about the aesthetic and procedural elements of digital entertainment in that she draws upon dance liberally as both a metaphor and a descriptive device for articulating the complexities of computer programming. More typical is the conspicuous absence of critical analysis of dance among the extant literature related to immersive design. It is challenging to parse chronologically the ways in which these forms influenced each other, with storytelling and theatrical conventions, including choreography, being always already connected and digital gaming employing both. And yet, an examination of choreography in relationship to digital storytelling and video gaming suggests that elements of these two genres have influenced the development of immersive performance.

Ubiquity and Invisibility

We have seen that choreography transfers the intention of the choreographer onto the body of the choreographed, and that this dynamic can occur in any number of different settings beyond traditional presentation platforms such as the proscenium stage, including in the digital world. Choreography's principles and practices have endured across centuries, not only influencing genres of live performance but also serving as a foundation for the evolution of new movement forms such as immersive performance. The vast reach of choreography can be seen by conducting a simple internet search for the term. One recent search yielded over one hundred million results to sources that associate the concept with a wide range of sectors of society far beyond the realms of dance. International banking, for example, makes use of what is called "service choreography." Cognitive science analyzes the "choreography of affiliation" and pro-social behaviors, while in the hospitality industry, chefs conceive of food production as choreographic, with some restaurants hiring choreographers to teach wait-staff to move efficiently through space in response to guests. Choreography is everywhere, and in many cases, it is explicitly labeled as such. And yet, as dance scholar Susan Leigh Foster has noted, even as choreography has managed to "proliferat[e]" as a term across multiple sectors of society, it has continued to be "ignored or suppressed" in other contexts (2011:15). For all its ubiquity in the world at large, choreography has gone largely unseen and unacknowledged by scholars outside of dance, and when it is applied in "real world" contexts such as customer service and food production, its practitioners are not necessarily aware of the broader choreographic tradition within which their activities fit. Since Arbeau's day, choreography has become so embedded in contemporary life, in our socialization, and in our ways of being in the world that it is largely invisible to us. Herein lies the paradox of choreography: while ubiquitous, its uses in many circumstances are unwitting, unconscious, or even—as in the case of immersive performance—intentionally obfuscated.

Given the wide and diverse application of choreography as both a conceptual practice and a term, it is critical to consider how and why choreography has been minimally addressed in some discourses surrounding immersive performance and invisibilized in others, and even obscured by practitioners themselves. As one example, Alston mentions choreography in relation to the work of Punchdrunk, and he describes an immersive production by Swedish artists Lundahl & Seitl (Christer and Martina, respectively) as "tightly choreographed and designed," questioning the freedom of the audience participants (2016:102). Yet beyond these references, Alston does not engage in theorizing choreography's role in these productions even though such a consideration of choreography as a technology to impinge upon audience agency could deepen his analysis of how immersive productions are designed to engender what he has called their "productive participation" toward "the objectification of experience as art" (7). Interestingly, in his discussion of SHUNT, another UK-based company renowned for its large-scale immersive projects and for choreographing the experiences of the audiences who attend them, Alston does not mention choreography at all.[51] In an anthology entitled *Staging Spectators in Immersive Performance* (2019), the term *choreography* is only mentioned once; in the first chapter, co-editor Doris Kolesch uses choreography metaphorically to say "immersion is much more about a subtle choreography of diving in and surfacing, about the play of illusionment and disillusionment" (9). In regard to practitioners, the hows and whys of choreography's obscuration are linked to the artistic intentions and aesthetic visions guiding the creation of immersive works, specifically in regard to audience participation. The specifics of production design will be discussed in the next chapter, but for now, it is worth noticing that choreography's invisibilization is made possible by the illusory nature of its function for spectators during performances.

The invisibility of choreography today can be partly explained by the notion of choreography as an expanded practice. Dance artist and theoretician Mårten Spångberg and Foster have each asserted that choreography is no longer bound to dance; rather, it has expanded beyond structuring the movements of dancing bodies into practices that have much broader applicability when guiding and designing different types of movement in the world (Foster 2011:15–72; Spångberg 2012). In explaining "choreography as expanded practice," Spångberg declares, "Choreography is today emancipating itself from dance, engaging in a vibrant process of articulation. Choreographers are experimenting with new models of production, alternative formats, have enlarged the understanding of social choreography considerably, and are mobilizing innovative frontiers in respect of self-organizing, empowerment, and autonomy" (Spångberg 2012). If Foster and Spångberg are correct that choreography has surged beyond the bounds of dance, and is indeed everywhere, then surely it can be used to organize the behavior of spectators such that they perceive themselves to be immersed in a production. I assert that one of the ways that choreography has expanded is in the creation of new audience engagement models such as immersive performance, which emerged from artists' interest in reconfiguring the role of audiences.

As immersive performance has emerged in the twenty-first century, it has needed resources that existing theater practices and dramaturgy could not provide. Only by turning to dance, drawing on choreography as a mechanism for facilitating audience immersion, could immersive artists create live productions that are *as immersive*, or approximate the immersiveness as other forms that audiences access on a daily basis, such as internet-based hypertext platforms and video games. And yet, despite choreography's role as a key structural mechanism in immersive theater, it often remains unacknowledged. While vital to the intentions of practitioners, its existence is hidden precisely because its obfuscation affords audiences the perception of a greater experience of agency in their own immersion. I argue that this obfuscation has not only perpetuated what André Lepecki has called the "subaltern position of dance in the general economy of arts" (2012:15, also 2016:15), but has also contributed to the ignoring of choreography in the discourses and scholarship surrounding immersive performance.

In the preceding pages, I have argued that even despite choreography's invisibilization, it has emerged as a critical structural mechanism for immersive productions through multiple historical and socio-political factors.

At this point, several questions surface: what are the social and political implications of these productions? What does it mean for practitioners to use the invisible mechanism of choreography to structure other individuals' embodiment? And to keep that work of choreographing spectators obscured during performances? It stands to reason that different kinds of people might be differently affected by such a power differential, pointing to the need for attunement to the ethical considerations involved in choreographing spectators. Such questions remain in the background throughout the discussions in this book. Recognizing the functioning of choreography in these productions is foundational to an understanding of how these productions work to engage audiences, meeting their desire to participate experientially through their bodies and to have experiences that are both personalized and shared. The breadth and depth of participation desired by present-day audiences is calling into question centuries-old ideas about artistic agency and authorship, prompting fresh conversations about what dance can be, and what it has already become without our even noticing.

2

Designing Differently with Dance

You are on a New York City street flooded with afternoon sunlight. A man to whom you have recently been introduced walks along the sidewalk in front of you, and you somehow understand that he means for you to follow him. He's dressed in a two-piece suit and a baseball cap, walking quickly and with purpose, his arms pumping so hard that the closed umbrella in his hand swings back and forth, tracing a tight arc in the air beside him (see Figure 2.1). The man approaches a street corner and stops abruptly, cutting the umbrella horizontally through the space in front of you. You, too, stop abruptly, as his umbrella blocks your path forward. The man keeps you in place with his umbrella as he peers around the corner of the building, gesturing for you to remain silent. You can't help but comply with the man's unspoken, physical imperatives for silence and stillness—and as you stand there, quiet and motionless, you begin to become attuned to the crowded city street all around you—seeing, hearing, and feeling the frenetic activity and loud noises. Suddenly, the man rushes diagonally across the street, glancing back to make sure you're following, and hustles down the sidewalk with you close behind. Halfway down the block, the man stops at the stoop of a brick building and gestures for you to climb the steps and enter the building. You obey, leaving behind the brightness of the street for the cool darkness of a small office.

A woman seated at a desk hands you a piece of paper. It is some sort of questionnaire, filled with cryptic queries like, "Why you?" and "Where are you going?" After a moment, you find yourself in motion again, curiously following one person's cues after another. There is a woman who engages you in a one-sided interview where she does all the talking. There's a gregarious woman in a garish floral blouse and gigantic red lace hair bow who intercepts you at a door back to the city street, chattering excitedly about being the center of attention as she leads you further down the street. And in the open doorway of a nightclub, there's a third woman, this one wearing a sleeveless tight-fitting black dress and gazing silently down at you from the first step of a tall, dimly lit staircase. The nightclub woman turns away from you, deliberately, and rushes up the stairs. You follow her deep into the quiet recesses of the building. When you catch up to

Tandem Dances. Julia M. Ritter, Oxford University Press (2021). © Oxford University Press.
DOI: 10.1093/oso/9780190051303.001.0001.

the woman again, she looks into your face and asks, "How would you like me to be for you?" Then she takes off again down the hall, full speed, leading you on a chase through narrow hallways lined with closed doors, and then down another set of stairs. At last, nearly half an hour after first you'd first met the man in the two-piece suit, you find yourself back out in the bright sunlight and cacophony of the city street.

So begins *YOU-The City*, a production that premiered in New York City in 1988 as "an intimate Manhattanwide play for an audience of one."[1] Written and directed by British-born artist Fiona Templeton, *YOU-The City* was an intricately designed, participatory, two-hour theatrical event that moved twenty-two audience members through fourteen one-to-one encounters in more than a dozen locations throughout Times Square and surrounding neighborhoods. While the term *immersive* had not yet surfaced as a descriptor for productions involving such spectator participation, Templeton's *YOU-The City* did immerse participants—or, to use her term, "clients"— within the landscape of the city through the use of choreographic strategies.

Figure 2.1 Thomas JF Regan III as Performer J—Crossover Minder, in Fiona Templeton's *YOU-The City* (New York City, 1988). Photograph by Zoe Beloff.

The production was an early, if not the earliest, forerunner of immersive theater in the United States.[2]

Given that *YOU-The City* was last produced in 1991, the only remaining opportunity to experience the production (at the time of this writing) is to watch the film version that Templeton made in 1989 in collaboration with Michael Ratomski, Jeff Preiss, and Mark Jay Schlossberg.[3] Further insight into Templeton's thinking in designing the production, though, can be found in her book, published in 1990, in which she extensively documents her creative process, including comprehensive notes on design and structure. The book contains the full script and performance photographs of the production, as well as the timetables, charts, and maps that Templeton designed in order to represent the choreographic pathways taken by both clients and performers over the course of the production. In the book's introduction, Templeton suggests that readers interested in what she calls the "details of the mechanics" should refer to a section discussing what she calls "Client Flow" and "Performer Shuttles." These are Templeton's terms for the "two types of movement," that is, choreography, that constitute *YOU-The City* (x).[4] Templeton's "Client Flow" and "Performer Shuttles" are analogous to what I have set forth in the two previous chapters as the track and score used by artists to craft immersive works in the twenty-first century.[5] The "Client Flow" and "Performer Shuttles" allude to Templeton's understanding of the conjunctive partnership between these two structures, and also between the individuals who instantiate them, that is, the audiences and cast members. Hence, I suggest that these artifacts are evidence that this early immersive production involved the intentional choreographing of the bodies of both performers and audiences in order to harness their corporeality into a kind of tandem dance (x). *YOU-The City*, having premiered in the late twentieth century, serves as an early case study in immersive theater, affording an opportunity to glimpse how artists, including Templeton, have pioneered the form over the past several decades. These practitioners have been designing differently through dance.

Further evidence of the impact of choreography on the early development of immersive performance can be found in the critical reviews and scholarly essays analyzing *YOU-The City* that call attention to the ways the audience participant/client is situated as a subject of choreography. Cynthia Carr, a reviewer for the *Village Voice*, reports being put into a car where "the driver choreographed me through rush hour" (Figure 2.2) to a different location, where she met another performer (Figure 2.3), "who walked me through a

Figure 2.2 Cecil Hedigan as Performer G—Meterless Charioteer, in Fiona Templeton's *YOU-The City* (New York City, 1988). Photograph by Zoe Beloff.

Hell's Kitchen playground in the rain" (1988, in 2008:161). Divulging that she arrived at the performance ready to be a "professional spectator," taking notes throughout the performance, Carr admits that she "couldn't write much of it down. I needed more distance for true spectating, and I'd been turned into a participant [. . .] I had become what the piece is about" (160).

In *ArtForum* magazine, theater critic John Howell writes that "the spectator was put into the performer's seat," claiming that "the performance was what you [the spectator] were able to *make it*, not what you were able to *make of it*" (1988:151, emphasis added). Theater scholar Stanton B. Garner Jr. recounts how "clients passed each other in an elaborately choreographed encounter on a basketball court; in a nearby apartment, encounters were staged with different clients and performers in the same room" (2002:104).

Another scholar, Elinor Fuchs, reflects on the production's "intricate geometry," imagining the impact of her body and that of her fellow "clients" in the space and time of the production. She states, "if all our movements could be incised into the urban landscape and the incisions seen *as* incised, what beautiful shapes and patterns we could trace" (in Garner 2002:118, emphasis original). The writings of these critics and researchers-as-clients reveal their

Figure 2.3 Nevenka Koprivsek as Performer H—Crossover Agent, in Fiona Templeton's *YOU-The City* (New York City, 1988). Photograph by Zoe Beloff.

interpretations of how *YOU-The City* was designed and how they themselves were choreographed, providing insight into how being-choreographed was, for them, a kinesthetic experience that shaped how they made meaning from their participation.

Importantly, Templeton's book includes "client" perspectives, albeit unattributed. One client observed that, "It is rare in this culture to be the object of the total attention of sixteen people, one right after another. You have to go into the hospital for major surgery for that. Particularly in theater, where you're used to thinking of yourself as the one who focuses attention" (106).

This reflection, in my reading, alludes to the ways that clients may have felt kinesthetically attuned within the space-time of the production, sensing the totality of their physical self—that which encompasses cognitive and perceptual faculties—as being an object of (the performers') attention (see Figure 2.4). The reason Templeton's client was able to perceive themselves as an object of attention is, I assert, precisely because they were transformed into a subject of choreography. A reflection from another client indicates that they felt obligated, somehow, to stay physically present with each performer: "In a theater you know you can leave. But here, yes, he's an actor, but . . . he's a person also trying to break through . . . When it's within a space declared as theater, that neutralizes it. Here though, it's primal, it's hard to let go of that other person. I just never considered leaving" (28). I surmise that due to the close proximity and intimacy of the client's encounters with performers, the client experienced a heightened sense of kinesthesia that inclined them to stay relationally engaged rather than depart from the performer. Their sense of being a kinetic agent, including the fact that they *could* leave if they chose

Figure 2.4 Greg Arciniega as Performer E—46th Streetperson, in Fiona Templeton's *YOU-The City* (New York City, 1988). Photograph by Zoe Beloff.

to, perhaps only intensified the sense of being physically and emotionally implicated within this designed, intersubjective exchange.

In Templeton's directorial notes, she offers the performers improvisational tactics that can be called upon during performances to assist them in guiding clients through the experience, especially to help them manage what she defines as the *unintendable*, meaning "what can't be planned, or what has a planned setup but deliberately no content. This is what is brought to the performance by the client, and in the case of this city performance, by passersby, or external events, or geography, or time of day, etc." (vii).[6] By acknowledging the "unintendable" as a factor in the production, Templeton follows in the footsteps of avant-garde and postmodern artists who embraced indeterminacy in their work. While Templeton had studied the methods of both Grotowski and Lecoq, two prominent avant-garde theater artists, she asserts that her work is more critically informed by visual arts and architecture, as well as postmodern dance. Templeton's work is best understood as part of a lineage of avant-garde art influence, as detailed in Chapter 1, rather than physical theater.

What Templeton was pioneering as an artistic approach in the late 1980s was a way of designing productions that foreground the audience member at the center of the action. As a kinesthetically intelligent agent who draws upon cues from performers and environments, the spectator can contribute to the overall structure and content of a production as a physically "productive participant," to use Alston's term. Templeton recounts in her book her interest in identifying performers who were kinesthetically adept at negotiating busy city environments, who could readily access kinetic strategies like peripheral acuity (indirect vision outside of the center of someone's gaze) and using a range of non-verbal, subliminal cues to orient clients through space. When auditioning performers for the cast of *YOU-The City*, Templeton chose New York City's busy Grand Central subway station as the audition location, a tactic that revealed "not only who [of the prospective performers] could retain focused individual attention in a large crowd, but who could take me where I didn't know I was going, without my feeling forced or lost" (145). Later, during the rehearsal process, she developed a range of techniques for guiding the audience in collaboration with her cast, some of which are detailed in her book. These techniques for performers range from directions for specific physical contact, such as "You touch the client's arm" (18), to others grouped under the label of "Interruption/Improvisation Strategies," such as "you will probably have to improvise physically, in manoeuvering clients"

(66). Other notes indicate where the audience as clients are choreographed so as to be situated relationally to performers and action. For example, a note for Act III, Scene I, reads, "the clients are *outside* of the centrifugal action" (66, emphasis original), whereas staging notes for a later scene directs two performers (Figure 2.5) to "move in all directions lightly around the client, now on both sides, now on the same, now one behind, now both well ahead and so on" (120). As Templeton explains, "immersive work is not work where you create the theatrical aspect and then add the audience. You begin thinking of the audience as part of the whole choreography; you have to start with them at the center" (interview with author 2019). *YOU-The City* provides specific examples that illustrate how choreography is intentionally deployed as a design technology for engaging audiences' kinesthesia and physical awareness, with the intention of attuning them to the intersubjectivity of their relational encounters as well as their larger embeddedness within the environments they move through.[7]

Figure 2.5 Jacqui Mulvey and Glen Venezio as Performers K—Twin Teenagers, in Fiona Templeton's *YOU-The City* (New York City, 1988). Photograph by Zoe Beloff.

In the Introduction, I proposed that immersive performance is experienced by audience participants first and foremost as a kinesthetic experience, namely through their being transformed into subjects of choreography. Chapter 1, then, established that choreography operates ubiquitously as well as often invisibly in many contexts. Now we turn to examining how choreography actually operates within immersive performance. In outlining how choreography functions as a design technology, I argue that what is being "designed" are choreographed structures and environments specifically intended to impact spectators' kinesthesia, that is, their affective experience of embodied movement. To support my claims, I draw on my theorizations of scholarship within the disciplines of dance studies and design studies. In addition, I rely on in-depth interviews with Templeton and analysis of audience reception data from her work to more fully understand choreography's operational role within immersive productions.

I analyze theater criticism and performance reviews to conduct reception research of these sources, alongside my first-person phenomenological research of productions I have attended or viewed on film. This first-person research is informed by a protocol now known as Spectator-Participation-as-Research (SPaR), a practice developed by Deirdre Heddon, Helen Iball, and Rachel Zerihan (2012) for analyzing one-to-one productions, meaning those that invite one audience member to experience a performance alone. According to Heddon et al., SPaR is located in the "experiential processes of reception" (5), and its "acronym intentionally signals the relational dynamic" of participatory performance. SPaR was later broadened through the theorizing of F. H. Babbage (2016), who frames it as an extension of practice-as-research, a "productive, valid, widespread and diverse mode of critical enquiry" used within arts and other disciplines to facilitate the function of audiences as researchers (1). To Babbage, audience-researchers are individuals whose practices of reception and spectatorship involve "watching, thinking, feeling, interpreting (and reinterpreting), and—sometimes—of moving, speaking, doing" (1). Templeton's inclusion of client/audience perspectives in her book aligns with the growing importance of spectator studies among theater scholars, and although her incorporation of these insights predates the coining of the term "SPaR" by several decades, her work can be understood as a form of SPaR. Overall, Templeton's prescience of the cultural shift towards increasingly participatory practices is evidenced in the design of both her production and the book that now serves as a documentary resource. The book is designed to allow the reader, whom Templeton calls the "vicarious client," to choose how to engage with its structure. The left-hand side of the book offers readers a running side-bar commentary of anecdotal yet critical observations from audience/clients and performers alongside Templeton's directorial notes, while the right-hand side displays the script (vii). This design affords the reader multiple pathways from which to approach how the production was designed, and then documented, allowing them to choreograph, so to speak, their own journey through the material contained therein. It is, as many books are, a *tandem* experience between author and reader. While she was not the first to design a book or production that prompts the reader/participant to choose how to engage, Templeton's inclination to do so signals her place within the rapidly burgeoning interest in designing participatory experiences in the late twentieth century.

While this chapter integrates discourses from dance studies and design studies in order to illuminate the role of choreography in immersive work, I am reminded of theater scholar Kirsty Sedgman's caution about identifying a causal relationship between design and audience immersion. She states, "[p]eople often talk about immersiveness and participation as if they were the inevitable outcomes of successful production design. Audience research unveils how these things are also the products of reception" (2018:291).[8] Similarly, immersive practitioner and scholar David Shearing warns that "[t]here is a danger in the discourse surrounding immersive experiences to consider enveloping design or participation 'as' immersive. Immersion is not an external experience given to someone. It is an internal state, built through an individual's sustained relational encounters with the world" (2018:291). With these cautions in mind, my aim here is not to argue for choreography as a *cause* of immersion; rather, in line with Shearing, I suggest that immersion surfaces from within, through the audience's participation, and does so specifically because of the ways that, following Sheets-Johnstone, choreography can "resuscitate" an individual's kinesthesia (2015:xvi). Choreography creates the shape and structures of productions that elicit participation. When choreography occurs in realms specifically designed to influence physical sensations, immersion can be the result. Through the rest of this chapter, I present an analysis of how immersive productions are designed such that their conditions orchestrate participants' movements, as a means of potentially inducing immersion. As we will see, the rubric of choreography offers a compelling way to understand what is occurring in productions that are intended to immerse audiences.

Interdependence of Dance and Design
in Immersive Productions

To establish that choreography is a design technology, I draw connections between the interdisciplinary discourses of dance studies and design studies. The latter, I understand as a field concerned with how design generates knowledge through both analytical and practical modes of inquiry. At its core is the concept of *design thinking*, analogous to the choreographic thinking discussed in the previous chapter. Design thinking has gained prominence since the 1960s as a problem-solving methodology that emphasizes multidisciplinary approaches to research and ideation, and prioritizes the needs of the people who will use the technology or product being created. Specifically, design thinking as a process draws upon techniques and skills from the social and computer sciences as well as from creative and artistic practices to ideate and innovate solutions. As both theory and practice, design thinking is widely applied by cognitive scientists and design practitioners alike, in fields as diverse as engineering, architecture, industrial design, fine arts, and business. A non-linear and recursive process, design thinking involves five iterative stages: empathize, define, ideate, prototype, and test.[9] The parallels between choreographic and design processes are the foundation of my argument that choreography operates as a design technology within immersive performances. It is the interdependency of choreography and design, as theoretical disciplines and as practices, following Elswit, that enables audience immersion to manifest in immersive productions.

In claiming choreography as a design technology, I readily acknowledge that there are no universally agreed-upon elements or principles of design for choreographic processes. Even the elements typically associated with choreography—body, space, time, energy, and relationship—are only contingent, culturally based heuristic devices for understanding different phenomena of structured movement. So, we begin by considering whether or how immersive practitioners themselves discuss choreography. Templeton's book on *You-The City*, discussed previously, provides some clues as to her own processes of choreography and design. In a similar vein, practitioner Maxine Doyle, associate artistic director and choreographer for Punchdrunk (UK), makes a more explicit statement: "Masked Punchdrunk shows are defined by the relationship between dance, design and site" (Doyle, in Machon and Punchdrunk 2019:88). By analyzing the work of different immersive practitioners, then, we can discern their distinctive aesthetic visions as well as the strategies they share in common. My key interest here is to analyze and theorize how, specifically, artists designing immersive performances capitalize on how dance can serve as a fundamental way of knowing and understanding the world. To draw upon dance as a way of knowing is to deploy choreographic concepts, that is, choreography as a technology, as a means of problem-solving. Immersive performance, as a form of live performing arts, can arguably be understood as being fundamentally concerned with what cognitive scientist and usability engineer Don Norman has identified as *experience design*.

In his classic 1988 text *The Design of Everyday Things*, Norman coins the term *user experience* (now known as UX), and argues that good design, meaning the conceptualization and creation of products and experiences that are both effective and enjoyable to use or operate, must take as its starting point the needs and psychology of human beings. User experience design is understood as part of the larger realm of Human-Centered Design (HCD), a design philosophy that, according to Norman, considers "human needs, capabilities, and behavior first, then designs to accommodate those needs, capabilities and ways of behaving" (8). With the human experience in mind, Norman establishes key principles of design, including "four classes of constraints," which he identifies as "physical, cultural, semantic, and logical" (125).[10] These constraints allow the designer to create a product or experience that "fits human desires, needs, and capabilities" (218). As Norman puts it, "After all, why do we make products? We make them for people to use" (218). For Norman, "constraints are powerful clues, limiting the set of possible actions. The thoughtful use of constraints in design lets people [users] readily determine the proper course of action, even in a novel situation" (125). The intelligent use of constraints, he explains, enables a design to guide its user to easily choose the correct action at the appropriate time. In Norman's framing of design thinking, he notes that the practice is not exclusive to designers; indeed, "all great innovators have practiced this, even if unknowingly, regardless of whether they were artists or poets, writers or scientists, engineers or businesspeople" (219). In my view, the work of choreographers can be analyzed under the rubric of design thinking.

Forsythe's concept of choreographic thinking, discussed in Chapter 1, is a useful starting point for understanding how choreography operates as a form of design. As an example of how Forsythe himself merged choreographic and design thinking, in 1994 he undertook an initiative called *Improvisation Technologies* that entailed the creation of a "digital dance school" comprising over one hundred video lectures on CD-ROM. The videos documented his pedagogical approach to improvisation as theory and practice, which was built upon the system of movement analysis developed by dance artist and theorist Rudolf Laban (1879–1958).[11] Forsythe, building upon the work of Laban, deployed a kind of cartography to digitally map his movement methodologies for the viewer/user, who could then use the methods to generate their own movement language(s). The parallels between design thinking and choreographic thinking did not begin in the twentieth century, however. They can be understood as stretching back through the centuries, since the very beginnings of choreography as a technology in which inherent constraints—arguably the precise constraints identified by Norman in his work on user-centered design—are deployed intentionally and intelligently to organize behavior.

As Norman explains, the paradox of technology is that it offers both solutions and limitations within processes of design. For Norman, the paradox lies in the fact that "the same technology that simplifies life by providing more functions in each device also complicates life by making the device harder to learn, harder to use" (34). In short, technology designs constrain even as they afford particular behaviors. Similarly, in immersive works, I argue, practitioners amplify the paradoxical nature of choreography by both liberating and controlling the user, that is, the audience participant. For instance, the directions that Templeton provides to her performers in her book illustrate different ways that constraints can operate within immersive works. In directions for a scene that occurs on a busy street, Performer F is instructed to speak so their "voice rarely rises above deep and low, occasionally a whisper" (32), suggesting that a client may choose whether to lean in and hear what is being said. In another set of directions, for Performer H, the performer is told, "You open the car door for a client," and in another moment, "Move behind the client" (44). The instructions have been designed to constrain, and thereby generate, speech and actions by the performer that will, in turn, afford particular responses by clients. The very properties of the choreography afford certain possibilities while simultaneously foreclosing on others.

Whatever functions a choreographic design may afford, when it is done well, the user/spectator is able to remain focused entirely on the experience of interacting with the product/production, rather than the process by which it was designed. Norman has asserted that "good design is actually a lot harder to notice than poor design, in part because good designs fit our needs so well that the design is *invisible*, serving us without drawing attention to it-self" (2013:xi, emphasis added). In a widely read 1991 *Scientific American* ar-ticle entitled "The Computer for the 21st Century," computer scientist Mark Weiser stated that "the most profound technologies are those that disappear. They weave themselves into the fabric of everyday life until they are indis-tinguishable from it" (1991:94).[12] The desirability of making design invisible shows up in both choreographic and design thinking and, as such, is seen in the creation of immersive performance. The processes of choreography and design are intertwined and interdependent, both having the power to op-erate as invisible undercurrents shaping how humans interact with and expe-rience the world. Yet, because of the paradoxical nature of choreography as a design technology, it is critical to consider how design thinking in combina-tion with choreographic thinking both enable and frustrate audience partic-ipation and agency in the new forms of performance known as immersive.

Discourses surrounding immersive performance, as well as the lan-guage used to publicize productions, often alludes to the absence of the fourth wall—that invisible, imagined barrier separating the audience from performers—and suggests that audiences will have opportunities to engage and take action as distinct from traditional performance presentations in, for instance, proscenium theaters. The fourth wall is a performance con-vention that serves as a design constraint, complete with its own physical, cultural, semantic, and logical implications, that engenders certain kinds of experiences and outcomes even as it (or because it) excludes others. If the fourth wall is "removed," then, something else is needed in its absence. Immersive performance's allowance for participation does not make it any less presentational, and thus the circumstances of its presentation warrant, even require, a boundary of some sort to distinguish between performers and audiences. I argue that in immersive performance, what has replaced the fourth wall is choreography, specifically because of its paradoxical functions as a technology. Choreography is the technology affording entry into the world of the immersive production, allowing audiences to be physically in-tegrated into the narrative. Choreography is installed as a sort of proxy for the fourth wall, affording spectators the perception of trespassing that wall. The constraints of choreographic structures impinge upon the movements of audience participants, thus securing it as the fourth wall. Artists making immersive work deploy choreography as a substitute for a more traditional barrier or demarcation between performer and audience, a function served in more conventional productions by the architectural structures of the proscenium or presentational stage.

Immersive practitioners' adaptation of experience design, also known as user-friendly design, has been critiqued by theater scholars Adam Alston and Jen Harvie, who express concerns about the productivity demanded of spectators. Both Alston and Harvie related user-friendly design to the concept of the "experience economy," as defined by economists B. Joseph Pine II and James H. Gilmore. First put forth in their 1998 essay in the *Harvard Business Review*, and then expanded in the 1999 book *The Experience Economy: Work Is Theater & Every Business a Stage*, Pine and Gilmore state that "*goods and services are no longer enough* to foster economic growth"; instead, an increasingly dominant business model for marketing a wide range of products is "the staging of experiences" (2011:ix, emphasis original). According to Alston, user-friendly design enables "the 'activation' of consumers as *producing consumers*, either in terms of affective engagement with a product . . . or in terms of consumer participation in the production of a product" (2016:146). While Alston states that not all immersive productions follow the dictums of the experience economy, he does claim that immersive theater,

> more so than any other kind of theatre . . . typifies this "genre" of economic production by targeting audience experiences as a centrally significant feature of a cultural product, especially by stimulating a range of senses in staged events; designing a cultural product around the involvement of an audience; and allowing audiences to shape their own experience of a cultural product. (147)

Alston's primary critique of the experience economy is its "romanticism of productivity and profitable co-optation of seductive consumer experiences," which, in turn, leads him to question how immersive theater may be contributing to the propagandizing of audience productivity as a supposed form of empowerment (148).

Similarly to Alston, Harvie claims that audiences of immersive works become "prosumers," or "combined producers and consumers who do for themselves what would formerly have been done for them . . . who fulfill their own needs by producing what they want to consume" (50). Drawing upon Adorno's concept of the "culture industry," Harvie asserts that immersive productions fall into "an entertainment market that offers its audiences no real power and actually deadens their awareness of the ways dominant economies enfold and exploit them" (Adorno, quoted in Harvie 2013:8). To some extent, my argument for how audiences are situated as subjects of choreography aligns with the claims of both Alston and Harvie. I agree that immersive theater can and does, in many cases, lead to the "commodification of experience" by relying on "a superficially empowering and 'active' engagement of consumers as productive participants" (Alston 2016:148). After all, I am arguing that audiences of immersive productions are operationally restricted by choreography as a powerful design technology, constrained within their abilities to contribute. Indeed, the design of choreography within immersive performance, as I have experienced it thus far, typically leaves little room for genuine innovation or individual agency on the part of the immersed spectator. And, yet, critically, choreography does inherently offer some space for agentive decision-making, specifically through the use of instructional, improvisational scores that are designed to enable and elicit action. This, then, is precisely the draw of immersive productions, and the experiences they seductively purport to offer: that spectators are really co-creators of the experience. At play, though, is a tension between structure and freedom, control and compliance, creativity and conformity. Here, as in Harvie's work on "prosumers," perhaps it is it is useful to think of audiences as becoming *proformers*, tandem-dancing alongside professional performers.[13] Rather than drawing upon the Latin meaning of pro-forma as "a matter of form" or suggesting audiences are "just going through the motions" (while this might well be the case in some circumstances), I use the term *proformer* to suggest we consider what prompts spectators to participate. Within the choreographed parameters of immersive productions, there is always the possibility of participating in a way that *makes something happen*, to paraphrase Maxine Sheets-Johnstone, and of at least perceiving oneself as having agency. Consider this line from one of Templeton's participants, or "clients," quoted in her book: "Not only did I feel like I was making it happen, but there was this role-reversal when the actor told me after the show 'You were great'" (132). This perception of agency is precisely why choreography can function as such a potent design technology for practitioners grappling with how to provide audiences with the participatory experiences they increasingly crave in this century.

Choreographing for Participatory Culture

The rise of what is known as *participatory culture*, which has been on the ascendant since the late twentieth century, is essential to understand when examining how spectators are designed into immersive performances. Participatory culture has arisen in a time of unprecedented engagement with technology and widespread, rapid learning of new capabilities in relation to digital design. The term and concept *participatory culture* is most closely associated with the work of media scholar Henry Jenkins, who established the term in his influential book *Convergence Culture: Where Old and New Media Collide* (2006). Jenkins situates participatory culture as an outcome of the emergence of the internet, framing the behaviors associated with it as "contrast[ing] with older notions of passive media spectatorship" (2006:3).[14] Jenkins characterizes participatory culture as having "relatively low barriers to artistic expression and civic engagement," while offering "strong support for creating and sharing one's creations with others," and functioning as a realm where "members believe their contributions matter, and feel some degree of social connection with one another (at the least, they care what other people think about what they have created)" (2006:7 and 2009:6). Describing participatory culture as characterized by previously unseen levels of interaction and engagement between those who create and those who consume, Jenkins acknowledges that the power held by the former renders the balance inherently unequal. When writing in 2006, Jenkins asserted that producers, including corporations, "still exert greater power [on culture] than any individual consumer or even the aggregate of consumers," and there is some question as to the verity of such a statement now given the prevalence of social media and the power its users can wield (2006:3). Yet Jenkins also notes, "not all participants are created equal . . . [a]nd some consumers have greater abilities to participate in this emerging culture than others" (2006:3). Nevertheless, for all its potential inequities, Jenkins emphasizes that participatory culture "shifts the focus of literacy from individual expression to community involvement" (2009:6). All participants may not have equal opportunities to express agency, but the potential exercise of agency has expanded in breadth. As a whole, participatory culture points to a broader expansion in participatory structures, part of the context in which immersive performance has emerged.

Insight into the nature and consequences of the participatory turn in culture and the arts can be found in studies on audience research. The 2011 study *Getting In on the Act: How Arts Groups Are Creating Opportunities for Active Participation*, conducted by the non-profit WolfBrown and published by the James Irvine Foundation, has been called the first comprehensive study on participatory arts practices in the United States.[15] While the study does not provide a precise definition of participatory arts practices or of immersive performance, it does definitively state that there has been a "seismic shift toward a participatory arts culture [in which] . . . people are engaging in the arts in increasingly active and expressive ways (Gauntlett quoted in Brown and Novak-Leonard 2011:2). The study discusses how participatory arts fit within a larger cultural context, one shaped by population diversification particularly in the United States. This diversification has, in turn, led to different forms of cultural production and consumption as well as increased interactivity enabled by Web 2.0. This report presents a model in which participatory arts practices are both acknowledged and situated alongside professional cultural goods and services within a larger sphere of cultural literacy (7).[16]

Following the release of *Getting In on the Act*, one of the study's co-authors, choreographer and scholar Shelly Gilbride, raised important questions on the connection between participatory arts practices research and the field of dance: "What are the consequences [of the participatory shift] to craft, technique and training? How does a dance artist engage with the public in dance-making and also maintain a sense of artistic empowerment? Can a dance artist maintain a sense of artistic integrity and create an atmosphere that encourages participation?" (2011). Underlying Gilbride's questions are certain presuppositions as to the values within the field of dance, which may or may not represent the aesthetic interests of immersive practitioners. Gilbride's second question, in particular, presents the notion that dance artists/choreographers prioritize maintaining an authorial role within their dance-making, which is not a universal goal for all. As she notes, the report challenges "the ingrained cultural hierarchy that prioritizes traditional spectator experiences" (2011). Yet her questioning itself suggests the difficulty in reframing the cultural hierarchies that have shaped the field of dance in order to understand the role of dance in immersive works. Immersive performance, having successfully harnessed choreography as a technology, has emerged from, and seen its popularity fueled by, the milieu of the experience economy and participatory culture. Whether immersive performance is understood within the genre of theater proper or some other cultural category, it is a form that uses dance in new and effective ways, sometimes resulting in outcomes that are commercially and economically successful. Underpinning these global developments is choreography, a powerful design technology that brings to the forefront the criticality of kinesthesia for understanding and negotiating our world.

"Resuscitating" Kinesthesia

"When man ceased to run and leap for his food, the decay of the kinesthetic sense began," and ever since, "nothing else about us has been so much allowed to atrophy" (Humphrey 1979:61, quoted in Sheets-Johnstone 2015:xvi). This statement, attributed to American choreographer Doris Humphrey in the preface to the fiftieth-anniversary edition of the groundbreaking text *The Phenomenology of Dance* by preeminent dance scholar and philosopher Maxine Sheets-Johnstone, is, she writes, an incisive acknowledgment of the "centrality of kinesthesia not only to dance but to life generally, calling attention to its neglect and our need to resuscitate it" (2015:xvi). The term *kinesthesia*, coined in the late nineteenth century by physician and scholar H. C. Bastian, refers to "sensations which result from or are directly occasioned by movements" (1897:6). Sense and sense perception have long been concerns of anthropology and philosophy, but in the early decades of the twentieth century, Bastian's notion of kinesthesia received little attention within academic circles, as scientists and scholars doubted its validity as a concept for understanding the moving body. In the field of dance, on the other hand, where kinesthetic experience is paramount, both conceptual and practical research on kinesthesia have been prioritized and pioneered since the early 1900s. It was not until the 1980s that interest in kinesthesia increased within other disciplines, resulting in the "corporeal turn" of researchers towards issues of embodiment and corporeality (Sheets-Johnstone 1990:19). Interdisciplinary research on kinesthesia is now prevalent across many disciplines, from cultural studies to politics, and from cognitive studies to neuroscience to psychology and sociology. Such expansive research on kinesthesia has yielded a wide range of diverse definitions for the concept, but broadly speaking, kinesthesia can be understood as an individual's sensing of the movement of their body in space and time.

In scholarship on immersive performance, kinesthesia has been cursorily addressed; Machon, for example, subsumes the kinesthetic within her theory of *(syn)*aesthetics. Machon's theorizing builds upon a metaphor to a rare physiological condition known as synesthesia, which she frames as a "neurological complication where there is a crossover between the senses" (2009:15). Machon's (*syn*)aesthetics, then, is a proposal that the five senses of the audiences of participatory and immersive productions interact with one another to affect cognition, physiology, and emotion. Here, Machon is hinting at rather than theorizing kinesthesia, particularly its pre-verbal and precognitive qualities, as possible driving factors of immersion as affect. While noting the importance of corporeality and emphasizing the sensorium of the spectator's body, Machon bypasses the importance of choreography and kinesthesia as contributors to the corporeal effects that audiences experience through such participation.[17] The kinesthetic *is* a sensorium, and choreography is an effective technology for cultivating that sensorium. Templeton, as well as other artists and scholars, including Machon, have emphasized the importance of centralizing audiences physically within environments created for their participation and designed to activate their sensory faculties differently from other types of live performance. I argue that the term *immersive* has evolved as a descriptor for such works, and thus, has enjoyed pervasive popularity in its application precisely because it accurately encompasses the sensorium that is activated by kinesthesia. Sheets-Johnstone's notion of "resuscitating" kinesthesia proves useful, then, not only as a launching point for restoring as well as foregrounding kinesthesia within the discourse, but also as a frame for my argument on the ways in which choreography as a design technology activates kinesthetic experiences for the spectator and on how kinesthesia may be contributing to audience immersion.

It is not surprising that Sheets-Johnstone finds such resonance in Humphrey's assertion of the elementality of the kinesthetic sense, as she (Sheets-Johnstone) has spent much of her prolific career arguing, cogently, for the importance of kinesthesia as the sense modality of human movement (2015:xxiii). Sheets-Johnstone foregrounds kinesthesia as a sort of sixth sense that is foundational to human consciousness and perception, definitively declaring it to be "the bedrock of our *learning our bodies and learning to move ourselves to begin with*, and of our learning new abilities and skills as we mature" (xix, emphasis original). More recently, though, Sheets-Johnstone has also commented on what she perceives to be the impact on kinesthesia of new twenty-first-century technologies and the human behaviors they generate, claiming that, "texting, twittering and facebooking have overridden the immediate tactile-kinesthetic-affective qualitative dynamics of everyday life" (2018:5). Sheets-Johnstone's speculations about the capacity of technology to impinge on sensory faculties find echoes in the discourses on immersive theater. Machon, for instance, suggests that "the alienation from real intimacy in our workaday lives, via such forums as Facebook, can be addressed by immersive practices, which demand bodily engagement, sensually stimulate the imagination, [and] require tactility" (2013:26). Machon's argument builds upon the research of architectural theorist Juhani Pallasmaa, specifically his assertion that technological culture is "causing sensory impoverishment" (Pallasmaa, quoted in Machon 2013:127). Yet such concerns regarding technology tend to foreclose upon *the possibilities afforded* by advancements in computing and leave little room for consideration of the resourcefulness of humans in navigating change, particularly within the participatory culture they themselves have ushered into being. Even in the face of such pressures, Sheets-Johnstone asserts kinesthesia's "insuppressibility," drawing upon neuroscientist Marc Jeannerod's claim that "there are no reliable methods for suppressing kinesthetic information arising during the execution of a movement" (2015:xxiii).

In response to speculations that kinesthesia is somehow subjugated within an increasingly technological world, I offer another perspective that, incidentally, further supports my argument that choreography is a design technology. If two realities are acknowledged as possibilities—if kinesthesia may be in some ways diminished or compromised by technology and nonetheless also exist as insuppressible—then it is possible to consider how choreography is deployed not only as a way of "resuscitating" kinesthesia, but also as a means of (a technology for) enabling new kinds of kinesthetic knowledges to occur through participation in immersive performance. Given that the emergence of participatory culture has fundamentally altered how individuals engage with culture, and specifically entertainment culture, immersive practitioners are pushing against the notion of spectators as atrophied entities by inviting them to "resuscitate" their kinesthesia through choreography designed to encourage their physical participation. The use of choreography by immersive practitioners is both a way of drawing upon the reality that humans are continually shaped by technological advances and computer-enhanced affordances and a way of drawing upon kinesthesia as a sensory modality that is, all the time, in every context, a way for knowing and functioning in the world.

The possibility of new kinds of kinesthetic knowledges being cultivated through different applications of choreography is addressed by Susan Leigh Foster in *Choreographing Empathy: Kinesthesia in Performance* (2011).

Deconstructing with precision the terms choreography, kinesthesia, and empathy, Foster recounts the historical emergence of all three as distinct concepts while also affirming their interconnectedness as constituent elements impacting how performers and spectators can experience movement in performance. Key to Foster's argument is the way that choreography, as a "clear cut technique for disciplining human movement" contributed to a "redefinition of physicality" over time in Western culture (176). From there, Foster systematically tracks choreography's role in redefining physicality through kinesthesia, from the sixteenth-century courts of Arbeau to the myriad venues of the twentieth century, situating along the way both kinesthesia and empathy as notions that hold both socio-cultural and political specificity (175). Foster supports her claims with observations from her experiences of kinesthesia and choreography as an audience participant in site-specific performances in the twenty-first century, namely the productions of *Call Cutta* (2005) by Rimini Protokoll (Germany) and *Cell* (2006) by Headlong Dance Theater (United States). While she does not identify these productions as immersive performance, Foster's descriptions of them include both conceptual and practical details that resonate as features often seen in immersive works. Both *Call Cutta* and *Cell* guide one audience member at a time through a city landscape, dislocating them from traditional spaces of performance and requiring them to physically invest as ambulatory participants. In this regard, these works bear resemblance to Templeton's *YOU-The City* produced decades earlier. The key difference, however, is that these productions choreograph the audience experience via instructions explained through the use of cell phones. Each audience member's experience is technologically mediated, and the intersubjective exchanges they have with performers are, for the most part, exclusively by phone. In Foster's view, such productions "require new kinds of competence from viewers," suggesting that these experiences are indicative of a "new kinesthesia" occurring between bodies and devices.

Foster's proposal of such a new kinesthesia is compelling, and I further propose that the use of such digital technologies may not be necessary to cultivate new kinds of competencies among audiences. Rather, it could be that the process of engaging in choreography as a design technology in immersive productions, regardless of how rigid or flexible the improvisational structures may be, calls for new kinds of kinesthetic awareness, even competencies, that are new for, and newly cultivated by, today's participatory audiences. Indeed, it seems possible that the choreography designed by immersive practitioners for instantiation by audiences is already contributing to redefinitions of their physicality. As audiences negotiate worlds saturated with movement, they are afforded opportunities to make meaning from what they observe around them as well as from the movement they themselves are performing. If part of the process of transforming spectators into subjects of choreography is a kind of resuscitation of their kinesthesia, perhaps this restored kinesthesia is precisely what affords them the sense of agency that enables them to function with new status as protagonists so that they can take on roles and responsibilities as physical, mobile, agentive entities during performances.[18] The resuscitation of kinesthesia through choreography, leading to redefinitions of physicality, may provide audiences the perception that they can, indeed, take on the opportunities offered to become both physically and creatively engaged during immersive productions. Because that physical and creative engagement occurs within productions that are social and potentially collaborative in nature, it is worth exploring how empathy, particularly *kinesthetic empathy*, functions within these experiences.

Kinesthetic Empathy

The concept of empathy, like kinesthesia, emerged in the late 1800s, proposed by German philosophers theorizing art and aesthetics. Robert Visher coined the term *Einfühlung*, or "feeling into," in 1873, and Theodor Lipps later applied the concept to how individuals make sense of the art objects they observe by projecting themselves onto the object of perception in order to understand it. As Foster puts it, *Einfühlung* suggests "a kind of physical connection between viewer and art in which the viewer's own body would move into and inhabit the various features of the artwork" (2011:10). Empathy's nineteenth-century conceptual origins were, therefore, "implicitly kinesthetic," with "visual objects . . . perceived in terms of movement dynamics" (Reynolds 2013:212). In the early twentieth century, these terms were coupled together as *kinesthetic empathy*, first surfacing within aesthetic discussions within the visual arts, and then later developed as a key concept within dance. The emergence of kinesthetic empathy as a concept directly reflects the development of new ideas from the first-generation avant-garde artists about evolving art to be an influential force for changing the hearts and minds of viewers and audiences (Jones 2012:10). While the concept of kinesthetic empathy is challenging to define, a brief historical overview of its usage lends insight into its usefulness for the discourses surrounding immersive performance.

The first prominent figure to associate the concept of kinesthesia with dance was John Martin, an American dance critic who wrote for *The New York Times* from the 1920s through the 1960s. Martin critiqued, chronicled, and analyzed the emergence of modern dance as a powerful new art form within the Western canon. Early pioneers of modern dance, such as the American Isadora Duncan and artists in Germany, wanted to distinguish their choreographic innovations from those of European ballet, which, up until that point, had focused on the communication of well-known stories through movement.[19] The aim of these dance artists, primarily women, was to create choreography that emphasized the medium of movement itself; dances could serve as means for the transference of emotions and concepts without offering any linear, definitive narrative. Martin, based on his own experiences as an audience participant and his observations of audiences around him, developed specific beliefs about how to attend to this new form of dance. Martin suggested audiences be aware of sensations such as "muscular sympathy" (1933:11) as well as the phenomenon of "inner mimicry," that is, the tendency to yawn when someone else yawns, or laugh when others laugh (1939:47). Martin declared, "we shall cease to be mere spectators and become participants in the movement that is presented to us, and though to all outward appearances we shall be sitting quietly in our chairs, we shall nevertheless be dancing synthetically with all our musculature" (1939:53). Martin reminded audience members that they already possessed what was needed to understand this new form: "[the] irreducible minimum of equipment demanded . . . [is] a kinesthetic sense in working condition" (1936:117). Thus, he urged audiences of dance performances to "carry along the expectation of response to movement and a reliance on the faculty of inner mimicry," a faculty he understood as an immersion of one's total self via physiological sensations to evoke the full emotional impact of the dance (Martin 1939:55, and Reason and Reynolds 2010:54). For Martin, audiences "could and should become by-proxy participants as well as observers" (Reason and Reynolds 2010:54). Yet Martin also suggested that through kinesthetic empathy, the viewer could somehow grasp what the choreographer intended, as well as understand the feelings of the dancer performing—debatable notions that have since been deconstructed by other scholars.

The main critiques of Martin's theorizing of kinesthetic empathy have been offered by Foster and by dance scholar Mark Franko, among others.[20] Franko notes the problematic tendency of dance artists and scholars of the modernist era, Martin among them, to "universalize and nationalize feeling" (2002:38). Similarly, Foster's concern is with how Martin's definition of inner mimicry promotes the assumption that responsiveness to dance is somehow generalizable. While acknowledging both physiological and psychological processes as important ways to analyze the performer–audience relationship, Foster nonetheless identifies such perspectives as multiple, shifting, and historically as well as culturally contingent. She resolves this complexity by defining empathy as contextualized within each individual performance event. It is, she asserts, a "pan-human but highly individualized phenomenon, produced through the individualized and culturally specific acts of each perceiver, including the full range of movement experiences that any given subject has undergone" (2011:168). Although Martin's work has been reconsidered and reconceived by subsequent scholars, it nonetheless remains foundational for any examination of audience experiences of dance.

Kinesthetic empathy featured prominently throughout twentieth-century dance scholarship on spectatorship, yet it was less present in scholarship from other disciplines. Empathy and spectatorship have been somewhat addressed within visual and performing arts disciplines for over a century, but it is only since the corporeal turn in the social sciences that research on kinesthetic empathy has gained momentum. Kinesthesia and kinesthetic empathy are now attracting increasing interest from theater scholars, specifically those engaged in cognitive studies, although surprisingly, much of the extant research on spectatorship references kinesthesia and kinesthetic empathy in limited ways, if at all. One exception is Bruce McConachie, author of *Engaging Audiences: A Cognitive Approach to Spectating in the Theatre* (2008), who draws upon the work of neurophysiologist Vittorio Gallese to consider the role of mirror neurons in empathic response. Others include Rachel Fensham, who proposes *embodied spectatorship* and *affective spectatorship* (2009 and 2016, respectively); and Garner, who developed the concept of *kinesthetic spectatorship* (2018).[21] Productive discussions led by these scholars have, over the past decade, shifted ideas about the body and spectatorship to the foreground of discourses surrounding theater studies.

However, even though practitioners and scholars have noted that the body of the spectator, that is, their physical presence, is key to immersive performance, neither kinesthesia nor kinesthetic empathy has been thoroughly analyzed in discourses surrounding immersive performance. If, given my argument, audiences are always already being choreographed when they encounter performances—whether they participate by sitting in seats in a proscenium theater or by ambulating around spaces designed to accommodate them as moving entities—then they are also always already embodied and experiencing kinesthesia. As Foster notes, "any notion of choreography contains, embodied within it, a kinesthesis, a designated way of experiencing physicality and movement that, in turn, summons other bodies into a specific way of feeling towards it" (2011:2).[22] Choreography, whether the spectator is being choreographed or watching the choreography being performed by others, serves as a stimulus and generator of affective responses, particularly within participatory contexts such as immersive performance. While both movement and choreography are fundamental to any live performance where the body is called upon as a medium of communication, in immersive works audiences are typically choreographed so they can participate in the action in closer proximity to performers and other spectators. This can provide opportunities for spectators to watch bodies move and perceive sensations with greater acuity, factors which might intensify their perception of sensations and responses such as kinesthetic empathy. Here we can see the importance of Elswit's call for cognizance of interdependency of forms, and for keeping discourses as open as possible between disciplines in order to build collective knowledge that helps to illuminate and sustain artistic practices.

With both practitioners and scholars of immersive theater emphatically claiming the centrality of the audience member as a physical subject who participates in performances, it is surprising that writings on immersive theater address kinesthesia and kinesthetic empathy only minimally. One rare instance is found in Biggin's discussion of Punchdrunk's work, where she suggests that "kinesthetic empathy is useful for considering immersive experience in interactions that are not naturalistic one-on-ones (where the audience member may more explicitly participate), but spectatorship in the presence of contemporary dance" (2017:17). What has yet to be recognized, though, is that the spectator is *never not* choreographed within immersive performance. Given my assertion that choreography has replaced the fourth wall, it can be presumed, then, that kinesthesia and attendant phenomena, such as kinesthetic empathy, can manifest whenever one person is intersubjectively engaged with one or more persons or environs. When we recall that the early origins of empathy are aesthetically oriented, it seems fitting that audiences of live performance are continuously engaged and interacting to some extent with the environment around them. As Martin has stated, kinesthetic response is not limited to "our relations to other persons; it applies to impersonal objects as well" (1939:48). Indeed, we even "respond muscularly" to architecture and to natural formations (1939:53).[23] Joslin McKinney has argued persuasively that scenography shapes audiences' experiences of live performance, including participatory and immersive works, citing the work of Punchdrunk in particular. She calls for an expansion of the discourse surrounding kinesthetic empathy beyond the focus on intersubjectivity (2013:221). These scholars' perspectives provide important insights into the experience of spectator immersion. Still, in order to fully articulate the connections between participating in choreography and watching dance, we must delve further into research that specifically explores kinesthetic empathy in dance, with particular attention to what might be happening for audiences in immersive performances.

For this, we turn to the work of theater scholar Matthew Reason and interdisciplinary scholar Dee Reynolds, who in the 2010s spearheaded a resurgence of scholarship devoted to kinesthetic empathy, notably through their *Watching Dance: Kinesthetic Empathy* project (2008–2011). This project, a multidisciplinary initiative involving collaboration across four institutions in the United Kingdom, aimed at "combining audience research and neuroscience as methodologies for analyzing how dance spectators respond to and empathize with dance."[24] It resulted in research available online as well as synthesized in their text *Kinesthetic Empathy in Creative and Cultural Practices* (2012) and, later, in individually authored essays (www.watchingdance.org). By analyzing qualitative data that largely consisted of writings collected from dance audiences, Reason and Reynolds concluded that as these audiences were watching others perform dance, they experienced complex processes of identification and mimesis, both physiologically and cognitively. Echoing Martin's concept of inner mimicry, mentioned previously, some of the spectators wrote about having "constructed an out-of-body experience" when imagining themselves as the other performing, while others felt extreme satisfaction in imagining themselves possessing the skills and talents they perceived in the dancers they were observing (2010:61). Reason and Reynolds extend Martin's idea of inner mimicry to issues of alterity and otherness, further situating the concepts of intersubjectivity and intercorporeality as critical to discussions around kinesthetic empathy. Their work lays a foundation for my own analysis of such processes in immersive productions.[25]

Within Reynolds's work, another critical distinction emerged, which offers further insight into audience reception of immersive works. Noting how empathy early on became associated with emotions rather than with kinesthesia, Reynolds has called for a decoupling of kinesthetic empathy from emotional response so that we can distinguish between "embodied responses which take the form of an 'affective encounter' rather than an 'emotional identification' with others" (2013:212). To refer to the former in relation to embodiment, Reynolds offers the term *kinesthetic affect*, defining affect as that which "is felt in the body but not yet 'captured' in emotion" (213). Reynolds draws upon discourses concerned with the affective turn of the 1990s and the development of affect theory, which in turn, is predicated on Dutch philosopher Baruch Spinoza's establishment in the seventeenth century of affect as concept concerned with embodied experience. Reynolds's association of kinesthetic empathy with affect rather than emotion follows the work of those who extended Spinoza's theories, including Bergson, Deleuze, and Guattari, particularly in her claim that kinesthetic empathy can be understood as "an embodied intensity that impacts the spectator kinesthetically" (2012:132). Reynolds is concerned with the tendency to overgeneralize and universalize kinesthetic empathy as a way to understand the emotionality of others, and particularly with the projecting of emotionality onto forms of contemporary concert dance (2013:213).[26] She suggests that, particularly in abstract dance contexts wherein narrative may not be the aim, kinesthetic empathy might be framed as an "engagement with kinesthetic intentionality, which inheres in the choreographed movement, rather than in the psychology of individual dancers or even the characters they may embody" (2012:124). While Reynolds did not theorize kinesthetic affect specifically in relation to immersive performance, her proposal has particular valence when considering choreography in these contexts.

Building on Reynolds's suggestion that we distinguish kinesthetic affect from kinesthetic empathy, and that we "think of empathy in 'affective' rather than emotional terms," I assert that in the context of immersive performance contexts, it is productive to consider these two concepts as distinct, phenomenological responses (124). This distinction is particularly useful when speculating on how spectators' experiences of movement—their own as well as that of others—contribute to personal perceptions of immersion. As they participate in immersive performances, spectators themselves have kinesthetic intentionality, performing as subjects of choreography to instantiate scores. Although immersive productions can and often do emphasize narrative content, the responses of spectators to performance content are not exclusively the result of emotional identification with storylines, narrative structures, and/or characters. As stated in the Introduction, spectators actually experience an immersive production first and foremost as kinesthetic activity. And following the ideas of Rethorst outlined in Chapter 1, what is known through the body, and what is experienced before both thought and feeling arise, has value. Being impelled to move and offered the permission and agency to do so, albeit limited by the parameters of the choreographic score, offers the potential for pre-cognitive understanding of experiences of immersive performance, before and beyond the consciousness of narrative. It is possible, then, to conceive of kinesthetic affect in these contexts as a response that manifests before kinesthetic empathy, with both forms of response serving as outcomes that are predicated upon the resuscitation of the spectator's kinesthesia through choreography intended to facilitate immersion. The kinesthetic affect that arises from the physical effort required to instantiate the choreography may be more impactful toward facilitating immersion as an affect than the encounters that spectators have with narrative elements and characters that prompt emotional responses.

One final point about kinesthetic affect and kinesthetic empathy bears mentioning here. Because affect and emotion are not binary opposites, as Reynolds points out, we must consider how these processes are not only distinct but also interconnected (2012:128). Kinesthetic empathy and kinesthetic affect may arise as independent responses and may also occur simultaneously and work conjunctively, *in tandem*, to influence spectators' perceptions during immersive performances (2012:128). In addition, both emotion and affect are inherently relational, following the work of Reynolds and philosopher Brian Massumi; we might, then, understand kinesthetic empathy and kinesthetic affect as relational processes that emerge through encounters with movement, including moving with others. Furthermore, as Massumi has asserted, because affect is relational, it is inextricable from politics and notions of power; his theorizing of the political nature of affect, as developed in his text *The Politics of Affect* (2015), is helpful when analyzing more thoroughly how audiences might be negotiating agency and action during immersive performances. Massumi centralizes what he calls the "deceptively simple" definition put forth by Spinoza that affect is "the capacity to affect or be affected" (2015b:91). He goes on to assert that Spinoza's framing is "proto-political in the sense that it includes relation in the definition. To affect and to be affected is to be open to the world, to be active in it and to be patient for its return activity"

(2015a:ix). Massumi argues that if affect is "the capacity to affect," then "to be affected" is a capacity as well; an individual has the capacity to resist as well as the capacity to acquiesce to affect, since, as he maintains, "power and resistance are two sides of the same coin" (2015b:92 and 104). Important for our discussion of audience agency is Massumi's suggestion that improvisation serves as an effective "relational technique" for modulating affect (2015b:96–97). The relationship of affect to power—the potential power and improvisational agency that comes with access to mobility and the possibility *to make things happen*, to borrow Sheets-Johnstone's phrase referenced in Chapter 1—can be a seductive draw and much desired by some audience participants. Massumi's ideas on the political nature of affect, particularly issues of power and agency, are taken up again in Chapter 4 when I introduce the concept of insider dynamics to illustrate the processual nature of affect, including the powerful desire for audiences to perceive inclusion within performance contexts.

Speculations

This chapter establishes a broad framework for how choreography as a design technology operates within immersive performance. Building on the idea established in Chapter 1 that spectators are transfigured into subjects of choreography who can instantiate the production as a work of art, this chapter's discussion of design enables us to see how choreography functions as an effective and essential technology for practitioners wishing to cultivate audience immersion. Choreography, as design, can serve to resuscitate kinesthesia, as well as activate kinesthetic empathy and kinesthetic affect. Because of choreography's convergence of three aspects of spectatorial responsiveness discussed here—kinesthesia, kinesthetic empathy, and kinesthetic affect—I suggest, speculatively, that choreography is an effective and essential component of immersive design. The convergence of spectator responses in choreography points to the kinds of outcomes that can result from designing dance differently. It also points to how choreography as design can serve the intentions of immersive practitioners to cultivate audience immersion.

As distinct yet interdependent phenomena, kinesthesia, kinesthetic empathy, and kinesthetic affect all emerge out of the processes of audiences being choreographed. These phenomena exist and function as conditions through which audiences potentially experience immersion as an affect.

Spectators, as subjects of choreography, are not only sensing their own kin-esthesia in motion, but are also watching, and even feeling, the dance of others in the space with them, including the performers and other audience members. The kinesthetic responses brought forth by choreography con-stitute a changed relationship of the spectator to experiences of immersive performance work, which influences their own consciousness and sense of physicality as well as how they perceive those around them.[27]

When writing about his notion of inner mimicry, Martin noted that indi-viduals typically go about their daily lives automatically reconciling their perceptions and their actions, but when they are engaged with art, they as-sume a fundamentally different stance. In such moments, he writes, "where perception is in a certain degree a conscious process, we are more than likely to concentrate our attention on the qualitative, the static element, leaving the vital factor of action virtually unperceived" (1939:52). We might consider, then, whether immersive performance activates perception of action. As a participant observer of immersive performances, I have found myself under-going what I can describe as a kind of a "doubling" of inner mimicry, wherein I was continually enmeshed in a type of perpetual feedback loop of affec-tive experiences that included watching, imagining, and performing move-ment. In many productions, I have felt equally *compelled* by observing the movements of performers and other audience members as I was *impelled* by my own movement desires and choices. This kind of kinesthetically charged participation offers spectators the opportunity to experience emotional real-ities and physical states via agentive action, in addition to experiencing-by-proxy, via kinesthetic responses. Building on my experiences and application of the Spectator-Participation-as-Research (SPaR) protocol method, I pro-pose that the impact of kinesthetic empathy and kinesthetic affect can be intensified in immersive productions because of the close proximity in which audiences often witness the movements of performers and other spectators. In addition, since immersive performance commonly involves some sort of narrative, in some cases more fractured than linear, it is possible that audiences may connect cognitively and emotionally with the circumstances of the characters, thus leading them to experience kinesthetic empathy.[28]

Rather than adopt a romanticized assumption that spectators are truly empathizing with dancers-performing-characters, though, it is important to remember, as Reynolds notes, drawing upon Lipps, "even if we had access to what the other person was experiencing, this would not be of interest, and in fact the more we ourselves are active, the less we are aware of what the other is experiencing" (2012:127). Indeed, we must be careful of the tendency to make assumptions about audience motivation and intention. When reflecting on my own participant observation of others in immersive performances, I have questioned my interpretations of their behavior, particularly when drawing conclusions that an audience member appears to be more immersed in their own agency and discovery than in attending to the action around them, including that of the performers. However, if the choreography of a production is optimally operative, that is, successful in capturing audiences as subjects, then it is understandable that they would be more attentive to and immersed in their own performance than that of others around them. Admittedly, even this notion can be questioned, though. For me, it is coun-terintuitive to presume that audiences are somehow less aware of others and their surroundings during their participation in an immersive performance, given my knowledge as a dancer/choreographer and audience participant. Rather, I maintain that being kinesthetically resuscitated means there may be an amplified awareness of the presence and activities of others around oneself. So, what does this mean for immersive performance? What is hap-pening here for audiences, and how it is happening? How are practitioners conceiving of and creating the conditions for productions wherein audiences can experience immersion? What can we make of audiences who are moving while watching, and what specific choreographic strategies afford them these opportunities? Chapters 3, 4, and 5 propose different strategies and processes to further untangle these questions.

Although my propositions about kinesthesia and related kinesthetic responses are speculative, given that conclusive evidence would require the undertaking of different kinds of empirical and qualitative studies that are beyond the scope of the current project, I nevertheless offer these propos-itions as a point of departure for the consideration of what might be going on in immersive performances. Reason and Reynolds's research has pro-vided evidence that audiences watching dance and theater in traditional presentation formats, such as proscenium theaters, can be compelled both by watching and by imagining participation. Immersive practitioners, I sug-gest, aim to go further, providing opportunities for agency by designing choreography that affords different kinds of physical participation, often through the construction and/or adaptation of spaces to accommodate the doing of performance. The permeable barriers and porous contexts for au-dience participants to play along the edges of being spectator, performer, and participant are only possible because of choreography. In the next chapters, specific productions are offered as examples of how immersive performance can be conceptualized and created so as to bring forth the convergence mentioned previously. Within this research is situated an overarching philosophical question concerning the nature of art itself, namely, the question of how exactly immersive performance functions as art. If we accept that art is by definition intentional, can a work of art absorb human beings into its physical instantiation without their conscious intent? Or, alternatively, how is the intent of audiences captured and absorbed into the art?

3

Elicitive Dramaturgy

Third Rail Projects' *Then She Fell*

I am led with two other spectators into a small, white-walled, closet-like chamber and positioned in front of a small window looking in on a bright, artificially lit room. Within this room, apparently unaware of our gaze, is a stern-faced woman in a red dress, poised rigidly on a stool at a dressing table. As each of us spectators watches her through our own tiny window, we can see her face reflected in the dressing mirror, her posture fully erect. As we observe, she suddenly sweeps her arm across the dressing table, sending objects flying across the room. One of these airborne objects is a bottle of pills, which scatters its jewel-like contents in an array towards the window separating her from us, creating a 3-D effect as they bounce off the glass inches from our faces. I realize in that moment that the windows between us are medicine cabinets built into the walls, which open like portals into her room. We watch through these portals as the woman launches into a wild whirling motion, spinning like a top, slamming into walls, and ricocheting through space. Her devolution is finally complete when her body abruptly decelerates and collapses onto the floor. After a pause, she slowly stands back up, meets our gaze through the portals, and walks to the door between our room and hers.

The woman opens the door and makes eye contact with each of us in turn. Alternating her gaze between each of us and a chair in the next room, she systematically guides us one by one to come in and sit down. Once all three of us are seated, she sits back down at the dressing table, opens a drawer, and retrieves three small cups. We watch her face in the mirror as she makes eye contact with us again through her reflection. Then, with an acute spatial clarity, she thrusts her hand behind her, holding out a cup for one of us, then the second, then the third. Given our individual responses, it seems we each know exactly which cup is intended for us. She whirls around on her stool to face us and holds up a medicine bottle before us. From this, she serves us each a portion of strong, red wine. Finally, after waiting for us to drink, she turns back toward the mirror, slowly begins to brush her hair, and speaks to us in a measured tone. Each word of her

Tandem Dances. Julia M. Ritter, Oxford University Press (2021). © Oxford University Press.
DOI: 10.1093/oso/9780190051303.001.0001.

*monologue is aligned to the deliberate, choreographed actions of her arrange-
ment of her hair. Speaking quietly yet emphatically as she spirals her tresses into
a tight bun, she states the importance of conducting oneself appropriately at
all times. Finally, having tucked in the last of many pins to secure her hair, she
looks at us again through the mirror, and flicks her hand behind her toward a
small bin. Without hesitation, we all stand up dutifully, turn, and line up to dis-
pose of our cups. When we are done, she opens the door and stands to one side
with her hands folded in front of her, staring straight ahead but looking at no
one. We know to take our leave of her.*

Immersive performance transforms the spectator into a subject of choreography. This much is evident from the scenario that opens this chapter, in
which my fellow audience members and I were introduced to the Red Queen,
as performed by Rebekah Morin (Figure 3.1), in the award-winning, critically acclaimed and long-running production of *Then She Fell* (*TSF*).[1] The
production was created by Zach Morris, Tom Pearson, and Jennine Willett,
artistic directors of the Brooklyn-based Third Rail Projects.[2] Based upon
the fanciful Victorian children's novels *Alice's Adventures in Wonderland*
and *Through the Looking Glass*, by Lewis Carroll (a.k.a. Charles Dodgson),
the production also draws upon the author's other writings and the details

Figure 3.1 Rebekah Morin (Red Queen) in Third Rail Projects' *Then She Fell*
(New York, 2012–). Photograph by Adam Jason Photography.

of his biography, especially his relationship with the real child who inspired the eponymous heroine, Alice Liddell (Figure 3.2). Now that the spectator is understood to be a mobile body whose movements and speech constitute part of the production itself, practitioners who design and present immersive performances must conceive of and plan for the spectator's role in ways unaccounted for by conventional conceptions of dramaturgy.

Drawing specifically on scenes from *TSF*, this chapter explores the dramaturgical dimensions of immersive productions in order to elucidate some of the strategies deployed by practitioners when accounting for mobile

Figure 3.2 Tara O'Con and Marissa Nielsen-Pincus (Alice) in Third Rail Projects' *Then She Fell* (New York, 2012–). Photograph by Adam Jason Photography.

spectators as part of a production. If we accept, following Gareth White, that the spectator becomes part of the aesthetic materiality of a production, how does the spectator's body figure into the processes of creative composition? What structures support audience participation of spectators such that their bodies are resourced, following White and Alston, to function together with the other elements—including performers' bodies, and the elements of time, space, and energy? How are the spectators' movements and speech coordinated, given that they enter a performance with little or no information about what they will experience during the production? And finally, what tensions emerge as spectators—having been given status and possibilities for agency—resist the structures that artists design for them?

In addressing these questions, I note that they intersect with questions posed by White regarding the nature of audience participation in participatory performance, including immersive theater. Specifically, White asked "how people are led to perform, [...] how far they can be said to be made to perform, and to give performances that have been conceived by theatre practitioners, [and] how people are able to give performances they invent themselves" (2013:27). White's investigation of these questions was built on a theoretical framework that provides a fruitful point of departure for my own discussion. White's argument is centered on his proposal of the "aesthetic act of the invitation," referring to the moment audiences are invited to participate, which he discusses in terms of two concepts; first, *procedural authorship*, a concept borrowed from Janet H. Murray, and second, his concept of a *horizon of participation*, which builds upon the writings of theater scholar Susan Bennett. Together, these three concepts—White's focus on an aesthetics of the invitation and his theorizing of a horizon of participation along with Murray's notion of procedural authorship—constitute a conception of how audience participation occurs.

White describes Murray's concept of procedural authorship as "the way that participation is manipulated by computer game designers to create a system with which players to [sic] interact, and designing the procedures that allow and respond to their activities" (31). While White acknowledges that Murray's coining of the term *procedural authorship* is linked to the creative practices of artists, for example, poets, novelists, playwrights, he neglects to mention that Murray herself likens the role of the procedural author to "a choreographer who supplies the rhythms, the context, and the set of steps that will be performed" ([1997] 2017 edition:187). Murray's term for the player of a game is *interactor*, which could hence be transposed for the audience participant in immersive performance. Murray further explains that "the interactor, whether as navigator, protagonist, explorer, or builder, makes use of this repertoire of possible steps and rhythms to improvise a particular dance among the many, many possible dances the author has enabled" (187). Murray's choice of dance-based language to describe how the procedural author functions reflects her recognition of the choreographic processes as inherent to the design of participatory projects. In White's adaptation of Murray's term, he defines procedural authorship through terms that allude to, without explicitly acknowledging, choreography. This omission points to a lacuna in the theorization of participatory forms.

White's second concept for understanding the nature of audience participation in participatory performance is that of the *horizon of participation*. Here, White builds upon Bennett's notion of a "horizon of expectations," which is an idea drawn from reader response theory that she describes as the kinds of anticipatory, "pre-activated receptive processes" that each audience member brings to a performance experience, as informed by their personal histories and cultural backgrounds (1997:104). White defines his idea of the horizon of participation as a "spatial, embodied, time-based response to an invitation (and henceforth a commitment) to act" (168), and claims that "becoming an audience participant involves perceiving a horizon, and accepting responsibility to act within that horizon, to make choices and to perform those choices" (164). In my view, this description alludes to the choreographic properties of an improvisational score, referring to the ways in which audiences, always already embodied and situated in space and time, "perceive" an invitation (i.e., are given scores) and choose to take action, or not.

White's conceptualization of the *invitation*, finally, is concerned with the moment "when an invitation to join the action of a performance is made and accepted, [and] the audience participant becomes material of a different kind, more carefully shaped and manipulated, more productive of signs and affects, more complex as a site of perception and action" (195). Again, I argue this language implies choreographic operations. Audiences are invited to participate when offered instructional, improvisational scores, and it is through these scores that audiences are shaped as materials and, in turn, are productive within performances via the movements they generate. Moreover, when White asserts that "the participant is simultaneously *the performer*, the one who enacts the performance through choice, *the performance* that emerges from their own body, *and the audience* as they view it," he is providing a description of improvisation as it happens in dance as well as theater (161). Improvisational scores provide parameters in which choices are possible, and when improvising, performers are simultaneously composing and performing while witnessing themselves in the moment. Hence, we can understand how spectators are resourced as subjects of choreography when given scores. The scores are choreography in and of themselves, which when enacted, provide spectators the opportunity to realize their tandem dances alongside performers.

While White's theorizing attends minimally to dance, I argue that the language he uses to discuss what he sees as processes of audience participation is consistently reflective of the choreographic. If spectators are already, in a sense, central to dramaturgy in theater and in dance, I suggest we aim for more specific terminology and analysis of the ways that their roles are made self-evidently even more critical within immersive performance. Given the emphasis on the spectator in immersive performance, I argue the form requires a new conception of dramaturgy, one that accounts for the important role of the mobile spectator. It is this new dramaturgy, which aims to orchestrate the mobilized audience, that I identify as *elicitive dramaturgy*. As a choreographically driven theory and practice of composing immersive performance, elicitive dramaturgy shifts the focus of the foundational dramaturgical concepts outlined in the Introduction—namely, the research of content and context to assist artists from the inception through the creation of a production, as well as theories such as White's procedural authorship— toward the ways in which the physical, enactive contributions of spectators are orchestrated through choreography during performances.

Contextualizing Elicitive Dramaturgy

Elicitive dramaturgy does not just surpass conventional understandings of dramaturgy; it also goes beyond other similar dramaturgies proposed in the past two decades, namely evocative, physical, and relational dramaturgies. It does so by prioritizing the efficacy of choreographic composition to engender audience responsiveness. First, *evocative* dramaturgy was posited by theater dramaturg and director Eugenio Barba in 2010 as a form of dramaturgy that aimed to evoke responses from spectators and produce intimate resonances within them (10). This "evocative experience" leads to "a leap of consciousness in the spectator; *a change of state*" (183, emphasis original). Barba suggests that dramaturgy has for centuries had the goal of instilling "the *permanence* of the performance in the spectator's senses and memory through the actor's action" (14, emphasis original). Such a conception of dramaturgy rightly attends to the power of theatrical stimuli to trigger affective responses. Yet, this notion of dramaturgy is limited in its focus on spectators' emotional and cognitive capacities and its neglect of their physicality. Through my own choreographic analyses of various immersive productions and interviews with practitioners, I understand elicitive dramaturgy as a process characterized by the deliberate efforts of artists to develop choreographic strategies, made effective through the skills of dancers, that go beyond evoking emotions to elicit physical and verbal responses from the spectator. The changes of state that a spectator can experience in immersive productions occur not only through the work of the actor/performer but also through the spectator's own entry into the performance as a subject of choreography and the work they perform as such. This change of state is demonstrated in the Red Queen scenario described previously, wherein my fellow audience members and I followed the performer's movement directives. The changes of state that are affected in immersive productions may at times even be permanent, in that the spectators' new states of being are not just leaps of consciousness but kinesthetic advances of self into the work. These advances are facilitated by choreographic structures that have been designed through elicitive dramaturgy to accommodate the spectators. If we accept Barba's claim that it is possible to affect the permanent resonance of a performance within the spectator, then it seems immersive practitioners expand even further on that potential to implicate the spectator as a subject of choreography who manifests the event itself.[3] Thus, immersive practitioners expand the possibilities for how the performance resonates or has permanence by using elicitive dramaturgy through the crafting of choreography that elicits spectators' physical and verbal responses. Spectators are resources as active participants in the manifestation of immersive performance.[4]

As noted previously, two other dramaturgies bear similarities to elicitive dramaturgy: *physical dramaturgy* and *relational dramaturgy*. Both have been proposed within the past two decades, the former to address issues surrounding movement-centered approaches to collaborative creation and the latter to account for the function of the spectator within performance. Physical dramaturgy appears primarily within the writings of theater scholars as a descriptor for how different kinds of body-based creative practices are used to create a wide range of live performance forms, including the production of classical dramatic texts (e.g., Shakespeare), as well as physical theater, performance art, dance, and immersive theater. Given the diversity of processes by which works of contemporary performance are conceptualized and created, scholars have been reticent to establish a fixed definition for physical dramaturgy. Theater scholar David Korish mentions physical dramaturgy in 2002 in relation to discussions around the "thin line which separates theatre and dance" and, in so doing, distinguishes between two kinds of dramaturgy in his efforts to analyze the "complicated relationship between the physical dramaturgy of the performer and the written dramaturgy of the written text" (284). Between 2006 and 2011, dramaturg Jeroen Peeters collaborated with choreographer Martin Nachbar on a series of practice-based workshops in Brussels on physical dramaturgy, describing it as that which "seeks to explore and exhaust the realm of meaning triggered by moving bodies, as well . . . as [by] the various materials and ideas that populate a creation process" (2011).[5] Peeters has written on both dance and physical dramaturgy, sometimes conflating the two, yet his theorizing of dramaturgy has focused on more conventional forms of contemporary movement performance during proscenium-based productions rather than on specific investigation of audience participation or on practices specific to immersive performance. A more concrete definition of physical dramaturgy is offered in *Physical Dramaturgy: Perspectives from the Field* (2018), where Bowditch et al. refer to it as "the process of *embodying* traditional dramaturgy" (2018:5, emphasis added). In staking this claim, the authors further distinguish between traditional and physical dramaturgy by describing the former as the "what" of conceptualizing and creating productions and the latter as the "how" (5). By contrast, in the case of immersive theater, the audience is conceptualized as a protagonist, that is, as a performer and contributor to the performance; thus, the "how" of dramaturgical practice involves a level of specificity related to the audience that is beyond what is used in conceptualizing other types of performance.

More relevant to a discussion of immersive performance is *relational dramaturgy*, a philosophical approach that has emerged within the past ten years to explain the ontology of the spectator in relation to performance. Proposed by theater scholar Peter Boenisch, relational dramaturgy is a "relational aesthetic practice" that "forges relations, changes relationships and calibrates a dynamic interplay" (227). In articulating the key theoretical concerns of relational dramaturgy, Boenisch draws from art critic Nicholas Bourriaud's concept of relational aesthetics, proposed in 1998 to describe the emergence of conceptual works of contemporary art that provide aesthetic experiences through socially engineered circumstances. As an example of relational aesthetics, Bourriaud identifies the work of Thai artist Rirkrit Tiravanja, particularly his *Untitled (Free)*, created in 1992, which involved the conversion of the exhibition space at the 303 Gallery in New York City into a kitchen. Visitors, rather than viewing paintings or sculptures displayed within the gallery, become part of the art, experiencing it through processes of gathering and interacting socially while eating the food cooked and served by Tiravanja himself. Boenisch applies his theory of relational dramaturgy to three works that have elsewhere been identified as immersive, including Belgian director Ivo Van Hove's *Roman Tragedies* (2012) and two works by UK-based immersive theater companies, namely *Hotel Medea* (2009–2012) by Zecora Ura (now known as ZU-UK) and *Money* (2009) by the London-based SHUNT collective.[6] In Boenisch's analyses, he rightly points out that such productions position spectators in a doubly implicated stance, where they are both spectating and being "acting agents" (240). At the most fundamental level, during these events in which they encounter a multitude of relational possibilities between a performance's materiality and semioticity, spectators must confront this double experience of the self as an entity that both spectates and acts (240). By pointing out the gap between what he calls the "spectating I" and "I of the spectator"—analogous to Jacques Lacan's theory of subjectification through language—Boenisch emphasizes the fundamental split between spectator and performer. The dance theorist and critic Gerald Siegmund articulates this split succinctly: "The founding principle of our Western theatrical experience is the split ... the institution of theatre as a split space" (2005:26). The split between performer and spectator is always there and cannot be erased; and yet, as Boenisch suggests, it may be "covered over" when spectators are "allowed to perform an action in accordance to a script" (238). It is precisely practitioners' strategies for facilitating such action, which we see deployed in immersive performance, that can "cover over" or bridge the split. Here, I theorize, is where choreographic thinking drives elicitive dramaturgy.

Although Boenisch and other scholars acknowledge the spectator's status as an intelligent interpreter of the production, they do not explore the spectator's kinesthesia (234). The practitioners featured in this book, however, not only affirm the audience's intelligence and interpretive capacities; they also make clear, in interviews with me, their intention to acknowledge as well as resource the kinesthetic intelligence of the spectator as a core function of cognitive and interpretative capacities. In 1983, Harvard professor of education Howard Gardner proposed kinesthetic intelligence as one of his multiple theories of intelligence, defining it as "control of one's bodily motions and the capacity to handle objects skillfully" (219).[7] It is this form of intelligence and these kinesthetic capacities that immersive practitioners wish to resource from spectators through their participation. As discussed in Chapter 2, the core conceptual tools of choreography can be understood as body, space, time, energy, and relationship; thus, when spectators are resourced as subjects of choreography, they are inescapably situated as part of the materiality of a work. The spectator is always in negotiation with their perceptions of self, as well as with their own bodies and those of performers and other spectators within the time, space, and energy of a performance. These concepts manifest themselves in the choreography, along with scenography, light, sound, and any other elements, such as text and video. These elements, in turn, inform the semiotic properties of a production—meaning the signs and symbols communicating ideas and influencing spectators' interpretations—and thus the spectators' relationships to content and meaning-making are constantly unfolding as they experience a work. By prioritizing choreographic compositional practices, practitioners endeavor to offer spectators access to physical knowledge to bring attention back to their bodies, as Leder put it, in order that the enacting of agency might allow spectators to find meaning through their positions as choreographed subjects. While spectators may be more or less choreographed (or to use Boenish's term, "scripted") in any given immersive production, nonetheless it is the practitioner's acknowledgment of the spectator's kinesthetic intelligence that is itself resourced as material for the performance.

In recognizing the resourcing of the spectator's kinesthesia, though, we confront the question of control and the illusory nature of agency. Does the spectator access their physical knowledge through being choreographed by the practitioner and thus made aware of their physical body? Or is the spectator actually under the practitioner's control, as their responses to the performer's choreography guide and choreograph them (the spectator) into particular responses? I argue that, in fact, both effects are occurring at the same time, working in tandem to create the kinds of performances in which audiences are resourced to perform through choreography that is intended to produce spectator responses. In immersive performances, the practitioners who create these productions, including those specifically fulfilling the role of dramaturg, overturn earlier conceptions of dramaturgy. By paying attention to spectators at a more granular level than is seen in any other form of live performance, these practitioners aim for a different degree of audience participation than is typically sought, one where spectators' physicality is fully engaged. This thoroughly realized physicality, then, is at the core of the new, new dramaturgy that I have termed elicitive dramaturgy (see also Introduction). As artists shift their focus from what happens onstage to what spectators do, they transform audiences and their bodies into stages of action. By adopting elicitive dramaturgical thinking, practitioners place implicit trust in the spectator's willingness to respond, building on the conceptual stance of confidence in body knowledge, corporeal capacity, and creativity to which all humans hypothetically have access. In this way, practitioners establish new expectations for spectators, raising the bar for their involvement and implicating them alongside the choreographers, directors, dancers, dramaturgs, and designers in the efficacious implementation of experiences of live performance.

To fully understand why *elicitive dramaturgy* is needed as distinct from physical and relational dramaturgies, it is helpful to look to the origins of the two latter practices in postdramatic theater. Arguably, physical dramaturgy and relational dramaturgy emerged from the discourse surrounding the theory of postdramatic theater in the late 1990s. German theater scholar Hans-Thies Lehmann proposed postdramatic theater in 1999 to acknowledge the shift in the mid-to-late twentieth century from the creation of performance works based on dramatic texts to those created through the use of diverse elements, particularly those emphasizing corporeality and imagery in performance.[8] Lehmann's concept of postdramatic theater materialized through his examination of trends and characteristics present in works of experimental performance from the late 1960s to the end of the twentieth century. The term *postdramatic* is meant to describe the new kind of theater—one that is *post*-dramatic, going beyond a framework in which dramatic text is the primary means of structuring content in order to prioritize other artistic elements as central within a production (2006:27).[9] Live performance, according to Lehmann, has evolved to be increasingly heterogeneous and interactive; importantly, however, text is not eliminated but relationally situated among different artistic disciplines. The multiple elements of a production are combined and interact in ways that "point simultaneously in different directions of meaning" so that the "consequence is a changed attitude on the part of the spectator" (87). A closer look at the postdramatic provides context on the emergence of new dramaturgies such as physical and relational dramaturgies, helping to differentiate elicitive dramaturgy as a distinct approach that emerged specifically within immersive performance.

Lehmann recognized that the artists in the early twentieth century (the first wave avant-gardes) grappled with the same kinds of tensions between text, theater, and body as the artists in the later twentieth century (the second wave avant-gardes, and physical theater artists), except for one key difference. The latter artists had to contend with what Lehmann calls the "caesura of the media society," by which he means the "the spread and then omnipresence of the *media* in everyday life since the 1970s" (22, emphasis original). The ubiquity of media and the possibilities that new technologies now presented for representation of text, body, space, and time have changed how artists conceptualize their work, and according to Lehmann, brought about an "influence of accelerated rhythms of perception" for spectators (134). Lehmann's suggestion of the caesura clearly acknowledges how changes in society instigate changes in theatrical styles, yet given that his text was first published in 1999, he could not predict the explosion of possibilities that came with the introduction of Web 2.0 in 2004. As the second generation of internet development, Web 2.0 brought forward a previously unknown level of user interactivity and collaboration, including new platforms allowing mash-ups, nomacity (the ability of users to connect to the internet from any location), social networking, crowdsourcing, user-generated content, and social curation sites like Reddit (2005) and Instagram (2010). Web 2.0 profoundly impacted behavior across sectors of society, including those involved in the creation and reception of contemporary performance. Jenkins's notion of participatory culture, as discussed in Chapter 2, is a part of this profusion of digital media, and practitioners across genres of live performance responded to this surge toward participation by adapting dramaturgical approaches.

Interestingly, within Lehmann's theory of the postdramatic, he himself proposed a new dramaturgy, stating that "[i]n place of a dramaturgy regulated by the text, one often finds a *visual dramaturgy*, which seemed to have attained absolute dominance especially in the theatre of the late 1970s and 1980s" (93, emphasis added). Lehmann situates visual dramaturgy as part of "the 'style' or rather the palette of stylistic traits [that] postdramatic theatre demonstrates" (86), while noting that "[v]isual dramaturgy here does not mean an exclusively visually organized dramaturgy but rather one that is not subordinated to the text and can therefore freely develop its own logic" (93). While Lehmann's theory of the postdramatic is influential and often cited, the term "visual dramaturgy" has not entered wide circulation. Instead, the concepts of physical dramaturgy and relational dramaturgy have seemingly taken hold in the discourse to describe the different kinds of dramaturgical practices required to produce works that can be understood via the rubric of postdramatic theater.

Lehmann's comprehensive theory of the postdramatic has indelibly impacted discourses surrounding contemporary performance, including those of immersive theater, with a handful of scholars situating immersive works within his theoretical framework.[10] Yet while his 1999 conceptual framework anticipates many of the approaches of immersive practitioners, Lehmann could not have predicted the impact of immersive performance nor the extent to which artists would reorient their attention from what was happening on the stage toward what could be made for and *made to happen by* spectators. The term *immersive* does not come from drama or dramatic structure; rather, it is a term that represents what the artists *hope to enable* for their audiences through their design of productions, which includes choreographing the parameters for audience participation during performances. These artists prioritize the responses of spectators, and through elicitive dramaturgy, they are finding ways to facilitate the kinds of responses that best suit the dramaturgical outcomes for which they have designed the production. Spectators themselves, in turn, not only understand but also expect elicitation as part of the experiential domain of immersive performance. Like postdramatic theater, immersive performance uses the tools of "theater after technology"—and yet the latter goes even further, putting the audience at the center of productions through designs which allow them to access live performances similarly to how they access technology in their daily life.

The postdramatic's lack of attention to the potential for spectators' embodied participation makes it a problematic rubric for analyzing immersive performance, and given my arguments thus far about the role of dance in such works, the problem is not resolved by considering Lehmann's treatment of dance within his theory. First, Lehmann makes multiple, explicit references to dance in his text, seemingly in an attempt to acknowledge the role dance played in the transformation of contemporary performance that he cites as fundamental to his theory of the postdramatic. For instance, he states, "[i]n dance we find most radically expressed what is true for postdramatic theatre in general: it articulates not meaning but energy, it represents not illustrations but actions" (163). With this, Lehmann acknowledges dance's creation of images conceived and generated through corporeality and visual methods rather than text. Lehmann also acknowledges that dance artists reoriented themselves from narrative and psychological approaches early in the twentieth century, far in advance of what he identifies as similar actions taken by theater practitioners (96). My stance, then, is that artists, working within the milieu identified as postdramatic by Lehmann, turned to dance in order to use choreography as a mechanism for facilitating immersion.

Statements such as these prompt Elswit to suggest that Lehmann is "hinting" that developments in dance presaged his claim for a postdramatic shift in theater (2018:58). Noting the widespread influence of Lehmann's theory, Elswit rightly calls for more critical analysis of the ways in which dance influenced and shaped his conceptualization of the postdramatic, noting that the lack of specificity around dance is yet another example of dance as sidelined in the discourses of contemporary performance. She argues instead for specificity, asking questions about "the ways in which dance has either been 'post' the dramatic for a long time, or perhaps was never dramatic in the first place, as least not in the way Lehmann means it" (59). Following Elswit's attention to these concerns, my theorizing, specifically my proposing elicitive dramaturgy within immersive performance, aims to foreground dance while acknowledging its interdependency with theater. Simply put, the postdramatic is not a sufficiently articulated rubric for the particularities of immersive performance. Physical dramaturgy as laid out by scholars thus far is not specific enough to describe the "how," following Bowditch et al., of immersive performance. As Elswit notes, we need to acknowledge the complex "tensions so we don't lose the opportunity" to better understand the interdependency of theater and dance, among other forms in the work of practitioners innovating new forms, including immersive performance. Specificity is important to getting to the core of developments within live performance, for understanding origins and comprehending complexity. Elicitive dramaturgy is a new way of working with the expanded form of immersive performance, applicable whether an immersive production is understood as more theater than dance or more dance than theater, following George-Graves' questioning of the "persistent resistance . . . between the fields of theater and dance" (2015:3). Elicitive dramaturgy is not merely about eliciting reactions to theatrical or choreographic content; it is, on a deeper level, about designing worlds in which the viewer perceives all the images and sensory information of the event in such a way that this content acts upon them so as to elicit their actions and reactions. Through the action and reaction, the audience then is part of making the work and draws meaning from it through the interdependent nature of receiving and responding.

Elswit's astute fleshing out of the problematic aspects of Lehmann's theory in relation to works by dramaturgs working across disciplines is helpful in reiterating the importance of dance and especially the choreographic process in contemporary performance, including works labeled immersive. For instance, dramaturge Synne K. Behrndt, writing about dance and dramaturgical thinking, states that in and of themselves, "the concepts of choreography and dance can be explored for their dramaturgical content" (2010:189). She notes that interdisciplinary scholar Bettina Milz has described the body as a "territory of research," and building upon this statement, she suggests that "it is possible to speak of the body as a dramaturgy in itself" (189). Choreographers, notably Bausch and Forsythe, among others, have long drawn upon the dancers they employ as primary resources through improvisation, generating performance material from bodies that are rich repositories of history, stories, politics, culture, and of course, movement. This resourcing of bodies is the dramaturgical work in dance; as dramaturge Hildegard de Vuyst, commenting on the work of choreographer Alain Platel, has noted, "the cast is the dramaturgy of the production" (de Vuyst quoted in Behrndt 189). If we accept that the cast (i.e., the dancers and performers) are the dramaturgy of non-immersive productions, then the statement is easily transposed and transcribed to serve this project: that in immersive works, audiences are the dramaturgy of the production. Thus, we can understand physical and relational dramaturgy as already existing within the choreographic processes used to create contemporary performance, including immersive performance, since choreography is the research of the body in motion. And elicitive dramaturgy is the necessary new framing for understanding how dance and theater intersect within the dramaturgical thinking surrounding audiences during the creation of immersive works.

Effectuating Elicitive Dramaturgy
through Action Frameworks

Once spectators have been resourced as subjects of choreography, they become, by default, part of the necessary materials required to create immersive performance. Practitioners are thus faced with a challenging task: to craft productions so that spectators willingly accept their positions within the choreography and experience their participation in ways that their actions, as well as their lack of action, can have value or meaning. This shift in the role of spectators has necessitated that practitioners develop drama-turgical ways of thinking that can account for and incorporate spectators' bodies, embodied knowledges, and corporeal capacities as part of the ma-teriality of a performance. In White's proposal of procedural authorship, he asserts "that work becomes meaningful through its aesthetic" and that "in order to understand an aesthetic we must understand its media" (2013:11). To this assertion, I pose a question: when the audience is the medium, how can you "understand" them, given that audiences are, as Profeta has estab-lished, an "unknown, irreducibly diverse, impromptu future collective?" (2015:88). I argue that perhaps the way to "understand" audiences, or at least to conceptualize them as active and mobile in immersive productions, is to actually choreograph them. Choreography is a time-tested method for the efficacious orchestration of bodies. As Richard Schechner, a pioneer of per-formance studies as well as founder of the form known as *environmental the-ater* (a precedent of immersive theater) has acknowledged, "spectators attend the theater unrehearsed," and for this reason, "they are difficult to collectivize and mobilize, but once mobilized, even more difficult to control" (1973:xxiv). I assert that choreography is what is deployed to control this mobilized au-dience. How exactly does choreography function so that spectators willingly respond to being orchestrated? As I conceptualize it, elicitive dramaturgy, as a choreographically driven theory and practice of composing immersive performance, involves the development of choreographic and theatrical structures that prompt and elicit specific audience responses. These chore-ographic structures, which I refer to as *action frameworks*, are the means by which practitioners actuate spectators and support their participation in the performance as mobile, agentive bodies.

An action framework comprises four components: (a) a narrative chore-ographic structure, often composed of multiple storylines; (b) a navigable space with alluring, tangible, and operable scenography; (c) character-driven choreography for dancers; and (d) improvisational scores for spectators. The first two elements establish the narrative and the space/venue wherein performances of the production will occur. Once these foundational elements are established, the actions and potential interactions between performers and spectators can then be imagined and composed. Specifically, these actions and potential interactions are defined by the choreography that structures the dancers' character-driven movements and speech, which is understood as the *track*, and by the improvisational *score* that structures the spectators' responses. Together, these two elements, the track and score of the production, define how the elicitive process plays out over the course of a performance. It is through these two mechanisms that exchanges between performer and spectator occur. By structuring these four elements of narrative, space, performers, and spectators, action frameworks effectively merge dramaturgy, scenography, and choreography—which are often understood as different aspects of a production—into a single cohesive whole. The process of composing action frameworks involves extensive investigation across source materials, as guided by the artistic research agenda of the practitioners. It is upon the composition of action frameworks that the efficacy of elicitive dramaturgy critically depends: through the action framework of a production, a world is constructed that expands the spectators' realm of participation, affording opportunities for them to move beyond behaviors of spectating into serving as subjects of choreography. Once the spectators are subjects of choreography, their engagement then assists in engendering immersion as an affect.

The first component of the action framework is a production's narrative choreographic structure, which serves as a primary mechanism for organizing and shaping content, and for communicating the specific information of the story or stories.[11] Depending on the production, such narrative structures may be sequential or episodic, chronological or non-linear. The most important feature of a narrative structure is that, no matter the production, it focalizes every element in the fictional world, as every aspect of the production arises from and fits within that narrative structure. In an immersive production, the narrative choreographic structure may be based on an existing, well-known text or set of texts, providing an accessible point of entry for spectators; alternatively, an original text may be devised by practitioners to invite spectators into the story world. As a component of the action framework, the narrative choreographic structure is conducive to multi-modal mechanisms for storytelling, as movement, text, and scenographic elements are utilized independently and in conjunction with one another to convey information.

The narrative choreographic structure of an immersive production manifests within venues chosen specifically for the navigability afforded to performers and spectators. Navigable spaces are essential since most spectator participation is predicated on their mobility—that is, their ability to travel throughout venues on journeys that are either self-guided or curated. For practitioners designing immersive productions, identifying suitable spaces often happens first or at least early in the creative process. A venue must either already be navigable or lend itself to adaptation and/or construction so as to render possible the choreographic form of the work. Practitioners identify and sometimes create surfaces upon which virtuosic movement can be effectively and safely executed by performers, and they organize spaces that will accommodate and keep from harm the perambulatory spectators. Productions vary in terms of the extent to which a spectator's journey is curated through the space, with some productions designed to guide spectators' movements and others affording a more autonomous experience.

By staging a performance in closed and contained spaces, often indoors, practitioners can design the choreography of performers and determine potential pathways for spectators who circulate or are guided through a performance. As spectators traverse the space, they encounter opportunities to interact with the environment. Often incorporating hyper-realistic scenography, these navigable spaces contain objects and ephemera representative of various narratives within the overarching story of the production, made available to spectators as tangible props to assist in deepening their immersion within the storyworld. For instance, audiences of *Then She Fell (TSF)* come across items such as teacups, letters containing correspondence between characters, and furniture such as beds, benches, and settees. When engaged with, these props shape how audience members move through each scene. Scenic designers capitalize on the attraction of analog materials in an increasingly digitized world by crafting environments that are accessible and attractive to spectators, affording them occasions to augment their understanding through touch and other sensorimotor capacities. Overall, the scenography serves the elicitive demands of the action framework by adding layers of multi-modal, sensory information in the form of tangible materiality so that spectators can establish relationships with the space and its content in their process of generating meaning.

Within these narrative choreographic structures and navigable venues, how are the performers and spectators actually encountering one another? The mechanisms that support the movements and speech of the performers and the spectators constitute the third and fourth components of the action framework mentioned previously: the character-driven choreography, which structures the movements and speech of the dancers (the "track"), and the improvisational score, which structures the responses elicited from the spectators (the "score"). Both the track and the score, as the mechanisms through which exchanges occur within performances, are critical to how the elicitive process unfolds between spectators and performers. I have described these structures in the Introduction and in previous writings as *tandem dances*, because when these structures are implemented, they form a partnership. By "occurring in conjunction with one another," they shape the overall production.[12] It is through this tandem dance, the interplay between the track and score, choreography and improvisation, that spectators find themselves enacting their participation in the production—audience participation taken to its logical extreme. The "improvisational score" side of that dual choreographic structure is crucial in providing parameters for structuring audience participation while also providing opportunities for audiences to negotiate agency through choice. Spectators not only observe the character-driven choreography of performers; they are also drawn into it themselves when offered proposals and deciding whether or not to respond. Fully situated as subjects of choreography, spectators are set in motion by improvisational scores that serve as tools to guide them in their own discoveries within the constructed world of the production.

The character-driven choreography—the track that structures the dancers' movements and speech—is the third component of the action framework. Because the performers are in most cases enacting characters derived from narrative sources, everything about them—their presence, actions, and interactions—is part of their character-driven choreography. Each character is conceptualized and designed to possess an identifiable, individual persona, which is then represented through distinctive choreographic vocabulary and physical mannerisms. Developed through elicitive dramaturgical processes, including movement improvisation and the exploration of existing or devised texts, character-driven choreography is the predetermined language of the performers. Character-driven choreography has existed across cultures for centuries, both in classical dance and in theater. It is similar to narrative-driven Western forms of classical dance such as ballet, as well as to dance-drama forms from South and East Asia. What is unique to immersive performance is that now, through elicitive dramaturgy, these characters are interacting with spectators with the intent of effectuating specific physical and verbal responses, in alignment with the dramaturgical frame of the fictional world. Immersive practitioners adapt the convention of character-driven choreography by assigning it dual-dramaturgical duties. In an action framework, a track does the work of *dance*, functioning in and of itself as a performance for the spectator to observe. As such, it can be replicated performance after performance, in addition to serving as the language through which choreographed movement and speech proposals are offered to spectators.[13] Each track is a rigorously crafted amalgamation of movement invention that ranges from abstract virtuosic vocabulary to specific pedestrian movements and perhaps more recognizable actions from practices of daily life. The distinct choreographic vocabulary of each character within an immersive production may include two types of proposals: those intended to elicit movement, and those eliciting speech. Jennine Willett explained that when crafting such proposals, she, Morris, and Pearson are "often trying to make choreography not feel like choreography" (interview with author 2014).[14] By this she means that the choreography—as it is both designed and meant to be performed—is intended to communicate its task-based intentions rather than abstract or emotional expression. Emotions and feelings may also be elicited, yet outcomes such as this are effectuated by the spectators' physical and speech responses to proposals. Built from improvisation assignments given by practitioners to performers during rehearsals, the choreography of the movement and speech functions through a sequencing of cause and effect, as a movement proposal (cause) by a performer hopefully leads to a response (effect) from a spectator.

The fourth component of the action framework, the *score*, accounts for the spectator's role within the performer–spectator interaction. The score comprises the instructional parameters that guide spectators' improvisational choices and decisions that will manifest the movements and speech they offer in response to the elements of the performance. In immersive performance, improvisational scores *are* choreography, following Foster's assertion that choreography can be "interpreted as a score or a set of principles that guide spontaneous invention" and that are, as such, the means by which spectators realize their dances in tandem with performers (2011:3). Together with the track (the performers' choreography), the spectators' score constitutes how they experience the production, including how the exchanges of the elicitive process play out. Instructions given to spectators at the beginning of a performance serve to both facilitate and delimit the volitional movement choices of spectators—including improvisational, pedestrian, and task-based choices—as they travel in a space, whether alone or in concert with other spectators, and as they respond to movement and speech proposals. When these improvisational scores are effective, the choreography is structuring not only the bodies of the dancers, but also those of the spectators. When the four elements of the action framework are working together to structure the bodies of the dancers and spectators alike, they represent an alternative approach to the conventional functions of choreography and dramaturgy. Blended into the cohesive whole of the immersive production, the narrative choreographic structure, navigable venue, track, and score combine to constitute the new elicitive dramaturgy.

We can see the four elements of the action framework operating within the scenario at the beginning of this chapter, in which I describe my encounter with the Red Queen. First, the elicitive dramaturgical development of the Red Queen character was informed by Third Rail's historical research on Alice Liddell's mother, Lorina Liddell, the wife of a prominent dean in Victorian England. Based on this research, Third Rail conceptualized Mrs. Liddell in accordance with conventional depictions of Victorian women, constructing the Red Queen character as someone who would adhere to strict norms and standards of behavior while expecting the same from everyone around her. My fellow audience members and I, as subjects of Third Rail's choreography, were staged as witnesses of the Red Queen's physical unraveling and re-composure. We were guided through choreographed gazes and gestures inside the tiny boudoir, a word derived from the French *bouder*, to sulk or pout, a setting that intensified the intimacy of this moment where we were invited to hear the private thoughts of a very public-facing woman. My established preconception of the Red Queen character had been the tired trope of an archetypal female villain, as informed by Carroll's texts and various film adaptations. This perception was reinforced early in the scene, as Morin interpreted the choreography and text with a high degree of muscular tension. The other spectators and I conformed to the score's design, responding immediately to the Red Queen's movement proposals that we sit, stand, toss our cups, and so on.

Our compliance was presumably due in part to Morin's dynamic, authoritative performance, but it was also due to the intuitive design of the scene. Centered around interactions that felt almost like ordinary, everyday encounters, the scenes evoked our movement and speech as naturally as they might arise in daily life from observing and reacting to the cues of other people around us. Importantly, though, Third Rail introduced another layer of meaning to what might have otherwise been a banal, if energetic, temper tantrum. The Red Queen delivers a feminist monologue in which she expresses concerns about gender inequity and the socio-political implications of women behaving contrary to conventions of their culture. By the conclusion of this intimate and carefully choreographed scene, spectators may perceive other dimensions of humanity latent within the Red Queen, and ultimately exit the scene feeling differently about the character. In this example, Third Rail set up a scene that progressed from observation to engagement through physical response. Through the Red Queen's carriage and choreographic vocabulary, spectators have the opportunity to perceive and understand both her status as a character—royalty, in this case—as well as their own status as subjects responding to her elevated status. In this scene, spectators watch her, listen to her, and respond to her upon command. We might describe spectators in this scene as somehow doubly subjectified. We are situated theatrically and narratively as "subjects" of a powerful Queen, while also "subjects" of the choreography within a tiny, repressive space.

Considerations in Elicitive Dramaturgical Thinking

Practitioners face a number of considerations when designing and iterating action frameworks for immersive performances. First, they determine what level of elicitation to seek from the production, that is, what types of responses and degree of responsiveness to attempt to elicit from spectators. Immersive productions can be designed with varying levels of intended spectator response in mind, which I refer to as the *spectrum of elicitation*. A second consideration for practitioners is how to achieve that desired level of elicitation, that is, how to craft productions such that they function as open systems that spectators can navigate intuitively, with their bodies as well as dancers' bodies being orchestrated by choreography even if unbeknownst to them. This type of intuitively navigable open system can only be achieved through iteration and experimentation, making greater use of test audiences than is typical in conventional theater. Finally, a third consideration for practitioners developing action frameworks is that choreography's command of spectators is not guaranteed. Practitioners must keep this fact in mind and take measures to recover or compensate when spectators are no longer functioning within the choreographic structure—when they "slip" out of or intentionally "escape" the capture, to use Allsopp and Lepecki's terminology.

A primary consideration for practitioners as they begin to build an action framework is what degree of elicitation they wish to seek from the spectators of the production. Practitioners engage in practices that are familiar in many creative processes of dance and theater—posing questions, designing tasks, and crafting improvisational scores as research assignments for themselves and the performers—and as they do so, they must carefully calibrate the choreography of the four components to set the conditions that will achieve the level of immersive experience they wish for their future spectators. With elicitation as the central goal, these action frameworks are designed to set the conditions for spectators to consent to participate and engage willingly. Yet, within every production there exists a spectrum of elicitation. Situations and scenes are designed at different levels of intensity, and the desired responses vary in terms of the type and degree of physical involvement. Both factors, the type and degree of participation that are desired, serve to support spectator perceptions of agency and volitional participation. At one end of the spectrum of elicitation, spectators may be enacting more traditional behaviors of spectating, such as observing choreography and action from a static, fixed position, which, as established previously, do fall within the choreographic realm in that they are specific embodied movements intended by the production's designers. At the other end of the spectrum, spectators may be fully involved as subjects of choreography, either through their scores or responding to movement and speech proposals. In some productions, audiences are afforded freedom to negotiate the spectrum, choosing when and where to observe as well as engage, while other productions are designed more stringently to control how spectators experience the work. Generally speaking, practitioners are not interested in forcing proposals upon spectators, and productions are designed to continue regardless of whether spectators offer responses to the proposals they receive. Of course, spectator responses are desired, and will only be possible if the elicitive dramaturgy is effective. It is for this reason that some practitioners are concerned with the "user-friendliness" of their productions—that is, with the extent to which spectators are able to navigate these productions as open systems using only their intelligence and intuition, rather than being given explicit instructions.

In addition to the spectrum of elicitation, a second consideration guiding the iterative development of immersive works is the notion of user-friendliness. In order for spectators to be immersed in these productions, their own intelligence and intuition must be sufficient to guide them in navigating the venue. The user-friendliness of an immersive production is achieved by incorporating feedback from test audiences in several phases. In an interview about the creation of *TSF*, Zach Morris, co-artistic director of Third Rail Projects, mentioned that he and his colleagues work to "craft a world where the audience intuitively knows what to do . . . so they're making the decision of where to go and not having us have to force them" (interview with author 2014). Intuition is generally accepted as a subconscious process that assists individuals in determining the correct action to take. In *TSF*, for example, the movement and speech proposals of the performers are constructed to enable audience members to provide responses that serve the performance, such as choosing the correct door from which to exit to another scene. These proposals also must be crafted such that audiences can understand when they are being asked to accomplish a task and how they can do so effectively in moving through the immersive world. Morris describes these precise, choreographic maneuvers as "intuitive modes of audience engagement" (interview with author 2014). He equates such intuitive structures with user-friendly design:

> If you can create that intuitive way that an audience can intersect with a work regardless of what the medium of the work is . . . then they can really find themselves in it, and I think that's incredibly powerful . . . if your piece is user-friendly—you can figure out really fast if it's not, because it'll blow up in your face. For me, it has become about an entirely different set of choreographic directorial controls that can create that intuitive audience engagement. In some cases, it is about what angle your sternum faces in relation to an audience . . . or . . . you hand them something . . . that then allows them to be a little bit lost or to lose themselves in the unfolding scene. It's about creating intuitive audience moments where our performers are able to be there, be who they are, do their jobs, do what they need to do in the scene . . . but it is in concert and collaboration with the audience and in conversation with the audience. (interview with author 2014)

Yet the goal of user-friendliness raises questions about what kind of collaboration, if any, may be occurring in these productions. As Frieze has noted, "in (most participatory performance) practice . . . collaboration is messy," adding that the script needs to be "flexible enough to allow for genuine collaboration" (2016:14). Otherwise, as Frieze points out, "complicity becomes coercion when the requirement to collaborate is limited by the requirement not to do anything that would stop the show from going on" (14). The notion that practitioners are designing productions to be user-friendly is in tension with the fact that the choreographing of the audience inherently delimits their choices, possibly foreclosing on the possibilities for collaboration. On the other hand, one might argue that the ways in which the proposals are offered are so intentionally and carefully choreographed, and the asks of the score are so clear, that the spectator is able to become a sort of "scene-partner," which is how *TSF* conceptualizes the participation of audiences (Pearson, interview with author 2014).[15] We might then understand the choreography in immersive productions as being designed to function in an intentionally playful way so that the design is perceived as accessible, that is, user-friendly, and thus can prove effective in eliciting certain kinds of responses. Audiences may indeed be calling upon their intuition when engaging with the characters, scenography, and other spectators in the production; they are subjects of choreographic scores which allow for some level of agency and afford various kinds of indeterminacy. However, the fact that choreography is indeed being deployed, very carefully and very precisely, underscores my argument for its fundamental importance within immersive works.

But how are the elusive qualities of "intuitive engagement" and "user-friendliness" to be achieved by the immersive theatrical practitioner? The answer is simple but difficult. Throughout the development of a production and during rehearsals, practitioners constantly explore the action frameworks through trial and error of choreography with performers. Equally important, they also engage in rigorous testing of the action framework by staging the production with multiple, broad test audiences when the work is at a far less completed stage than what is usually seen in previews of conventional productions. Producers in the performing arts have long deployed preview performances as a way to determine whether or not a production is compelling and to generate advance publicity from reviewers, but the practitioners featured in this book integrate test audiences into their dramaturgical processes in novel ways. They regularly invite groups of test audiences consisting of family, friends, associates, long-term fans, and donors into rehearsals, providing early-stage test performances that enable practitioners to assess the effectiveness of (what I term) the action framework and make adjustments before opening night. The extensive pre-testing of immersive productions demonstrates how the collaborative, process-oriented nature of new dramaturgies is functioning in these performances, and it also serves as evidence of yet another level of the dramaturgical thinking of the "first spectators." By opening their work to a larger group of individuals and soliciting a greater depth and breadth of information about user experience, practitioners are enlarging the pool of possible responses and gaining feedback in real time with test audiences. Practitioners and performers can, then, learn through interfacing with multiple and diverse spectators whether or not the character-driven choreography is having the impact they intend, as well as whether the scenography is sufficiently alluring, whether the score is intuitively navigable, and whether the proposals are sufficiently elicitive to prompt spectators to the desired responses.

A third consideration for practitioners of elicitive dramaturgy, in addition to elicitation and what is called user-friendly or intuitive design (Murray suggests transparency), is the possibility of choreographic drift or, to put it in other words, failure of design.[16] Action frameworks are not foolproof structures. Though designed to be intuitive, they may not succeed in their intended choreographic elicitation, and spectators can drift choreographically and/or fall out of its capture, either willingly or unwillingly. Proposals can fail to achieve their purpose at moments when the instructions of the scores are not operable as intended, when spectators lack the understanding or miss the cues of a proposal, or when choreography itself fails in its design to allure and then elicit specific responses, or even any responses at all. One way that scores can fail is by being too open, with too few instructions for spectators to understand what to do, where to go and when to take action, such that they are overwhelmed by the abundance of possible choices. In a sense, then, the constraints of a score perform a critical function, supporting spectators' perceptions of agency by providing a structure that guides their choreographic potential. A similar challenge occurs in traditional dance contexts when improvisational scores are used to generate movement, which is why instructions must be clear for dancers and the range of their choices must be delimited. A related way in which action frameworks can fail is if a spectator misreads or accidentally misses a movement proposal, fully willing yet unable to provide a response. Perhaps the choreography of that particular proposal was poorly designed or incomplete, or it may have been performed imprecisely or incorrectly, or the spectator simply missed the cue and the performer had to continue with the performance. Whatever the cause, in cases where the edges of the immersive world begin to unravel, the potential for spectator immersion is diminished, thus allowing for choreographic drift.

Choreographic drift is common parlance in the field of dance to describe when a performance deviates gradually over time from the original predetermined choreography. As choreography is repetitively performed by dancers over many months or even years, it can transform into movements and expressions other than what was originally designed and intended by the choreographer. In the case of immersive performance, the performers might execute a movement or gesture countless times over the course of their occupying a particular role. For example, Elizabeth Carena (Figure 3.3), who originated the Hatter in *TSF* and performed the role over 533 times between

Figure 3.3 Elizabeth Carena (Hatter) in Third Rail Project's *Then She Fell*
(New York, 2012–). Photograph by Rick Ochoa.

2011 and 2014, reported she had opportunities to "look into the eyes of literally thousands of audience members" (Carena 2014). Immersive performance requires that performers repeat the same movement numerous times
within each performance, with every audience member they encounter,
with a higher degree of precision than may be necessary in conventional
productions. The exact manner in which a performer executes a proposal
can determine whether or not a spectator responds. Tom Pearson, who originated the role of the White Rabbit (Figure 3.4), explains how he experienced
this kind of drift in one of his performances of *TSF*:

> It gets so precise. You can do something over a hundred times and then all of
> a sudden—the other night, they [the audience participant] didn't want to sit
> when I pulled the chair out. And I thought, "I'm doing something different,
> but I don't even realize I'm doing it. What have I changed? I'm pulling this
> chair out now and they won't sit. They always sit. What am I doing?" I do
> that scene four times a show, and [have performed it] a thousand times.
> I eventually figured it out . . . it was because I used two fingers instead of
> four. And that made all the difference. (interview with author 2014)

Figure 3.4 Carlton Cyrus Ward (White Rabbit) in Third Rail Projects' *Then She Fell* (New York, 2012–). Photograph by Adam Jason Photography.

When an action framework is poorly designed or incomplete, spectators may not be able to interpret what is being asked or what is being proposed to them; and, as per White, sometimes the execution of an invitation, regardless of how well it is choreographed, may simply be unclear. From the performer's perspective, choreographic drift on the part of the spectator may require additional drift on the part of the performers. In these moments, performers often must deviate from the original choreography even further in order to improvise movements or speech that will elicit specific kinds of spectator responses to advance the scene and get it back on track.

While it is possible for spectators to resist or deviate from the action framework unintentionally, it is also possible for them to willingly disregard the performers' instructions and consciously subvert the proposals. These instances of choreographic drift can be understood as spectators intentionally slipping out of the apparatus of capture. According to Allsopp and Lepecki, improvisation is the means by which performers may break out of the command of choreography, and I argue that in the case of spectators who are choreographed, they may take up improvisational behaviors outside the parameters set by the practitioners in order to test the limits of their agency and assert authorial control that supersedes the notion of coauthorship discussed in the Introduction.[17] Instances of choreographic drift of this kind suggest that the spectator has chosen to operate within an improvisational zone that primarily serves the spectator's own self-interest. Spectators who make such choices move from displaying disinterest, in the classic aesthetic sense of impartial or objective regard for experience, to a more self-oriented perspective, seeking to acquire experiences for themselves personally with minimal regard for how their actions impact others. In these cases, spectators may demonstrate a lack of awareness of or interest in the theatrical intent of the practitioners and the social and relational aspects of such productions.

In immersive productions, the behaviors of any one spectator can impact the experiences of those around them. When an audience participant experiences choreographic drift, then, this can compromise other participants' sense of immersion in the production. For example, an interview with Micah Edwards, an audience participant who attended *TSF* multiple times, revealed that the behavior of other audience members sometimes distracted him during performances. He stated, "If you're not paying attention [as an audience participant], that's rude. . . . I've watched people. There's a big scene going on, and there's someone rummaging through the drawers. I'm sure whatever is in the drawers is very interesting, but these are live performers. They can see you. People are doing something here. Recognize that" (interview with author 2014). On the other hand, intentional choreographic drift may also enable spectators to engage in the production in ways they might find more satisfactory or fulfilling of their desires than if they were to remain fully subjects of the choreography. For example, a comment from Gunny Scarfo, another *TSF* audience member whom I interviewed, provides insight into the reasoning behind participants intentionally deploying tactics to assert agency that might be perceived as intentional choreographic drift: "I remember talking back to the Hatter and I remember trying to negotiate. I didn't want to become this automaton controlled by the performer. I wanted to maintain my unique identity and bring my own flair to it" (interview with author 2014). Scarfo goes on to say, "I wanted to play along, but I didn't want to lose myself by playing along. I think that it was . . . definitely sort of [a] tension that I had. And, you know, that's part of the fun" (33). However, at the same time, by evading or slipping out of the choreography, spectators may lose access to the opportunities offered by the action framework and thus negate the chance to be something other than audience members, to be subjects of choreography and perceive themselves as protagonists of their own journeys. While these audience members may willingly slip outside the action framework, they can never completely escape their own positions as audience members, since the spectrum of elicitation is designed to accommodate a wide range of behaviors, from observation to participation. Pearson, describing how Third Rail recruits and trains their dancers to engage with audiences, says they look for dancers who "can be in that scene with [the audience participant] . . . [and] just talk to them. And if it's funny, you laugh. And if it's disturbing—take care of them and honor their choices, but listen" (34). These acts of honoring and listening allow the performers to stay in an improvisational performance mode that is open to many possibilities and to remain at-the-ready to create new moments of performance alongside the spectators.

A fundamental challenge of elicitive dramaturgy is that this practice brings forth not just the conditions of designing proposals and the considerations of responding but also the ethical concerns of how these two actions are to be undertaken. When engaging in the elicitive dramaturgical thinking necessary to create action frameworks, including movement and speech proposals, it is important to acknowledge that the inherently kinesthetic nature of immersive performance is something that not all audiences are comfortable with or desire. Immersive works draw heavily upon intimacy, including close proximity of bodies and, at times, physical touch. My data has revealed that practitioners take great care in training performers to respect the bodies of spectators. However, on the other hand, the issue of consent, or lack of it, has surfaced in relation to spectators inappropriately touching performers. This potential danger has prompted companies to provide clear policies and guidelines for acceptable behavior. The kinds of behaviors that go beyond choreographic drift and manifest as unwanted and un-elicited are *non-consensual* behaviors, reflecting the non-consensus (e.g., lack of general agreement) of some audience members to conform with structures designed to facilitate their experiences of immersion. This area of consideration is taken up further in Chapter 4, where I discuss the inclusion of audiences in immersive performance.

In considering the notion of choreographic drift in particular, the research of theater scholar Nicholas Ridout on theater and ethics is helpful. Ridout reminds us that ethics is inevitably concerned with "how we organize the ways in which we live with each other" and that "our actions always have consequences for people other than ourselves" (12). I suggest that the use of choreography to organize the bodies of spectators in immersive performance reflects how practitioners deploy dance for making "social and political arrangements that minimize the negative consequences of one's individual actions" on others (12). In other words, choreography is an effective method of organizing audiences as mobile participants so that their actions during performances function for the "good of all." Pointing out that "how shall I act?" is a foundational ethical question, Ridout goes on to pose the following question: "Can we create a system according to which we will all know how to act?" (12). In the case of immersive performance, at least, the answer to this latter question is, of course, no. The choreographic drift of spectators described previously, as well as the issue of non-consensual/non-consensus behaviors I take up later, provide evidence of the inherent imperfection of any system, however carefully designed and executed. So perhaps we might consider choreography as it functions within elicitive dramaturgy as an *attempt* to devise a system in which a certain conceptualization of ethics guides audience participation. In the case of *TSF*, at least, I argue that following the intention of the choreography can be understood within an ethical framework, in that the "greater good of the production"—the intention to guide audience participants through a carefully curated narrative experience—is best served if audiences respond within the parameters of the choreography as designed. Of specific interest here are the paradoxical and ethical challenges that practitioners must contend with when asking audiences to respond, while at the same time hoping they will respond in certain ways and attempting to choreograph them to do so. As practitioners work to develop, iterate, and assess the effectiveness of immersive productions, they must confront these considerations and contingencies.

Desire and Delimitation in Elicitive Dramaturgy

The notion of choreography exerting power over the spectator may at first seem to suggest a sort of control that is negative or even oppressive. Why actuate the bodies of spectators merely to then capture them as subjects of choreography? Yet, we find that the captivating potential of choreography is precisely what enables it to function as a *generative* constraint for spectators. Through the choreography in action frameworks, spectators are *provided cues for* contributing (not *coerced into* contributing) their speech and actions to the production. For spectators of immersive productions, being captured as a subject of choreography can afford new experiences of performances, fulfill desires, and lead to the self-perception of being agentive within performances and engaging in encounters that are intimate and interactive. Because practitioners manage the implementation of their productions' action frameworks such that spectators feel engaged in processes of discovery, the spectators' perceptions of intimacy and interactivity, as outcomes of the choreography, are unsurprising. Spectators who choose to attend these productions generally *desire* to be a part of the performance, to engage in the fantasy; and for this reason, they willingly submit to the choreography as an apparatus of capture. In most circumstances, the artistic directors of immersive productions do not intend for spectators to labor as strenuously as the dancers do, or to feel as if they are oppressed by the choreography; after all, the majority of these events are conceived as and offered under the auspices of entertainment. Nor do practitioners want audiences to get so lost and befuddled within a venue that they are unable to follow a narrative or construct one. Indeed, the sustained creative efforts and strategies of practitioners who produce immersive works speak to the extent to which they as artists are willing to innovate in order to accommodate the desires of the spectator to take on new roles and responsibilities within performance.

The various dimensions of dramaturgical thinking are still evolving in immersive performance, and it is likely there will never be one definitive process for composing such productions. Nevertheless, my participant observation of multiple productions has led me to understand many of the ways in which elicitive dramaturgical activity, particularly choreography, assists the spectator in transitioning across the threshold from outside the fictional world of the production to its most intimate interiors. Throughout history, creators of live performance have developed numerous practices for inviting audiences into the world of a production, and immersive performance brings a whole new set of strategies for doing so. By deploying elicitive dramaturgy, practitioners endeavor to construct action frameworks for spectators as bridges for traversing the historical "gap" or "split"—as per Boenisch and Siegmund, respectively—that has traditionally positioned the audience as passive and the performer as active. Admittedly, none of these attempts can entirely dissolve the divide between performer and spectator; the continued existence of that split is confronted regularly within the practices and discourses surrounding immersive performance, particularly in regard to spectatorial agency and perceptions of interactivity. Still, through elicitive dramaturgy and the choreography of the action framework, practitioners can and do demonstrate their interest and skill in taking into account the bodies of performers *and* spectators as sites of research and possibility. How immersion manifests and reveals itself in performances, what it looks like and how it feels for spectators to be immersed in such a production, will be the focus of the second half of this book.

4

Insider Dynamics and Extended Audiencing

Punchdrunk's *Sleep No More*

A scene of violence erupts, and a crowd gathers around the commotion. A pregnant woman, alone with a suitcase in an ornate lobby, has just been viciously attacked by a man from behind. The woman attempts to flee, weaving through the lobby furniture, putting obstacles between herself and her pursuer. He charges toward her, overturning the furniture right and left, as people in the crowd jockey for a view of the action. Some scale the furniture as others step aside, shifting their own bodies out of harm's way, allowing the man's frenzied assault on the woman to play out in front of them. The man captures the woman in a chokehold and slams her pregnant belly against a wall. Confident that his savagery has killed her, the man loosens his grip, and the woman's limp body slides to the ground. The crowd stops jostling and becomes absolutely still; the room is silent except for the thud of the woman's body as it drops heavily upon the floor and the raspy breath of her murderer. He pauses over the body and then turns quickly and leaves the scene.

Moments later, another man enters the lobby, sees the woman on the ground, and rushes to her side. Realizing she is dead, he gathers her body in his arms and rises slowly to a standing position, still cradling her in his arms. Weighted by grief and her pregnant body, he lurches toward the bystanders surrounding him, beseeching them to witness his sorrow. One woman, seemingly empathizing with the scene in front of her, takes a step forward from the crowd and places her arms around the dead woman's body, sharing his burden. The duet becomes a trio in a gentle moment of love after death, as the man and the woman slowly rock the deceased woman's body across the divide from the world of the living to that of the dead. Wordlessly, they seem to decide together when her soul has gone, and they carefully separate. The woman releases the body to the man as she steps back into the crowd.

Tandem Dances. Julia M. Ritter, Oxford University Press (2021). © Oxford University Press.
DOI: 10.1093/oso/9780190051303.001.0001.

The woman who had stepped forward into the death scene was an audience participant during a pivotal moment in the UK-based Punchdrunk company's New York production of *Sleep No More* (2011–present, hereafter *SNM*). Designed to immerse audience members into a silent film noir, *SNM* is enacted solely through movement, involving a mashup of Shakespeare's *Macbeth* with the films of Alfred Hitchcock (specifically *Rebecca* [1940] and *Vertigo* [1958]), and the lesser-known yet true story of the late-seventeenth-century trial and execution of the seven "Paisley Witches" in Scotland. Just moments before including herself in the scene, the woman had been complicit alongside other audience members when witnessing Lady Macduff's death at the hands of Macbeth (see Figure 4.1). Yet in beholding Macduff's

Figure 4.1 Emursive Present Punchdrunk's *Sleep No More*, New York (2011–). Jenna Saccurato. Photography by Giafrese.

subsequent arrival and ensuing sorrow, this woman seemed to be drawn into his grief and responded instinctively, pushing her body forward into the action. The participation of spectators in *SNM*, especially their inclusion in its choreography, has been a focus of my research since I attended my first performance in 2012. Analyses of specific scenes allow for consideration of how the choreographic thinking and choreographic practices of *SNM*'s creators contribute to audience immersion, specifically through a process of affective engagement that I have identified in previous writings as *insider dynamics* (Ritter 2016).

The production company Punchdrunk, founded by artistic director Felix Barrett in 2000, has created over seventeen productions since its inception, with *SNM* thus far achieving the greatest critical and commercial success. The New York production has attracted an unparalleled level of mass attention from international critics, scholars, and the public, and received two prestigious New York theater awards in 2011, including the Drama Desk Award for Unique Theatrical Experience and the Obie Award's Special Citation for Design and Choreography.[1] An internet search of "*Sleep No More* Punchdrunk" yields several hundred thousand references in the form of critical reviews and essays, as well as blog posts and mentions across different social media platforms. Simple arithmetic suggests that the New York production has been performed over five thousand times since its premiere in 2011, with millions of audience participants having attended. Drawing upon the success that *SNM* has enjoyed in the large metropolis of New York, Punchdrunk premiered a new version of the production in Shanghai, China, in December 2016, furthering the reach of their aesthetic to a new, and potentially larger, population of international audiences.[2]

SNM's popularity and longevity as a production in New York, and its subsequent expansion to and success in Shanghai, is likely due in large part to the ways that choreography has been established as central to the Punchdrunk aesthetic. From the very first Punchdrunk productions, Barrett was engaged in choreographic thinking when conceptualizing the role of the spectator (interview with author 2015a). It was his introduction to choreographer Maxine Doyle in 2002, however, that irrevocably defined the company's vision and creative processes. Doyle, a choreographer skilled in a range of modernist and postmodernist dance practices and already exploring audience participation in her own work, has been instrumental in helping Barrett fulfill his vision of a type of performance that would "locate the audience at the epicenter of the experience" (Doyle et al. 2012).[3] Together, Doyle and

Barrett have refined a way of using choreographic thinking toward opportunities for audience participation. Choreography is firmly established as a central feature of Punchdrunk's work, with Barrett and Doyle each applying it in distinct, yet intertwined, ways toward the shared intention of potentially facilitating audience immersion.

Doyle's choreographic thinking involves a complex, two-fold process of conceiving and crafting choreography for dancers to perform; it communicates their relationships and interactions and is the primary means of storytelling for the fractured narratives that play out across the performance spaces. Barrett, meanwhile, is primarily concerned with the movement of the audience as they journey through the space and time of the production, seeking out the bits and pieces of the multiple stories that the creative team has embedded within the large-scale architectural sites that they collectively transform into seemingly endless worlds. I have argued previously that the collaboration between Barrett and Doyle, particularly in the creation of *SNM*, constitutes its own kind of tandem dance; further research reveals how the interdependency of their choreographic thinking is integral to Punchdrunk's works. Barrett's fracturing and adapting of dramatic texts across the *SNM* landscape is a way of making space for and encouraging the movement of performers and audiences. His strategy works in conjunction with Doyle's choreography for dancers as relational partners to the audiences as well as to the buildings and spaces wherein Punchdrunk's works are typically staged. Barrett and Doyle's choreographic thinking entwines to create the theatrical environments and relational structures that support the tandem dance between dancers and audiences of *SNM*. I understand the tandem dance of *SNM* as comprising parallel and intersecting performer–audience worlds that were conceived and designed through Barrett and Doyle's incorporation of different approaches to performance, including elicitive dramaturgy, as discussed in Chapter 3.

SNM's success and longevity are significant, and arguably rare, within the world of immersive theater.[4] Having premiered in 2011, the New York City production continues to offer eight performances per week to date, with a similar number of performances currently running each week in Shanghai. These factors have established *SNM*, in both locations, as productive sites of research for many scholars, including myself, as well as for audience participants. Those with resources to attend repeatedly are afforded opportunities to observe scenes more than once, as performed by a rotating cast of dancers and in the company of different audience participants. *SNM* is a fruitful site for observing the repetition of choreography and its impact on audiences.[5] As a scholar interested in how the moving bodies of performers and audiences are prioritized, privileged, and contextualized through choreography, *SNM* has provided me with a wealth of primary source material, including opportunities for choreographic analysis and observations of the interactions between performers and audiences, as well as those among audience members themselves. Interviews with Barrett, Doyle, dancers, and audience members have provided further insights. In addition, my background as a choreographer has further amplified the perspectives from which to explore choreography as an element of the production, and to observe my spectatorship as well as that of my fellow audience participants.

In what follows, I examine the processes of spectator immersion. First, building on the previous chapter's treatment of elicitive dramaturgy, I describe how this new form appears in the choreographic processes of Barrett and Doyle. Then, I explore how spectators' experiences within *SNM* are facilitated by *insider dynamics*, which I identify as occurring in four phases: complicity, porosity, contagion, and inclusion.[6] Each is illustrated with description and analysis of four scenarios that I witnessed as an audience member in the production. Finally, I consider the *extended audiencing* that characterizes many spectators' experiences of the production long after the performance has ended. As I show, participants transform their physical and emotional experiences of the production into cultural discourses that extend their audienceship (see Ritter 2016 and 2017). These actions and behaviors include spectators' repeated attendance at *SNM* performances, engaging in face-to-face conversations with other audience participants, and sharing their creative responses about experiences across myriad online platforms in the forms of blog posts, online commentary, and artistic expressions, including photography, video, cartoons, digital art and drawings, fan fiction, poems, collage, and sculpture.

Choreographing *SNM*: Setting the Conditions for Insider Dynamics

British choreographer Maxine Doyle has long explored the ways in which "dancing has an effect on audiences" through "intimacy of the setting" (interview with author 2013). An early choreographic commission in 1998 provided what she describes as her "first foray into shifting the proximity of audience to performer," choreographing dancers among the patrons sitting at tables and chairs in a crowded bar (interview with author 2017). In 2002, Doyle had just put her dance company on temporary hiatus when her company manager Colin Marsh introduced her to Barrett, with whom she "hit it off," and began working, as he had been seeking a choreographer "because he was feeling that words weren't working within his vision [yet] didn't have the skill set to know what to do with movement" (2013). The initial meeting between Doyle and Barrett led to their collaboration on the first version of *SNM* in 2003 in London, which was staged in the Victorian Beaufoy Building, a former boys' school. As Doyle explains:

> Felix had no real interest or desire in directing [the first version of *SNM*]. We did direct it together, but his focus was very much on the space and the music and the sound installation. It was the first time he'd worked with dancers. So he let me do what I wanted to do, which was really just my work that I'd been doing [previously] . . . I felt like we were on to something—the combination of choreography and dance and visceral theater in relation to architecture and space with this sort of fluid audience relationship felt like [a] really interesting formula. (2013)

Doyle was instrumental in situating dancers, rather than actors, as the primary performers of *SNM*, believing that "the body often can be more expressive than language—certainly in [the Punchdrunk] world, where you need to be able to convey the essence of a scene very quickly" (Symonds 2011). The London version was Doyle's first choreographic work for an entire building, and her approach to Barrett's vision of centralizing audiences within performances was critical to their collective discovery of a creative process that offered the promise of continued productive potential. As Doyle explains, her mission when starting *SNM* "was to search for a physical language which would complement a building, or a site" while "questioning how abstract I could be" when crafting movement for dancers so they could convey the narrative elements conceived as imperative to the production (interview with author 2017).

Barrett began presenting works in 2000 in the United Kingdom through a theatrical approach to transforming large-scale architectural sites into seemingly endless worlds that serve as performance spaces. When founding Punchdrunk, Barrett was primarily interested in "deconstructing classic literature and layering these elements into environments," with the company's earliest productions prioritizing spoken text (in Doyle et al. 2012). However, as Barrett explains, he learned through building his initial productions that "words couldn't match the experiential scale of the work" (interview with author 2015a). Spoken text delivered by actors failed to resonate with the impact Barrett envisioned within the epic spaces he conceptualized and constructed with his team. Words were not sufficient in establishing the kinetic atmosphere Barrett desired for audiences, one that would prompt them to move through the performance and evoke the feeling of "floating through a dream world" (interview with author 2015a). Upon meeting Doyle, Barrett came to understand the power of choreography as a technology to catalyze audience response. Doyle, in discussing Barrett's vision, asserts that the choreography of the audience is "all Felix" (2017). She explains,

> Felix's reason for making theater in the beginning . . . was about shaking up an audience experience, moving them away from the passive, making them engage *by having them do*. That all comes from him; I can't take any credit there. [What] I could see was how dance just engages [the audience] much more immediately than words do. (2013, emphasis in speech)

While Barrett was already foregrounding the experience of the audience, Doyle introduced the choreography of dancers as a means for drawing audiences further into the *SNM* scenes.

Barrett's design of audience experience in *SNM* and other Punchdrunk works is not typically recognized by scholars or critics as the choreographic thinking that I suggest it is. Rather, his application of such thinking is, I argue, sometimes misunderstood or misconstrued as tactics meant to shock or scare spectators.[7] Yet Barrett's own accounts suggest his thinking is indeed choreographic. For example, Barrett explains that his decision to maintain low light levels in the performance spaces of the McKittrick is not meant to evoke terror in audiences, like a haunted house. Rather, he explains:

> The use of darkness in *Sleep No More* is not about fear—it is about slowing down the bodies of audiences . . . if they get through the space too quickly, then it loses its layers of complexity. If the audience can see too far ahead of them, then there is no reason for them to go there . . . the darkness slows the audience down so they are wary, curious. This way, [audiences] tune into the tempo of the piece and are able to experience its layers of complexity. The scenes and performers are important, but the impact of the work

comes from the way everyone *moves through the space*. (interview with author 2015a; emphasis in speech)

As Barrett explains, he has designed the darkness throughout the McKittrick as a kind of choreographic object, following Forsythe's use of the concept, as a way to delimit certain kinds of movement in order to manage *how* and at *what speed* audiences travel through the McKittrick. In another example, Barrett's choreographic, elicitive dramaturgical thinking manifests itself through the presence of discreet, black mask-wearing staff, known as "stewards," on each floor to also manage and direct the movements of spectators. Stewards are choreographed to serve as barriers to staircases or rooms and as frames through which audiences can safely spectate the full-bodied, vigorous dancing of cast members. Stewards also give participants someone to follow; they rush through quiet areas of the space to locations where the action is unfolding, functioning as a kind of scenographic corps de ballet. Though the stewards are background figures, they are essential in the overall scope of the performance, assisting audience participants in negotiating the specificities and sensitivities of the site and being available for those participants struggling with their reactions to the sensory nature of the space. Audience participants acknowledge the bodies of the stewards as choreographed signs expressing "Do Not Enter" or "Wait Here," rather than relying on speech or written signifiers to manage their journey within the space. Stewards may step in to assist a performer by guiding spectators away from critical areas and also directing spectators by enabling and disabling access to spaces in the building, essentially rerouting spectators to different locations throughout the performance. This is particularly true toward the end of performances, as the space seems to close in on itself as stewards manage an intricate choreography of closing and locking doors in order to funnel spectators as a group into the ballroom to witness the final scenes of the production.

Working together in the United Kingdom between 2003 and 2008, Barrett and Doyle developed multiple projects through "processes that put the audience and the performers in a shared environment where the boundaries are fluid [. . .]. The world itself is 360 degrees, and the audience exists within the 360-degree sphere, where there's an absence of [a] front and the performance can be anywhere" (Doyle, interview with author 2013).[8] While Barrett continued to refine strategies for shifting the "audience into a particular state of disorientation, of otherness" as they journey through different scenographic and sonic atmospheres, Doyle was experimenting with methods for training dancers to be effective performers within immersive worlds (interview with author 2017). Two key practices that Doyle has incorporated into her work with Punchdrunk's cast members are the "Seven Levels of Tension" method from physical theater practitioner Jacques Lecoq, and the use of contact improvisation to interact with the space of the production.

The Seven Levels of Tension method is used to train actors to quickly access a range of emotional and physical states of being (1998:89).[9] To master this scale, performers begin by learning to embody level one, which is a state of no tension (relaxed, exhausted). They then progress systematically up the scale, with each level an expression of increasing intensity until they physicalize level seven, which is a state of solid tension (highly pressurized, bound emotionally and physically). Performers skilled in the Seven Levels can shift across the scale seamlessly to express numerous levels of tension within mere seconds, modulating the intensity of their muscular tone and the rhythm of movement in order to best communicate through their physicality whatever needs to be expressed to fulfill the scene. Drawing upon Lecoq's ideas, Doyle has developed a choreographic version of the Seven Levels, which she calls States of Tension, to train Punchdrunk dancers to access "a more articulate body" within immersive performance (interview with author 2017). Doyle finds the States of Tension essential to problem-solving the kind of artistic challenges presented by Barrett's desire for the audience to be mobile during performances—namely, how to train dancers to perform their choreography with a kind of qualitative specificity that would impel audiences to move as well. In this way, Doyle's choreographic language—a mix of compositional skills from dance and performance methods from physical theater— functions as an essential component of the Punchdrunk aesthetic.

Doyle utilizes her States of Tension as a language when crafting choreography and directing dancers to perform so as to guide them to build their "sensitivity to muscular tone and rhythm as useful ways of inviting, suggesting, manipulating, leading an audience" (2017). While performing, dancers draw upon Doyle's choreographic version to perform with the kind of qualitative specificity that will capture the attention of audiences and garner responses from them; how a performer moves can effectively energize the space between them and the audience, thus harnessing the audience members' capacity to function as moving entities across the venue. She explains further that because audiences are often in close proximity to the dancers, this vantage point "sort of blurs the way that [audiences] look at movement. Movement becomes less full, becomes less clear when you're really close to it, and energy and dynamics take over" (2017). Doyle's choreography, when instantiated by a dancer, elicits a "kinesthetic response in an audience member" and functions to catalyze audiences into motion (2017). Doyle suggests that when dancers perform her choreography via one of the levels in close relation to audiences, "something automatically shifts in the [spectator's] physiology" (2017). By this, Doyle means she has observed marked differences in the physical reactions of audience members when encountering a performer who is in state one versus state six, when "auditing" a performance as a masked participant herself. In other words, Doyle suggests that how a dancer manifests tension in the body when approaching an audience member and interacting with them, as well as when interacting with props or other scenography, is key to guiding the spectator through their experiences of the performance.

Doyle's States of Tension method, key to the audience experience of moving through the spaces of the venue, is also critically linked to "the choreography of objects," by which she means the bona fide items installed as components of the production's highly detailed scenography (2017). The McKittrick encompasses six floors and over one hundred rooms, each of which are sites for scenes designed via elicitive dramaturgical thinking to prompt participation, such as demonstrated by the woman described in the opening scenario in this chapter.[10] Yet the "realms" of *SNM* are also intricately designed and furnished to encourage interaction with and exploration of scenographic spaces and contexts, allowing audiences individual opportunities for discovery, participation, and connection.[11] Objects such as a glass of whiskey, a table set for tea, or a file of detective's notes, and performance spaces designed variously as a sweet shop, detective agency, or hospital ward, may all attract and entice audience participants. Doyle's choreography involves dancers interacting with multiple objects of different types and sizes, ranging from a fragile drinking glass to a heavy wingback chair. Such objects and spaces may prompt responsive action from spectators, as they then follow a performer or mimic another audience participant who has recently touched the object or inhabited the space. By emphasizing choreography over spoken text in *SNM*, Punchdrunk establishes a fluid space in which hundreds of spectators are encouraged to move while accessing their imaginations and resourcefulness to discover multiple narratives, which are woven into the dancing and the hyperrealistic scenography.

In addition to Doyle's use of her States of Tension in composing immersive productions, she also draws on the concept and practice of contact improvisation. Both she and Barrett find dancers to be particularly suited to immersive performance because they "tuned into a particular way of experiencing space and experiencing other bodies in space" (interview with author 2013). Doyle is especially interested in casting dancers with contact improvisation skills since Punchdrunk performers must be able to "use space in the same way that they use a partner. So a wall becomes a body, or a chair, or an edge of a surface. All of those contact principles of being a good partner are transposed to the space" (2013). Dancers in contact improvisation draw upon their skills in order to kinesthetically sense and interact with people, objects, and scenography within their range of motion. While, for the most part, spectators are not engaged in the kinds of contact improvisation performed by the cast members, such as weight sharing and partnering, they are indeed adapting to other bodies in space, negotiating situations through action and response, and exploring the ideas that there are no leaders and partners may be interchangeable as they move along pathways that are not predetermined.[12] In addition, contact improvisation can be applied in order to minimize physical boundaries between spectators and dancers and encourage explorations of the space, its structure, and the objects therein. Many spectators come into contact with furniture by sitting on it or moving it; some can be seen applying weight and testing its stability in processes similar to those of the cast members; and still others may find themselves climbing over the furniture or on top of it in order to make way for a duet or trio of dancers, or simply to get a better view of the choreography, as in the opening vignette describing the murder of Lady Macduff.

Through their tandemized choreographic thinking, Doyle and Barrett have established the conditions for audiences to discover the stories embedded within SNM by observing the movements of dancers and engaging in their own movement. The dancers, for their part, hold the dual responsibilities of performing choreography to convey narrative and performing choreography to cultivate the responsiveness of the audience specifically through movement. Since audiences are masked, they make sense of physical action and reaction, rather than responses through speech. Both Doyle and Barrett underscore the need for the choreography of dancers in SNM to have a rigor and exactitude. According to Barrett, because "the audience is free-form . . . the performers need to be absolutely precise" (interview with author 2015a). Barrett describes the production as "meticulously choreographed . . . every single beat, even though it feels like it is a flippant bit of improvisation, a brush, a glance, is set, and it kind of has to be . . . be-cause . . . the performers have a lot of power and so do the audience" (Barrett 2015b). Throughout their development of SNM, Doyle and Barret have en-gaged in choreographically informed, elicitive dramaturgical thinking in order to catalyze and structure the movement of audiences, creating the conditions for their experience of insider dynamics.

Insider Dynamics

I suggest that in addition to contact improvisation, Punchdrunk's work is founded on several other postmodernist dance practices that Barrett and Doyle effectively adapt and extend from the dance studio to the sites of their immersive productions: pedestrianism, chance operations, and site speci-ficity. *Pedestrianism* refers to the commonly known non-verbal tactics and physical norms for negotiating space in Western society, of which most au-dience participants would be cognizant, such as walking on one side and passing on the other, or communicating through eye contact in addition to speech. These norms are complicit in a common language of pedestrian movement and used by audience members to communicate bodily know-ledge in space with others while moving within, through, and around the realms of the production. *Chance operations* are reflected and permitted by the score, which enable the spectators to be generally free to improvise their movement paths or contacts and pursue individualized chance oppor-tunities. The performance of the woman who responded to the grieving Macduff in the opening scenario of this chapter illustrates Barrett and Doyle's extension of postmodernist dance practices as elicitive dramaturgy; the score offered the woman the chance opportunity to enter the dance in the lobby through ordinary pedestrian movement and to engage in a mo-ment of contact improvisation when sharing the weight of Lady Macduff's body. Another postmodern dance practice, *site specificity*, or as Doyle refers to it, *site sensitivity*, is used to create possibilities for artists and audiences to experience each performance space differently.[13] Spectators roaming throughout the building are pursuing their own creative agency to the de-gree they desire within the context of SNM by shifting between roles of au-dience participant, creator, spectator, curator, and performer. Adaptation of postmodernist dance practices creates conditions for site-specific, choreographed, improvised, pedestrian, and chance spectatorship designed to stimulate and sensitize dance audiences beyond their usual visual, aural, and kinesthetic experiences.

Barrett and Doyle's extension of these postmodernist dance practices is, I argue, one way in which they apply elicitive dramaturgical thinking, creating optimal conditions for a process of affective engagement that I have identified previously as *insider dynamics* (see Ritter 2016). While audience members are engaged within insider dynamics, their experiences are transformed through moments of individual discovery and agency. Spectators move, literally and figuratively, throughout the performance from states of unknown to known, and then yet farther into the unknown. Arts education scholar Graeme Sullivan's comments about practice-led research are instructive in illuminating how the insider dynamics operate within an *SNM* performance. Like practice-led research, the choreographic structure of *SNM* is "purposeful yet open-ended, clear-sighted yet exploratory" (Sullivan 2009:49). The *practices* through which audiences engage in participatory spectatorship in *SNM* are different from other forms of spectatorship. Sullivan also asserts that "creative options and new associations occur in situations where there is intense concentration [. . .] within an open landscape of free-range possibility" (48). The opportunities to explore and discover in *SNM* are multiple, and all the participants place themselves at crossroads—places full of risk and potentiality.

I have identified four progressive stages of insider dynamics by which spectators become and remain involved in the production: *complicity, porosity, contagion*, and *inclusion*. Through these stages of insider dynamics, audience members have multiple opportunities to transform their spectatorship experiences and meaning-making, thereby experiencing a blurring of boundaries between their objective and subjective identities and becoming immersed within the production that has been designed with this intent. Insider dynamics is a conceptual framework offered to illustrate the operational nature of affect in immersive performance.

Complicity

Complicity is typically understood as collusion, that is, involvement with co-conspirators towards some nefarious end or wrongdoing. Complicity as a concept in Western theatrical practices has a long history, with roots in the

very first live performances; audiences who attend a performance are implicated alongside the performers within the imaginative space and time of a
production that bends or even suspends the rules governing daily life to present other worlds onstage, whatever that stage might consist of and wher-
ever it may be located. In discussing immersive theater, Machon frames
complicity in relation to "co-creation and agency, risk, and investment"
(2013:150). She suggests that audiences in immersive performance need to
first be complicit in accepting "the invisible rules of the space" through implicit performer–audience contracts or, in the case of *SNM*, explicit directions
given by hosts before audience participants enter the performance space
(2013:41).[14] Another perspective can be found in the insights of educators
Jan Meyer and Ray Land; through their work, it is possible to understand
complicity as a "threshold concept," which they define as "akin to a portal,
opening up a new and previously inaccessible way of thinking about something. . . . It represents a transformed way of understanding, or interpreting,
or viewing . . . without which the learner cannot progress" (2010:1). In addition, educational researcher Glynis Cousin asserts that the "grasping of a
threshold concept [such as complicity] is transformative because it involves
an ontological as well as a conceptual shift in the learner" (2010:2). In immersive productions such as *SNM*, complicity acts as a threshold or portal
allowing audience participants to learn new ways of participating, including
different modes of spectating. This dynamic can also transform their participatory agency by opening them up to an experience of playing with their
identities and moving deeper into the performance.

If complicity is a threshold *concept*, the mask worn by audiences in
Punchdrunk's productions is a "threshold *object*," following Janet H. Murray's
coining of the phrase, that assists in facilitating audience complicity.[15] In
SNM, all audience participants are required to wear masks that resemble
the *bauta* masks donned by eighteenth-century Venetians. Audience
participants essentially become replicas of one another in a participatory
process of mimesis (Figure 4.2). This masking serves multiple functions: it
accentuates the alterity of the unmasked performers versus the collectivity of
the masked audience while also incorporating the audience participants into
the scenography. Theater scholar Gareth White, discussing Punchdrunk's
practices previous to *SNM*, describes masked spectators as "part of the
scenery," claiming that the "audience is prevented from doing what they
might in another promenade performance: looking at each other's faces for
reaction to the play" (2012:224). *SNM* has redefined the impact of masking

Figure 4.2 Emursive Present Punchdrunk's *Sleep No More*, New York (2011–).
Matthew Oaks. Photograph by Yaniv Schulman.

on communication and hence on the spectator's experience of complicity. White's assertion that "communication is *inhibited* by the lack of visible facial expression" (224, emphasis added) does not hold true for the performances of *SNM* in which communication via the reading of *bodies* is paramount. Facial reactions are of minimal import when non-verbal gestures, postures, and choreographed movements are the primary communicators of the narrative in the performance. Embodied communication in *SNM* affords audience participants visceral and sensate comprehension beyond the usual visuality, aurality, and more restricted physicality of other theater productions. The mask doubles as a kind of "free pass" for audience participants, behind which they can become physically engaged in movement and shifting identities at will, as they play within and outside of social and theatrical conventions.

Ushered Across the Threshold

I have been asked to enter a small, dark room with twenty-five other people. While watching faces, I feel the proximity of our bodies as whispers and nervous giggles are shared among the group. The room quiets when our host, a Punchdrunk company member, welcomes us and gives instructions. We are asked to put on a mask and to stop speaking. Our bodies change immediately. Some people adjust their posture and straighten up, while others fold arms protectively across chests. Suddenly, our host bangs loudly on one wall of the room, and it slides open to reveal an elevator with another company member, an usher, who has come to take us up to another floor in the performance space. The usher sweeps his arm open to reveal the empty elevator and we, the audience participants, step silently into the elevator one by one until all are corralled inside. The door slides shut, and the elevator begins to ascend.

Porosity

In defining *porosity* as an operational element of insider dynamics, I propose that it extends beyond the discourse of "porous" boundaries between performers and audiences to include the conceptualization of porosity as an essential component of spectators' negotiation of affect within immersive performance contexts. Porosity, I suggest, encompasses and extends the notions of kinesthetic empathy and kinesthetic affect, as historically framed within the context of live performance and theorized in Chapter 2, given that audiences are themselves choreographed within immersive performances. In a production such as *SNM*, audience participants, having crossed over the threshold of complicity, are presented with performance environments and circumstances that are richly constituted by myriad possibilities for social, psychological, and physical agency and adaptation. Porosity is not passivity, however; instead, the kinds of adaptation made by audience participants and the levels of engagement experienced are facilitated by the ways in which an individual spectator modulates their porosity along a spectrum ranging from absorbent to resistant.

Porosity, then, is a concept inextricable from philosopher Brian Massumi's notion of the politics of affect, as put forth in Chapter 2, and, as such, includes the ways in which both cast members and audience participants possess the capacities to affect and be affected, as per Spinoza. Although Massumi addresses affect in relation to larger issues of the political in society, including democracy and capitalism in his 2015 text, his theorizing around the politics of affect is useful when clarifying the concept of porosity in immersive performance. As he states, "in the heat of the encounter, we are immersed in eventful working-out of affective capacities," which includes the capacity to acquiesce to affect as well as to resist it (2015b:93). While the elicitive dramaturgical thinking deployed to create *SNM* can lead to processes of insider dynamics, audience participants are always modulating the impact of affect while moving through the stages of insider dynamics. This is particularly the case during the stage of porosity, as spectators are negotiating how they receive and/or reject the activity happening around them and how they themselves contribute. Critically, as spectators adapt their decision-making through improvisational choices, some may expand their porosity to initiate their own creative, pleasurable, or productive responses while others, for multiple reasons, have difficulty processing and/or integrating their experiences within the immersive world. Through individual porosity, each audience participant finds themselves confronting interpersonal (between self and other) and intrapersonal (within self) boundaries of, or barriers to, engagement. Massumi's concept of the transindividual, which he defines as "what is passing *between* individuals involved, which is reducible to neither taken separately," has particular resonance in relation to interpersonal, intersubjective relations in immersive contexts (94, emphasis in original). It is this transindividuality that speaks both to the relational nature of affect—our capacity to affect and be affected—as well as to the ways in which bodies engage in "a joint activity of becoming" during encounters, which are always moments of transition (95). When offered opportunities to interface with performers, spaces, objects, and other spectators, audience participants may or may not make space within themselves, that is, adjust their porosity, in order to allow changes in their emotive, active, and reactive states of being.

Lady Macbeth and Her Mistaken Consort

Lady Macbeth is spiraling down a long hallway, her circular movements carving the space as a physical metaphor for her uncoiling sanity. Suddenly her eyes fix on one of the spectators in the crowd, and, in her deluded state, she addresses him with mumbled words and grasping hands. She clearly mistakes him for someone else. To whom does she speak with such distress? Is it the ghost of Duncan or of Banquo? Pressing one of her hands onto his shoulder and grasping his arm, she runs back and forth in the dim space, pulling him along behind her. Is the physical contact and human connection with the mistaken consort stalling or quickening Lady Macbeth's descent into complete madness? The man obliges Lady Macbeth by offering his arm for support, but he appears also to be reacting cautiously, reflecting an awkward paradox of vigilance and powerlessness while witnessing her body mirroring the unravelling of her mind.

Porosity enables this man who has been randomly chosen from the audience to physically and emotionally connect with objects, spaces, and performers. The dancer performing Lady Macbeth used several tactics to "read" the porosity of the man she ultimately chose to be her spontaneous consort, and made decisions as to how she might affect him by eliciting responses. First, she crossed the boundary of social space through his personal kinesphere to test the perviousness of his intimate space.[16] She moved in close and directly addressed him with eye contact just inches from his mask, a moment that framed the two of them in a cinematic "close-up" shot for those of us observing. The man's accommodation of her body into his territory with no resistance allowed her the opportunity to move to her next tactic of engagement: physical contact. She pressed her hand onto his arm to gauge his resilience to touch and pressure. With his acceptance of contact, she advanced to the final level, which was to have him invest in his own movement by joining her in an improvised journey up and down the hallway. And yet this man's capacity to be affected and to affect is part of this particularly interpersonal exchange as well. His willingness to move alongside her advanced the action and allowed him to contribute another moment of improvised movement performance within the production.

It is within porous moments such as this one in SNM that audience participants may seize on the opportunity to apply improvisation strategies used by dancers to move skillfully through space and time. Like the dancers, audience participants can improvise movement on the basis of breath timing, awareness of overlapping kinespheres, use of eye contact as visual code, and physical feedback from the responsiveness of other bodies in close proximity.[17] Audience participants who observe and experiment with these strategies increase their porosity within the structured improvisational score so as to be more effective in managing their movement and engagement in and through scenarios. For example, in the scenario with Lady Macbeth succumbing to insanity, audience participants were choreographing the space through their improvised movement around Lady Macbeth and her consort as they made way to accommodate the spatial changes happening between the two. Tori Sparks, who has performed the role of Lady Macbeth, contextualizes the energy and interactivity between performers and audiences in SNM as "co-existing with the audience. It's not interactive in the sense that if an audience member were to come and pick up your prop that suddenly . . . your story would change. It's not interactive in that way. However, their energy is feeding your energy and the space and everything around it" (Doyle et al. 2013:8). This audience energy is an integral aspect of SNM. Participants are observing affect arise within themselves in response to their participation in the choreographed scenes. They improvise reactions and responses within their embodied awareness, thus becoming part of the choreography.

Audience engagement is enhanced by such agentive actions and by how far participants will let themselves go in trying, feeling, and doing something new. The shifts in the spectating experience really happen when participants are attuned to and allow themselves to be affected by the bodily sensed knowledge that develops from their movement as well as that of performers and other spectators.

Contagion

Dance critic John Martin put forth the term *contagion* in relation to dance in 1946 when theorizing kinesthetic empathy, claiming that a spectator can experience "sympathetically in his [their] musculature the exertions he sees in someone else's musculature" (1946:105. See also Foster 2008). I utilize contagion in relation to immersive performance to describe how emotionality and behavior are influenced by an individual's porosity or openness to the changing course of experiences offered within a participatory event. Contagious behaviors include physically following performers and other audience members across spaces as well as enacting repetition of specific actions and reactions to extend situations and scenes within performances. The choreographic device of canon (analogous to singing in a round, as in the songs "Frère Jacques" or "Hot Cross Buns"), can be witnessed as contagious activity in *SNM*. Both choreographed dancers and audience participants catalyze canon choreography. Lady Macbeth's lying down in a bathtub in her apparent attempt at cleansing away her guilt can inspire repetition in audience participants who have witnessed her (see Figure 4.3). On the fourth floor there is a row of empty bathtubs, and if, as an audience member, one remains long enough, they can witness spectator after spectator climbing in and out of the bathtubs. Is each repetition a transformation of the choreographed material they witnessed performed by Lady Macbeth, which somehow ripples on through subsequent participants' re-enactment of it? Or is the choreographic placement of the empty bathtubs, in itself, enough to impel spectators to move in and around them? If the former, then spectators may observe the bathtub movement motif without ever having seen Lady Macbeth's original performance of it, as the choreography continues to be interpreted through contagious action. Alternately, a spectator's decision to pick up a book or wine glass can trigger a contagious reaction in others, who repeat the action, which extends the potential for the movement motif

Figure 4.3 Emursive Present Punchdrunk's *Sleep No More*, New York (2011–). Paul Zivkovich and Sophie Bortolussi. Photograph by Driely Schwartz.

to be picked up by yet others over a temporal delay. The efficacy of dance as a catalyst for spectator agency and engagement, as in the bathtub example of contagion in *SNM*, seems confirmed by Punchdrunk's choice to structure their subsequent 2013 production, *The Drowned Man*, via similar choreographic inventions. Therefore, my experiences of *SNM* are not congruent with theater scholar Gareth White's claim about Punchdrunk's other immersive productions, of which he says, "a crowd does not form," and "faceless strangers mill around, each having very individual experiences" (2009:224). Other reflections I have gathered from audience participants attending the New York production similarly contradict White's claim. In witnessing the contagious contributions of audience participants to the choreography and action throughout *SNM*, I can clearly see when choices of one participant inspire action in others, resulting in the production of a collective composition.

Unmoored by Macbeth

I am in a long corridor facing a graffiti-covered wall flanked by exits. I am alone and am trying to decide which way to go. Suddenly, there is a gentle but firm grip on my shoulder. I am being purposefully moved aside as the dancer performing Macbeth rushes past me. I am unmoored for a moment; I was alone and now I am not alone. There is tremendous action taking place just inches from me as Macbeth launches himself against the wall, executing explosive movement that erupts across its surface. However, the touch on my shoulder signified not only Macbeth's presence but also danger, because coming on the heels of Macbeth is a mob. It is Macbeth's retinue of masked spectators, who are full of competition and hungry for a piece of the king. Macbeth's touch now means much more to me—it signifies through him the presence of his pack of followers as they engulf me.

Dancer Paul Zivkovich's virtuosic performance as Macbeth transforms him into a huge celebrity this evening, and the masked audience, fueled by their fanaticism, are accomplices to the murders he committed while in character (Figure 4.4). I have to make a decision: am I going to stand here, bracing against the rush of the crowd, or will I escape? Or, am I going to follow, watch, and thus collude in Macbeth's crimes? What lies ahead if I exit or if I choose to be a co-conspirator? What are the political implications of my choices? In the presence of Macbeth and this contagious crowd, I feel both empathy and anxiety. *SNM* participants get caught up in such "contagious flight" at many times in the performance as the exit of one or more performers from a room impels twenty, fifty, perhaps one hundred or more spectators to physically follow them. The dancers literally amass a following, giving sensorial materiality to the concept of *having a following*. Spectators learn that to be swept up by the actions or enthusiasm of the crowd can lead to further experiential rewards. Interestingly, a spectator who did not directly witness an event may still have a sense of it from a distance, through the bodies and reactions of others, in a kind of participation-by-proxy. This "by-proxy participation" extends the action in a wave-like undulation beyond the actual moment of initiation and results in the inclusion of more spectators in the scene (Reason and Reynolds 2010:54). Ultimately, the contagion among audience participants, whether they follow pathways or repeat patterns of choreographed action, is mediated by the attraction of being included.

Figure 4.4 Punchdrunk's *Sleep No More*, Shanghai (2016–). Paul Zivkovich. Photography by Yuan Studio.

Inclusion

As an overarching operation of insider dynamics, *inclusion* integrates the other three concepts—complicity, porosity, and contagion—thereby offering opportunities for audience engagement in collectivity, corroboration, and even conspiracy. Audience participants who both experience and facilitate inclusion in an immersive event like *SNM* find themselves tracing the paths of others in an effort not only to embed themselves within the culture but also to explore alterity with respect, and recognition without appropriation. Thus, these audience participants expand their understanding of the *SNM* culture through all their efforts. Inclusion is motivated by more than FoMO—fear of missing out. Inclusion entails that audience participants move emotionally, physically, empathetically, and cognitively deeper into the action of an immersive performance in order to connect with content, performers, and fellow audience members. In so doing, they gain more experiential and meaning-making benefits. The term "inclusion" might be construed as having some semantic overlap with "immersion," given their definitional contexts related to being enclosed, absorbed, or contained within. I suggest, however, that these two terms actually refer to distinct aspects of what occurs within immersive performance, and I posit that some level of inclusion is required as a precondition for individuals to experience immersion.

As an agentive action, inclusion allows audience participants to reroute themselves from exclusionary outsider positions into more inclusive insider perspectives in their spectatorship and participation. As they do so, spectators experience the affective benefits of feeling acceptance and belonging during a performance. This, in turn, promotes perceptions of collective composition and co-creation while also challenging existing paradigms in which artists and audiences are separate entities. An experience I had during participation in *SNM* and subsequently interpreted as co-creation and inclusion occurred when I entered a long hallway of storefronts, including a tailor's atelier, a detective agency, and a sweet shop.

The Candy Man

Wearing my mask, I enter through the sweet shop door. A wall lined from floor to ceiling with shelves holds jars filled with sweets. On a long counter in front of the wall are a cash register and a measuring scale. These are all props set out for use by any audience member to improvise a scene. Another masked participant is behind the counter. I watch the fine articulations of his upper body, his arms carving through space as he shifts jars from side to side along the shelves. I stand and wait for my cue. He looks in my direction. I slide through the space toward him. Just as I reach the counter, he is opening a jar of sweets, perfectly on cue. Two quick shifts of weight and a turn of my body brings me around the counter to stand in front of him. I strike a pose, just inches away from him with my hand extended. He pauses for one, two, three beats and then drops a wrapped sweet into my palm. My fingers close around it and we stand there staring at each other. One, two, three beats more. Then I turn and dash across the space and out through the same stage door. Our scene together is over.

The "candy man" and I were not company members of Punchdrunk in this production of *SNM*; rather, we were both audience participants and complete strangers to one another. And yet, we were indeed performers in the *SNM* context. Our costumes were the masks we had been given and were required to wear throughout the performance. As I exited the sweet shop into the hallway, I realized that other audience participants had spectated our danced exchange through the plate glass window of the shop. With no "official" dancers, that is, cast members, present in the space, we two audience participants had constructed a dance, having stitched ourselves into

the fabricated sweet shop of the *SNM* performance, albeit for just a moment. It may be argued that inclusive immersion in its most actualized form
occurs when audience participants, having taken on new identities within
the performance, are completely absorbed and engaged in co-creation and
invested in performance by and for themselves, without the presence of paid
performers.

In proposing *inclusion* as a fourth and culminating stage of insider dynamics, I acknowledge that this term also has important resonance within
contemporary discourses referring to the need to foreground marginalized
groups, particularly in terms of access and representation. The immersive
productions I have experienced thus far, *SNM* included, have been designed
to accommodate individuals who are able-bodied and neurotypical. Many
of the performance spaces within the McKittrick, for instance, would be
challenging, if not impossible, to navigate with an assistive device such as a
wheelchair, and the atmospheric elements such as flashing lights and loud
soundscape could be uncomfortable for individuals who are neurodivergent.
Furthermore, inclusion through the representation of marginalized groups
has also been problematic due to the tendency, to date, of immersive
practitioners drawing upon literary narratives from the Western European
canon that prioritize the experiences and perspectives of white cisgender
males.[18]

Acknowledging these significant physical and socio-political concerns
regarding access and representation, however, there is another question of
inclusion to consider in relation to immersive performance: namely, the
question of what happens when inclusion mutates into a sense of entitlement in audience behavior that presents ethical and moral concerns in relation to other audience members as well as performers. To understand how
inclusion might become entitlement, we must consider the larger cultural
context of *curationism* in which *SNM*'s insider dynamics occur. As art critic
and editor David Balzer suggests in *Curationism: How Curating Took Over
the Art World and Everything Else*, since the mid-1990s, there has been an
"acceleration" of the "impulse" to select and arrange elements of culture according to one's own liking (2015:2). Balzer connects the term *curator* to
improvisational practices, specifically that of *bricolage*, from French ethnol-
ogist Claude Levi-Strauss. Balzer suggests that the bricoleur is "a tinkerer, an
improviser working with what was at hand, cobbling together solutions to
both practical and aesthetic problems" (Wilcken quoted in Balzer 2015:23).
Because spectators in *SNM* have the freedom to improvisationally roam

the spaces of the McKittrick through choreography that permits proximity to dancers and scenography, they can act as bricoleurs/curators collecting different experiences. The curatorial amassing of experiences can lead both to extended audiencing, which will be discussed in the next section of this chapter, as well as to what I identify as coauthorality, by which I mean the sense of being a co-author of the production, as will be discussed in the next chapter. Yet such curatorial freedom, while potentially leading to inclusion and immersion for audiences, can also lead to a sense of entitlement that plays out across a wide range of behaviors amongst audience participants of immersive performance.

In *SNM*, the mask is a kind of meta-level criterion for inclusion; individuals who take their masks off flout the rules governing the space and risk being ejected from the performance. Other behaviors with far more serious ethical and moral implications also breach the implicit norms of appropriate conduct within the immersive worlds created by practitioners. In the case of *SNM*, instances of aggressive behavior, such as elbowing others out of the way to better witness a scene, surface in the blogs written by fans of the production, who call out what they have deemed as inappropriate behavior by other participants in attempts to regulate the performance environment to keep it safe for performers and other audience members. Furthermore, a widely circulated article published online in 2017 by *Buzzfeed*, an American digital media company, reported on instances of sexual misconduct as perpetrated by audience participants toward *SNM* performers and staff. The author of the *Buzzfeed* article cites the convention of masking as a possible contributor to such behavior, suggesting that the anonymity the mask confers upon audience members spurs them to engage in behaviors, such as inappropriate touch, that they would not in other contexts. Alston has noted that this stance suggests that "the fault is with the performance rather than with an opportunistic audience member" whose expectation of inclusion is, as I would argue, representative of a sense of entitlement (Alston 2019). Such entitled behaviors on the part of some spectators are in tension with the idea of being complicit with the rules of the performance.

Theater scholar Keren Zaiontz lays out some of the reasons why spectatorship and participation within immersive theater might migrate into expressions of behavior that demonstrate apparent entitlement. Indeed, she suggests that some audience members adopt a "presumptive intimacy," by which she means "an entitlement to the artistic production through material and multisensory encounters" (2014:410).[19] Zaiontz also suggests that such work "frame[s] reception as a thing that participants not only consume, but own" (424). This, then, is the very tension that exists in my argument for how spectators are choreographed in immersive theater: if people are *being asked to do*—as Doyle has suggested Barrett wants audiences to feel empowered within Punchdrunk productions—then it is natural they will take some ownership over that doing. The problem, then, is when the doing of an individual encroaches upon the safety, well-being, and rights of another person sharing the same time and place of performance, namely performers and other audience members. Here we see how kinesthetic empathy and kinesthetic affect, as outlined in Chapter 2, resurface as important concepts within immersive performance. If the kinesthetic empathy and/or kinesthetic affect are catalyzed for audiences through both watching the movement of others and performing movement oneself—as evidenced by the woman in the opening scenario who, moved by the gendered violence she witnessed, stepped forward to share the burden of Lady Macduff's dead body—how might the production best manage such moments of inclusion by audiences? Choreography sets up a perennial tension between being controlled and/or authored by the apparatus of choreography, following Lepecki, and knowing there is the possibility of slipping out of the control of the apparatus.

Insider dynamics in immersive performances such as *SNM* operate through agentive action and engage multi-directionally across performers, audience participants, spaces, and scenography. Insider dynamics also allow audience participants to forge self-curated identities that are hybrid, reconfigured amalgamations of the self. Such amalgamated identities afford inclusion in multiple domains, not only surfacing in the initial performance context but also developing within post-performance products and personas. Audience participants are invested in negotiating power, ownership, authorial control, creative action, and curatorial agency, becoming whomever and whatever they wish, both during and after the performance. Experiences of immersion within *SNM* do not, it turns out, end when the audience exits the building. Rather, after encountering *SNM* as a highly sensory, nonverbal, and choreographic event, the immersive effects of the performance stay with participants, preoccupying their imaginations and catalyzing their actions for months or years afterward. The immersed state of being continues and even deepens through *extended audiencing*. This ripple-effect phenomenon manifests itself in various forms of actions and behaviors *around* immersive productions. These audience extensions of a curated self, during performance events and surrounding them, are undertaken with the intention of becoming somehow "more"—more differentiated, more actualized, more immersed, or more oneself than is usually possible in other sectors of life or within other spectating experiences.

Rendering Dance through Fandom: Extended Audiencing

Critically important to the success of *SNM* are the ways in which spectators continue their experience of the production long after departing from the venue. Across social media, blogs, and websites, as well as print media, they share their perceptions and experiences, engaging in forms of *extended audiencing* that have contributed to the development of fan communities, or fandoms, dedicated to the production. The premiere of *SNM* in Shanghai in December 2016 at the McKinnon Hotel, the "sister" venue to the McKittrick Hotel, has generated new fandoms and catalyzed a new generation of artists in China who are dedicated to immersive performance, as evidenced by international news reports and the writings of cultural critics.[20] These practitioners are now developing a distinct canon of immersive productions that reflects their exploration of China's literary and storytelling traditions and foregrounds Asian identities, offering insight into the international impact of the production and Punchdrunk's work on a global scale.[21]

Media scholar John Fiske coined the term "audiencing" as a verb in 1992 as a cultural studies concept relating to the consumption of popular television. Fiske argued that "culture is a continuous process of the social circulation of meanings and [. . .] 'audiencing' is part of that process" (1992:345). For Fiske, audiencing is something that is done in relation to others, such as groups of people coming together because of shared interests, in particular television shows. As a term, "audiencing" reflects the "process of producing, through lived experience [. . . ,] social identities and social relations" (353). In a similar vein, sociologist Eran Fisher later commented that "audiencing begins when one connects with other audience members, becoming, in fact, *their* audience. Audiencing on social media, then, is entwined with creating networks among members" (2015:63, emphasis in original). Cultural critic and media scholar Nick Couldry introduced the term "extended audience," applying it to examine the "whole spectrum of talk, action, and thought that draws on media, or is oriented towards media" (2005:196). Building on Couldry, I propose *extended audiencing* as a term for an agentive, multipronged phenomenon that is perpetuated through behavioral responses of fans who repeat-attend, create art inspired by the production, and share their creations within the public sphere of the internet. The concept of extended audiencing is especially useful in relation to immersive performance as a nonsequential, recursive process that regenerates and perpetuates itself through behavioral responses of repeating, sharing, and creating (see Ritter 2016 and 2017).

The most direct form of extended audiencing occurs when audience members attend *SNM* performances dozens, even hundreds of times despite ticket prices over $100. Another, less direct form of extended audiencing occurs when individual hear or read about, and thus indirectly experience, a performance via a friend or critic through either the print media or online content of websites, blogs, Facebook, or Twitter. The extended audiencing of *SNM* includes the continued interpretation of the event through the re-enactment of scenes and performance moments via multiple artistic media such as photos, videos, cartoons, drawings, writings, poems, and musical compositions.[22] While audience members are complicit in the posting and sharing of experiences online, they demonstrate porous, contagious, and inclusive behaviors through social media outlets with their agency as spectators spilling over into a kind of post-performance continuation of their state of immersion online. Spending three hours experiencing moments in *SNM* builds up tension, suspense, and an immense desire to share one's excitement with others, as is indicated by the explosion of fan blogs, particularly in the United States, and the postings of fans of the Shanghai production on the Weibo and WeChat platforms, primarily. *SNM* fan blogs came about through audience participants' hyperawareness of the reality that participation in *SNM* is not only a highly individualized but also a shared event.

Such fan creations function as a creative medium for audience participants to both process their experiences and share and compare them with others via extended audiencing. These reconstructions of memory allow audience participants to extend their own audiencing while also providing others, who may or may not have seen the event, an extended-audiencing experience as well. Audience participants witness the inventions of others and further extend them through dialogues and social media "witnessing," by which I mean users of such platforms, acknowledge, like, and repost the content of others. This extended audiencing constitutes the epistemological framework through which individuals increasingly understand themselves in the world. Walter Benjamin notes humans' "powerful compulsion . . . to become and behave like something else" (quoted in Taussig 1992:19), and indeed, the abundance of social media outlets enables not only the marketing of *SNM* but also the post-performance sharing of spectating experiences and responses. Audience participants can share how they risked immersion in a performance culture via their attempts to cross over and enter the immersive world, and they reveal how it felt to do so.

Fan blogs, social media, and artworks inspired by *SNM* all demonstrate a sort of democratization of spectatorship and the development of fan communities, that is, fandoms. Many of these spectator-generated materials are posted online for anyone to access for free, and consumers of these cultural products can identify with a blogger's experience and apply that blogger's point of view, whether or not they have attended *SNM*. Moreover, the anticipation and excitement created by these blogs radiate to others and, even before prospective audience members have attended the performance, allow them entrée to the fan community. Among *SNM* fandoms, the shifting boundaries around the communities can mean one might feel a sense of inclusion during one performance and not in another; similarly, a spectator might drift in and out of the fandom, being part and not a part, depending on their level of interest and access at any given time. What can be learned from the agency that audiences exercise here and from the shifting perspectives of individuals as they move within and between the roles of audience participant and performer, individual and fan community? It is my contention that the attraction to *SNM* is catalyzed by elicitive dramaturgy and fueled by insider dynamics, which in turn drives the agency of extended audiencing. Extended audiencing can therefore be understood as an energetic radiation amplifying immersive experiences and practices beyond the event of *SNM*. These echoes of experience are re-orchestrated into new creative expressions, which, when shared online, attract attention and stir curiosities.

In Biggin's discussion of the fan community of Punchdrunk, she reports on her analysis of one hundred or so comments (curated by Punchdrunk for their company archive) from the many sent by audiences to the company's website (http://www.punchdrunk.org.uk/) following their productions of *Faust* (2006–2007) and *The Masque of the Red Death* (2007–2008) in the United Kingdom. Acknowledging that these particular responses were mostly written specifically for Punchdrunk and "not intended to be read by an outside party," Biggin notes how the commentary explicitly reveals positive biases, since "negative experiences would be unlikely to be communicated or archived" (101).[23] Nonetheless, she finds, as I have through my research of *SNM* fan activity, that "fans often have a highly sophisticated critical gaze towards the work they love—rather than the passive non-critical adoration of the fan stereotype" (98). Biggin rightly notes that such commentary by fans serve as more than a "honorary curtain call or giving of thanks. It functions as a means of claiming ownership over immersive experience and a means of effectively beginning dialogue or conversation—initiating interactivity—with a production, theatre company or other members of the fan community" (98). For Biggin, some of the fan commentary she has analyzed indicates that immersion has a kind of stupefying effect on certain individuals, resulting in a "immersive theatre hangover" that is the result of experiences that have left audiences "physically changed" (106). I argue that such physical changes for audience participants are the direct outcome of the kinesthetic impact of choreography, that is, given their situated status as subjects of choreography who experience the resuscitation of their kinesthesia, alongside the sensation of attendant phenomena, such as kinesthetic empathy and kinesthetic affect. Although some audiences may perceive the affective impact of immersion as all-encompassing and even overpowering, Biggin points out this does not mean that they cannot also simultaneously maintain critical distance from the event and their experience of it. Indeed, I agree with Biggin's assertion that "immersion and [critical] distance do not work as a binary, but instead have a reciprocal relationship, informing one another in the moment," not only during performance but also in the post-event behaviors I identify as extended audiencing (111).[24]

In fact, I argue that the creative output generated by fans—in particular such non-verbal artistic expressions as cartoons, digital art and drawings, collage, and sculpture—can productively be understood as representations of critical distance as manifest in physical forms. These works of art reveal how audiences, searching for a way to understand and reckon with what they perceive as immersion, have chosen artistic expression as the most effective and appropriate means for reflective processing of their experiences as subjects of choreography in the hours and days post-event. While such fandom is not a new phenomenon in the history of the performing arts—one recalls the besotted fans who purportedly drank champagne from the discarded pointe shoes of nineteenth-century Austrian ballerina Fanny Elssler and the throngs of admirers who crowd the stage doors of twenty-first-century Broadway productions—in the context of immersive performance, the specific experience of being choreographed as mobile entities intensifies the impulse for participants to extend their feelings of inclusion beyond the event itself by generating their own creative responses (Anderson 1986:68–69).

Punchdrunk's skillful fracturing and inventive reassembly of multiple stories in order to imaginatively restage them thus compels spectators to themselves experiment creatively with how to extend the fantastical storyworlds of the production. The performance space serves as a research site for spectators—as incidental and intentional ethnographers—as the instructions offered before entry to the elevator become their parameters for conducting participant observation. The spaces are designed to encourage audiences to gather tactile feedback by engaging directly with the scenographic elements. When the tactile elements of the scenography are experienced simultaneously while in motion, they can be inspirational to spectators, not only within the time and space of the performance, but also when reflecting (and acting) on experiences in their post-performance extended audiencing. As sociologist Kathy Charmaz writes, what an ethnographer should study in the field is, "Whatever is happening there. By remaining open to the setting and the actions and people in it, ethnographers have the opportunity to work from the ground up and to pursue whatever they find to be of the greatest interest" (2006:21). Spectators conduct bodily ethnography through the movement they perform while following their impulses during performances. Not expected or required to perform the dance language, spectators must nonetheless involve themselves in a bodily experience to fully immerse themselves in the performance. Thus, their movement experience and their awareness of the action around them is a primary ethnographic tool for collecting their data and making meaning of performances. Running, climbing stairs, being lost, being in close proximity to dancers and other spectators, touching the scenery, and smelling the atmosphere are the ways they make meaning from this performance that serves as the realm of their research. By taking time to explore the space and observe through kinesthetic and bodily awareness their actions and those of others, spectators begin to understand the environment they temporarily inhabit as ethnographers practicing participant observation. Punchdrunk has established conditions that capitalize on the abstract and interpretive nature of dance, a form that lends itself to the development of imaginative interpretations by fans in their responses to performances. The choices spectators make—what they choose to see, whom they follow, where they stand, how they express their body language and behavior—allow them to become elements in the fluid environment of the work, making the experience of the performance all the more engaging.

While I was unable to obtain concrete data on the percentage of spectators who make return visits, the discovery of the fan community, or fandom, devoted to *SNM* provides evidence of numerous individuals attending multiple times.[25] In addition, analysis of fan data gathered from the internet and from interviews supports my argument. Often, fans return to gain more inspiration for their individual creations, such as drawings, sculpture, and fanfiction; they want to engage in online *sharing* that ultimately leads to more information about the performance and to both elaborations and reinventions of that information. Fans create their own meaning in the real time of performance via their individual journeys, then transfer their *choreographed* and *ethnographed* experiences—their accounts of embodied participation and spectatorship—through the creation of post-performance cultural products that manifest as art objects and/or creative writings. Located primarily on the social networking site Tumblr, the *SNM* fandom has generated so many online fan blogs devoted to the production that a blog directory has been compiled (see behindawhitemask 2012). Notably, the fans who create the blogs on Tumblr, or on WeChat or Weibo, the platforms popular with fans of the Shanghai production, in turn, amass their own audiences.[26]

Reflecting and Rendering: Inspired to Create by *SNM*

Returning attendees whom I interviewed had diverse agendas for their repeated viewing, a chief one being that because there is simultaneity of action throughout the performance venue and spectators explore at will, it is impossible for anyone to witness every scene during a single performance. Although it is possible that spectators who follow only the dancer performing Macbeth may experience a sequential storyline similar to Shakespeare's original play, they are freed from linearity of narrative and from the physical immobility encountered in more traditional live performance settings. Just as ethnographers visit a site more than once to collect data and develop ways to present their findings, so do many repeat attendees return to see scenes they have missed, to encounter specific performers, and to explore the scenography in greater depth.[27] Interview data with fans reveals that the ethnographic exploration serves spectators' interests and processes of extended audiencing.

One such repeat attendee is Dee Anne Anderson, whose first visit to *SNM* was six months after its premiere in 2011, when she was invited by a friend who told her it was about *Macbeth*. A high school English teacher whose curriculum includes the play, Anderson was curious how Punchdrunk's production would impact her analytical understanding of the story and assumed she would take her usual cerebral approach to the work. However, Anderson found herself "confused and intrigued" as well as "completely stunned by the emotional impact" of the production (interview with author 2017). Her experience was "emotionally gripping and I was 100% engaged with everything that was happening around me," yet she was compelled to return more than a hundred times because she understood she was "able to focus only on a small percentage of what was going on." She decided, "I want to learn this, and I want it to become my space, a place that I explore":

> the one answer that I give to people when they ask, "Why do you go so much?" is that I've never seen the same show twice. I've seen 130 performances of *Sleep No More*, and not one of them has ever been the same. There's this juxtaposition of text and intention and audience that's just fascinating and, in my opinion, unique to immersive theater and immersive dance in ways that are just fascinating to me as a literary theorist and educator. (2017)

Anderson acknowledges that she is now strategic in return visits, choreographing herself during the performance so as to witness specific scenes:

> I know if I stand in a particular space or if I move in a particular way, I'm able to experience parts of the performance that I hope to see, [and] not to lose the performers when they move quickly. At any particular moment, I know the choreography; I know where a character is coming from, and I know where a character is going. (2017)

She adds, "immersive theater as a genre is still being defined, but it is hard for me to imagine that definition not including dance in some way. The intimacy of dance in immersive space is such a beautiful thing and so different from proscenium dance performance" (interview with author 2017). Anderson started blogging about *SNM* under the name "readwithjoy" in 2013, and she estimates she has created approximately 450 posts specifically about the production.[28]

Many fans, such as Anderson, produced fieldnotes (known within this fandom as "recaps") far more comprehensive than mine. These spectators are the first-generation bloggers of *SNM*, individuals who have invested thousands of dollars of personal income and copious time visiting the site of the McKittrick over the past six years. Laura, a blogger known by her first name, is a director of online production at a global cosmetics company. Having been active in fandoms before, Laura knew to begin researching online after her first performance in April 2011 to find information about the production. She followed the fan community on Tumblr for a year before establishing her own blog, drinkthehalo, in summer 2012. Since then, she has created hundreds of posts documenting her thoughts about the show. On her one hundredth visit, Laura posted the following: "It pretty much comes down to: blame the last four years and tens of thousands of dollars on the Boy Witch" (Laura 2015a). As she explains in another post:

> Three and a half years ago, when I went to *Sleep No More* for the first time, Conor [Doyle]'s Boy Witch was the only thing that kept me from leaving early. I didn't like the show at first. It seemed wrong to do Shakespeare without dialog. Dance was not an art form that I appreciated. I stayed at the show and followed the Boy Witch [and he] became my favorite character for a bunch of reasons. He runs an emotional gamut [. . . ;] the way he teases and plays with his audience is so much fun, and just observing the crowd dynamics around him is fascinating. (Laura 2014)

Laura's writing here provides some insight into Conor Doyle's performances, his play with the States of Tension, as mentioned previously, and qualitative aspects of the choreography as strategies for attracting and sustaining the attention of audience members. Another example of her commentary on individual performers is this interpretation of a performance of Macbeth by Paul Zivkovich:

> With Paul's Macbeth, though of course he executes the major choreography beautifully, it's the smaller moments that make the performance exceptional. There was this little moment one time, right after he'd killed Lady Macduff and they were both on the ground, where her hand had landed next to his—and for a brief moment he clutched her hand. I hadn't seen that before and it went right to my heart. And I'm always riveted by how he stands, starts to leave, stops, and goes back to pull down her dress for

modesty. It's so heartbreaking to watch. I've seen versions of that scene where you can't really tell what Macbeth is thinking—is he contemptuous? just glad she's dead?—but with Paul's Macbeth you can't possibly miss the guilt coming off him in waves. (Laura 2016)

When I asked her about the significant amount of fan-driven creativity around *SNM*, Laura replied, "I think the stereotype of fans is that they're passive. They just receive what they're given and they worship the creators, but that's not true at all. We reinterpret and we create responses" (interview with author 2017). The issue of stereotyping of fans within fandom studies has also been discussed in the writings of Jenkins; he actively pushes against "the social stereotype of 'the fan' as masculine yet emasculated, overly emotional yet analytic and socially inept, educated yet enraptured with the detritus of the popular" (2011). These posts are typical of Laura's writing throughout her blog; her primary interests are analyses of characters and thick description of performances by certain dancers.

Another fan, known as Lindsey in the *SNM* fandom, is a fashion designer based in Shanghai who has attended more than thirty-eight times since the production's premiere in 2016. Lindsey recaps her visits in Mandarin and posts them on Weibo, one of the largest microblogging websites in mainland China, with over 445 million monthly visitors. While not familiar with Shakespeare's play upon her first visit, Lindsey subsequently purchased a copy of *Macbeth* translated into Mandarin in order to seek out connections between the original source material and her experiences of the production. She explains that "with an interpretation of the original text, I can find out how they redesigned the stories and the relationships between characters in *Sleep No More*" (interview with author 2017). Lindsey revealed that, even though she had not previously been a regular attendee of dance performances, "after many *SNM* visits, I have more interest in contemporary dance and I have since gone to the Shanghai Grand Theater to watch dance" (2017).[29]

Lindsey's posts on Weibo are textual, consisting primarily of written posts, much like those created by Anderson and Laura on Tumblr. Yet many *SNM* blogs function as visual ethnographies as well; through their extended audiencing, fans have created digital and visual forums devoted to *SNM* that feature images—in the form of reposted and remediated *SNM*-related fanart, photography, GIFS, and videos—that illustrate and visually comment on the production. Because Laura and Anderson are well known in the New York fandom for generously answering anonymous logistical and practical questions posed by other fans, as well as for engaging in interpretive discussions, their blogs still receive heavy fan traffic as of this writing. They are also instrumental in disseminating the work of artists who create fanart inspired by *SNM* that is evocative of dance in ways that writing is not.

One such artist is Gina Maria Hayes, a director and playwright who first attended *SNM* in 2012 and since that time has attended more than thirty-five times. As of 2014, Hayes had completed more than 160 digital drawings related to the production (Figure 4.5). Hayes reflects on her experience of *SNM*:

> I came out of the first performance at one o'clock in the morning [. . .] and when I came back home, I was like, "I have to, like, get this out of me somehow." Normally I would write, but it felt wrong to do something textual or verbal, because *Sleep No More* is not that. I had this sketching app on my iPad and I just started, like, sketching all of these images. I think I drew for two or three hours that first night. (interview with author 2014)

Figure 4.5 *Banquo on Pool Table*. Digital watercolor by Gina Marie Hayes. Image courtesy of Gina Marie Hayes © 2013.

Figure 4.6 *Sexy Witch*. Digital watercolor by Gina Marie Hayes. Image courtesy of Gina Marie Hayes © 2013.

Hayes provides a description of the choreography that inspired one of her digital drawings of the "Sexy Witch" (Figure 4.6):

> The Sexy Witch is behind the bar, and she gets her hair wet [. . .] then it's almost like a dolphin or a whale coming up as her hair does this amazing arc and it splashes the audience watching her. Drawing dance is really challenging for me—I'm not a trained visual artist, but I'm trying to capture the movement of it and not just static scenes. This is one of the few drawings that I've done where I feel like I have captured the motion. (2014)

Tina Lam, a graphic designer based in New Jersey, attended fourteen performances of *SNM* between 2012 and 2014. Lam's interest in the Boy Witch character (Figure 4.7) led her to concentrate on his track during her many visits.

> I like to follow the Boy Witch because he's such an unpredictable, wild character and the role involves really complex choreography [. . . ;] the way

Figure 4.7 *Boy Witch*. Digital illustration by Tina Lam. Courtesy of Tina Lam © 2012.

he throws his body around without hurting himself is impressive to watch. There is one scene—it's supposed to be the prophecy but we call it the rave scene because of the strobe lights and everything—and it seems like the other witches throw the Boy Witch into the rave in order to set their hold over him, like it is an intense initiation. He is possessed but not totally willing. He has periods of lucidity in his dancing, where he resists their pull but then periods where he would just go in on the madness. I was able to watch a full loop of dancer Austin Goodwin perform the Boy Witch right before making that piece and I was really inspired by how unwilling he seemed as a participant. That piece was supposed to be sort of like a play on his sensuality, but makes it so it doesn't seem like he's a willing participant. I really love that kind of vulnerability that Austin brought to the arc of that role. (interview with author 2016)

In her blog post titled "Boy Witch Is a Difficult Character to Get Right," Laura analyzed Goodwin's interpretation of the role and used fanart—including Tina Lam's depiction of Goodwin—to illustrate her argument that he excelled in the role by balancing "the duality of Boy Witch, that he is both a monster and a victim" (Laura 2015b). Both Laura's writings and Lam's fanart comprise analyses of dance and performance, establishing a trail of spectator-generated description, contextualization, and evaluation of choreography and performance—and importantly, an example of spectators audiencing each other's creative research—that underscores the discourse developed and sustained through the extended audiencing of *SNM*. The audiencing of the fan works by other fans through both cross-referencing and re-posting illustrates how the community functions, and it has contributed to the fandom expanding beyond New York to connect with fans in Shanghai.

Another fan artist, who goes by the name Arfman, is a financial professional in London. Arfman has seen the New York production of *SNM* eight times since 2014.

And after my first couple of Punchdrunk shows [. . .] I did a lot of research online, as you do, because their shows are so overwhelming and complex. The one thing I discovered was that there are so many passionate fans out there—they obviously love the shows very much. Being a fan on social media was something new to me—I'd never followed any sort of fan group or forum for theatre before. There are so many articles written by fans online about their experiences. I followed a few blogs, some written and some with mostly artwork. I've always been interested in art [. . .] but I'd never really received any sort of formal lessons or training in art since high school. It was something that I wanted to pick up again and I guess you could say that immersive theatre was a muse and inspiration. (interview with author 2016)

Arfman describes how a private interaction with the dancer performing Lady Macduff during a one-on-one influenced the creation of his painting *Sofa* (Figure 4.8):

Figure 4.8 *Sofa*. Digital oil painting by Arfman. Courtesy of Arfman © 2015.

I was chosen for Lady Macduff's one-on-one. She was sitting on the sofa, turned and looked at me, and then led me to another room for the highly emotional interaction. So the sofa in the Macduffs' living room was a memorable space for me. This is a still life piece, with no one present, but it's a space where some amazing dance is staged. So I tried to give a more worn look to it, an object that a family would have owned for a long time and is well used, comfortable. It represents a sort of very still, very calm, perhaps even a safe space. [. . .] And there are not many of those in the McKittrick. (2016)

Having attended several consecutive performances of *SNM*, Arfman explains how one space, the speakeasy (Figure 4.9), inspired another work and its title:

I spent quite a bit of time in the speakeasy—it's a space [where] people converge [both . . .] characters and audience. And there is a lot of action in that room. The Boy Witch has a beautiful dance with Bald Witch there. There's not much color in that room—it's dark, it's dim, it's all cardboard boxes

Figure 4.9 *Speakeasy*. Digital oil painting by Arfman. Courtesy of Arfman © 2015.

and wood chips on the floor. So the image of the pool table—a big, green, smooth, velvety flat surface that is floating, ethereal, levitating in that space—I thought it would come out well in a painting. One of the things that I try—with my photography, especially—it's all about capturing light and color, and how you sort of play around with them. So, lighting, for me, it's very important in a set, and I think Punchdrunk does it very well. (2016)

Lu Zhihao (surname Lu), who works in advertising in Shanghai, attended the version of *SNM* in that city several times in 2016 and 2017. After performances, he has done many sketches of scenes in a notebook, sharing them on Instagram and offering them as gifts to performers. Lu's renderings of *SNM* performers tend to be detailed pen and ink portraits with a semblance of realistic caricature while he depicts himself via more simple cartoon line drawings (Figure 4.10).

Lu's first immersive experience was with an "Escape the Room" event in 2011. Lu notes that while escape room events have been "popular in China

Figure 4.10 *Jude as Malcolm*. Pen and ink drawing by Lu Zhihao. Courtesy of Lu Zhihao © 2017.

in the past couple of years," in his estimation, "a meticulous performance with such a magnitude like *Sleep No More* had not been seen before" in the country (interview with author 2017). Lu cites the opportunity to be in close proximity to performers as having compelled him to return, stating, "the actors' expressions and dances are so close to me, I can feel the tension of [the] art performance to the greatest extent possible, and I can feel the same strong emotions as the actors; I never had this experience before . . . this is fascinating" (2017). Commenting further on dance, he specifies:

> There are not many lines of text in the performance . . . the characters' emotions, as well as the emotions between the characters, need to be expressed through the dance form. Moreover, in this particular environment (dark, background music, open performance space), using body language to express this art form which is full of tension and beauty is more appropriate and exciting. In the whole drama, the artistic approach of using different types of dance . . . for different roles is very helpful to allow the audience to understand the character and follow along [with] the story line. (2017)

Lu is motivated to return repeatedly in part because "different actors on the same role in the dance performance [are] different, which brings me different surprises each time I view the same scene" (2017). When describing why he began making sketches, he recounts:

> I was shocked by the performance of this drama, [being] so close to the actor's expression and emotions, this is very amazing, which prompted me to try to catch the moment of that emotional feelings [and to] use another artistic form to describe this unforgettable art moment. I like this piece of work a lot (*Sleep No More*), especially the feeling after the interaction with the actor, so I would like to use my own way to record and express. Of course, in order not to reveal too much about the plot so as not to affect the experience of other viewers, I will not deliberately depict the scenes, but I will express the unique interaction, the emotions and the feelings in my painting. (2017)

Lu believes the popularity of immersive will be ongoing:

> I think this form of performance is very attractive, I believe it [has] a very broad prospect and bright future. In China, especially in Shanghai and Beijing where the intense influence of international culture, immersive production[s] will be very popular. (2017)

As suggested by the images described here, there is a broad spectrum of artistic works created by fans of *SNM*, one that ranges widely in style and composition. In the works of Gina Hayes, as well as those of Lu Zhihao, we see the depictions of both dancers and spectators serving as witnesses to each other's presence and movement. Lu's work is distinct in that he depicts himself in his interpretations of various scenes, revealing his experiences of movement through space as well as his relationality to performers and their physical interactions (Figure 4.11).

Having myself attended several performances of *SNM*, I had immediate recollections of the choreography and action performed on the sofa and pool table when I first saw how Arfman depicted these scenes in his art. Arfman's images make evocative use of light to illuminate the surfaces upon which choreography *has just occurred* rather than representing the actual dancers in motion. With his art, Arfman offers viewers of his work an opportunity to create their own reconstructions of memory—Lady Macduff in a moment of

Figure 4.11 *Speakeasy*. Pen and ink drawing by Lu Zhihao. Courtesy of Lu Zhihao © 2017.

domesticity, moving calmly across her sofa; dust rising from the pool table that has just served as a stage for both an erotic dance among the Witches and a fight to the death between Macbeth and Banquo.

Spectators working as *incidental* and *intentional* ethnographers search and observe in the constructed habitat of *SNM*, which teems with energy via particular scenographies and characters. In their roles as researchers during the performance, and through the extended audiencing that follows, spectators create maps of meaning through visual ethnographies that reflect the processes of their own sometimes very private and intimate exploration, both during and after the performances they experience. The choices they make within the immersive domain of the performances extend outside the performance venue into their own personal spaces and the public spaces of the internet where they share their critical and artistic responses. *SNM* fanwork—in the form of writing and fanart—is evidence not only of the enormous popularity of the production but also of a particular kind of perceptual framework that immersive choreography evokes in its spectators. Reflecting upon what they witnessed as participant observers and drawing upon their embodied experiences, spectators transform participatory movement and dance languages into other artistic media, as their own creative research. What is compelling about the *SNM* blogs is how they serve as examples of fan-driven creativity that are inspired, informed, and shaped by dance, while demonstrating how the imaginative output of spectators is both prolific and ongoing.

In the case of the *SNM* fandom, we can see how the realm of critical and theoretical studies of performance, traditionally occupied by critics and scholars, is now shared by spectators, whose analytical examinations of dance and performance can be found in their writings and artworks posted on blogs. *SNM* bloggers are extending the work of the critic and scholar; in addition to posting their analyses of performances, bloggers also answer the questions that other fans pose, often anonymously, about the production. These questions from fans are another way that the production comes to be understood, and it is precisely these dialectical relationships among fans that reveal how extended audiencing serves as a recursive process through which information is shared and constructs knowledge about the production. The visual ethnographies and artworks emerging from the extended audiencing of the *SNM* fandom demonstrate that the discourse surrounding performance is taking on new forms and characteristics, stretching beyond conventional scholarly articles and essays to include the voices of spectators whose creative output constitutes discursive practice as well as a form of creative research in and of itself.

5

Coauthorality

bluemouth inc.'s *Dance Marathon*

Dear Dance Marathon,

Thank you. I know we only spent a few hours together but I wanted to let you know how wonderful you are. Despite my aching calves and mysterious bruise, I miss you. You were a joy to be with. The friends I made through you might not last a lifetime but, for that one, lovely night, they meant so much. You made a team of two from strangers; we laughed, we tried, and held on to each other.

At first I thought you were too good to be true and in a way I was right. Your trickery at first was subtle but once I realised the kindness in your lies I knew I had to forgive you. For some you made them feel inadequate; for others you gave them the courage to shine. And even though we floundered and fell, after knowing you for such a short time we all became champions. Even when our number was up we spurred each other on. Even when you stripped me of my purpose; an indignity which led me to the regrettable act of betraying my sister, still then, I fought on.

I saw so much through you. I witnessed amateurs evolve into experts. I saw kindness morph into competitiveness. I sensed strangers becoming friends and family turn into temporary enemies. You made me race to the finish line, flail in an attempt to regain my status, squish my sweaty body against an unknown other. And even though you may have turned me into a loser, well, I forgive you. You showed me humility; the sigh of relief in letting go of hopes of a trophy and cheering for our new, winning, friends.

So thank you Dance Marathon. Thank you for the fun, thank you for the music. Thank you for the artistry, thank you for the effort; I'm sure you must be tired so please go and take a long and well deserved rest. But know that—If we meet again—I'm on to you. And as I have already proved, I'm not above doing whatever it takes to leave our next night together as your dancing queen.

Love and very, very sweaty hugs,

Your not-so-bitter Loser

Tandem Dances. Julia M. Ritter, Oxford University Press (2021). © Oxford University Press.
DOI: 10.1093/oso/9780190051303.001.0001.

This ardent, lovelorn missive was written by Bella Fortune, writer-in-residence for Theatre Bristol, who participated in bluemouth inc.'s production of *Dance Marathon* (*DM*) during its run at the Mayfest contemporary theater festival in Bristol, England, in May 2015 (Fortune 2015).[1] Fortune, in describing her sense of investment in the event, reveals her enthusiasm for *DM* as a durational immersive performance based on the competitive dance marathons popular in the United States in the 1920s and 1930s. Bluemouth inc., an award-winning collective based in Toronto, Canada, created *DM* in 2009 through the national commissioning program of Toronto's Harbourfront Centre.[2] *DM* is bluemouth inc.'s most widely toured and commercially successful work to date, with over fifty international performances involving more than seven thousand participants.[3]

While some audience members are aware in advance of the interactive nature of *DM*, most discover only when they arrived at the venue that by purchasing tickets, they have registered as contestants in the marathon. Over the course of the next three hours, audiences are given lessons in various dance styles and have the opportunity to practice them as part of a group of 150 increasingly sweaty participants (Figure 5.1). In addition to dance lessons, there are "dance times" during which audiences may dance improvisationally

Figure 5.1 Contestants in bluemouth inc.'s *Dance Marathon*, Vancouver, Canada, 2010. Photograph by Janet Baxter, 2010.

and recreationally, as if at a dance club or party, to carefully curated playlists featuring popular hit songs from the 1970s through the early twenty-first century. Participants find themselves dancing to the Bee Gees' 1976 "You Should Be Dancing" one moment and Sophie Ellis-Bextor's 2002 "Murder on the Dance Floor" the next.

Bluemouth inc. uses dance to guide the participants literally and figuratively step-by-step into movements that are increasingly physically grueling while introducing scripted theatrical content that reveals the past histories, dreams, desires, and fantasies of the bluemouth inc. performers. The components of *DM*—dance lessons, improvisational dance sessions, elimination contests, and predetermined choreographic and theatrical content—recur throughout the production. Theater scholar and practitioner Bruce Barton, who worked with bluemouth inc. as dramaturge during the creation of *DM* in 2009, describes the production as "part play, part relational event, part performance installation, part concert, part dance party, and part athletic competition . . . an endurance test of dancing, foot races, choreographed routines, vaudeville performances, special guest appearances, trivial pursuit, and one wild bumper-car ride" (Barton 2009a:582). In each performance, audiences are challenged to consider how they will respond to the content offered, which in turn influences how they will experience the event. For audiences who choose to invest fully, there exists the possibility for full immersion through the physical exertion and expression of dance while their senses are barraged via Artaud-style production elements, including choreographic and theatrical material as well as sound, video, and lighting design.

Bluemouth inc.'s core members are Stephen O'Connell, Lucy Simic, Richard Windeyer, Sabrina Reeves, and Ciara Adams. The former three met in the early 1990s during their studies in interdisciplinary arts, dance, and music composition at Simon Fraser University in Vancouver, Canada. They met Reeves through a mutual friend who also attended Simon Fraser. Adams was invited to join bluemouth inc. as an associate artist in 2003 and became co-artistic director in 2009. Bluemouth inc. has collaborated with numerous guest artists since 1998; in particular, actor Daniel Pettrow contributed to the creation of *DM* and is now a bluemouth inc. associate artist.

In the early 1990s, O'Connell, Simic, and Windeyer all worked, in different capacities, with Radix Theatre, a Vancouver-based company dedicated to collective creation.[4] Reeves and Simic are credited with collectively creating bluemouth inc.'s first project, *Mapping Currents*, which they presented at the Edgy Women Festival in 1998 in Montreal. After *Mapping Currents*, bluemouth inc. established itself as a collective of "artists trained in various disciplines, brought together by a common vision of sharing our diverse creative practices and forging a new language" (bluemouth inc. 2015b). Bluemouth inc. adopted collective creation as their preferred method for developing projects, drawing upon the experiences with Radix and their subsequent experimentation with the method. O'Connell describes *collective creation* as "vitally specific to Canadian sensibility," noting that the term is preferred by Canadian artists to the terms *devising* or *collaboration* (email correspondence with author 2016).[5] Through email discussions with Adams, O'Connell, Reeves, Simic, and Windeyer, I learned that bluemouth inc. does not have a fixed definition of collective creation; rather, they have a set of aesthetic principles and a philosophical stance that guides their work. The following is a synthesis of those discussions:

> Collective creation is a dynamic form of creative collaboration in which hierarchical structures are replaced with egalitarian processes that reflect the shared agreement to serve, encourage, and support what has been collectively identified as the "best idea." The removal of hierarchical structures is predicated upon the desire to challenge and facilitate the creative ingenuity of the group as a whole while celebrating and encouraging individual expertise and excellence. Through experience, bluemouth inc. has observed that despite attempts to avoid hierarchy, imbalances of power can emerge that are situational to the individuals comprising the collective or project. When imbalances of power are identified, the group works to actively dismantle them in order to create space for all voices and opportunities for all members to contribute in the conceiving, building, and producing of art. (email correspondence 2016)

Collective creation is not the end goal of their work but rather the means to make "immersive site-specific performances by marrying choreographed movement, text, immersive sound design, original live music, video, and film to create a cohesive, multi-sensory experience" (bluemouth inc. 2015b). In all their productions, the collective aims "to reach beyond boundaries of conventional performance to create site-specific interdisciplinary art that leads audiences and artists alike into new forms of play" (bluemouth inc. 2015b). However, *DM* is distinct within bluemouth inc.'s oeuvre for multiple reasons. First, when creating *DM*, the collective prioritized dance as both context (dance marathons), during which the core members guide audiences to play with content (dancing generated during the marathon). They do this by introducing dance styles and creating an environment that encourages interpretative and generative dancing by audiences. Second, because of the ways in which audience participation is essential to the manifestation of each performance, artists and audiences must dance together in order to manifest each performance.

In this chapter, I describe how the bluemouth inc. as a collective situates audience members as protagonists and actuates them to dance during performances of *DM*. By introducing the term *actuate*, I call attention to ways in which artists, including the members of bluemouth inc., "stir into activity" and "enliven," as well as "set in motion, energize," and "animate" audiences within the context of immersive performance.[6] Finally, I introduce the term *coauthorality* to describe the way audiences, alongside bluemouth inc.'s core members and embedded dancers, generate and perform dance content that shapes *DM*.[7]

Contextualizing Dance Marathons and *Dance Marathon*

In her book *Dance Marathons: Performing American Culture of the 1920s and 1930s*, theater scholar Carol Martin examines the development of dance marathons as part of the economic cultural background of the United States at the beginning of the twentieth century. Her in-depth analyses of the form acknowledges marathons as "extremely complicated performative events" (1994:xvi). While first structured as nonstop dancing to live music, dance marathons developed into professionalized, grueling, gladiator-style competitive events with longer durations and additional challenges for participants (xix).[8] Promoters hired "plants"—professional performers who traveled with the promoters from town to town—to participate as contestants. The plants were privy to and complicit with the promoters' aims, and functioned accordingly to manipulate the outcomes of the marathons so that they—as well as their employers—benefited. Competing along with the plants were individuals in dire financial circumstances who signed up as contestants in hopes of winning monetary prizes. Equally important for these individuals was the promise of a daily meal and a roof over their heads for the duration of the marathon (49). Marathons were extended over months, requiring audiences to return multiple times if they wished to follow the action and narratives of the contestants.

The promoters, being savvy, understood that the spectacle of endurance dancing alone would not sustain the interest of audiences or ticket sales (5). With this in mind, they sensationalized the marathons by incorporating various "elimination contests" to reduce the number of contestants and to put pressure on the remaining dancers to perform (55).[9] Promoters also publicized performances by popular contestants and local celebrities, and when audiences dwindled, they staged mock weddings of contestants to reinvigorate interest (42). Such tactics served to serialize the marathon as an ongoing dramatic event in which human suffering was a feature of live performance.

Establishing that they would collectively create a dance marathon as a participatory event, bluemouth inc. researched the history of marathon dancing and outlined their goals for *DM*: "to contribute to the historical development and perception of performance; to collectively renegotiate the role of the viewer in performance; and to devise performance in a truly egalitarian environment where the project is always best served by the best idea" (bluemouth inc. 2009). In pursuit of these goals, bluemouth inc. set up conditions to enable audiences to participate in an egalitarian environment, so audiences would take on active, cooperative roles and acts of "doing" in the moment to contribute to performances through their presence, and especially through their dancing. While bluemouth inc. may have used historical accounts of the early marathons as inspiration, their approach to creating and staging *DM* differs radically from those of the original competitions, which, according to Martin, "were modeled on a version of social Darwinism" and where only the strongest—and the most strategic—dancers became winners (Martin 1994:xvi).

First, bluemouth inc. determined the size and scale of the audience that would be dancing during each performance. As Simic explains, "We read *The Tipping Point* and [author Malcolm Gladwell] talks about how you can only really create community with 150 people. Anything more than that and you start to feel like you're just one of many.... With 150 people there is the feeling that you can actually know or remember everybody.... There's something about that versus the indifference of 200 people, or 500 people" (interview with author 2014). Adams supports this strategy of limiting the audience to 150: "One person described our work as we create instant communities and I think that's a really valid way of describing it" (interview with author 2014). Bluemouth inc. found this limit is effective in guiding audiences toward an atmosphere of cooperation and community during performance.

Understanding that the dance marathons of the 1920s and 1930s had distinct players—emcees, promoters, and contestants—bluemouth inc. debated what roles they and their audiences would assume in performances. The collective established three groups of primary performers in *DM*—bluemouth inc. core members, embedded dancers, and audience members.[10] Bluemouth inc.'s performing members are referred to throughout this chapter as *core members* but are also identified by specific "names" that indicate either function or persona. The role of each core member is designed to sustain audience participation in a specific way, and members fulfill their functions by performing predetermined choreographic or theatrical content. For example, Adams is known as Lady Jane, the lead singer of the *Dance Marathon* band, and her voice, energy, and charisma motivate and guide the audience to participate in dance lessons and other dance-related activities (Figure 5.2).

Unbeknown to the audience at first, O'Connell and Simic, as the characters Little Stevie and Ramona Snjezana Knezevic, respectively, are "embedded" as contestants.[11] Under the guise of being contestants, O'Connell and Simic function as partners of audience members and exemplars for the audience to follow during dance lessons. As the MC, Reeves is host and steward of the marathon. Pettrow, as the Referee, or the Ref, enforces the rules of the

Figure 5.2 Ciara Adams as Lady Jane in bluemouth inc.'s *Dance Marathon*. Photograph by Janet Baxter, 2010.

production (Figure 5.3). Windeyer, known by his nickname, "Rocket," is situated behind his drum kit onstage with the band during performances; as bandleader, sound designer, and DJ, he manages the sonic environment.

Keeping in mind that "historically, the economic success of dance marathons relied on promoters hiring and embedding eccentrically skilled performers among the actual dance contestants to create unusual and exciting situations" (bluemouth inc. 2009), the company constructed the role of embedded dancers as hybrids of the historical use of plants and "eccentrically skilled performers" in dance marathons of the past. Before each *DM* tour, bluemouth inc. recruits fifteen to twenty volunteer dancers from communities where productions will be shown. The company welcomes all levels of dance experience; some volunteers have professional backgrounds and degrees, while others may be avid recreational dancers. This diversity contributes to performances in multiple ways. The embedded dancers meet daily with Adams, O'Connell, and Simic for a week before performances to rehearse the choreography and learn about their functions in the production—the most important being to work with core members to encourage audiences to overcome their inhibition and perform dance.

Figure 5.3 Sabrina Reeves as the MC, with a *Dance Marathon* contestant, and Daniel Pettrow, on the left as the Ref in bluemouth inc.'s *Dance Marathon*. Photograph by Janet Baxter, 2010.

While the core members and embedded dancers perform the choreography and are featured in "spotlight" moments via their singing or dancing talents, they are not the protagonists of the marathon. Rather, as Adams explains, each audience member is his or her own protagonist: "In *Dance Marathon*, you're the protagonist. You're actively in the piece. Without the audience there, the piece doesn't exist; it can't. So, every single aspect of it, and every single moment of the piece is designed to immerse the audience member in an experience. We're carefully conducting the audience member through this experience" (interview with author 2014). By casting audience members as contestants—protagonists—in the marathon, bluemouth inc. assumes that audiences possess skills, particularly in dance, and implement tactics to convince audiences to draw upon these skills during the performance. If they accept their roles as contestants, audience participants understand from the start that there is an expectation of engagement beyond observation. They thus participate knowing their obligations and responsibilities, and (hopefully) assume ownership and accountability for their actions.

Bluemouth inc. provide limited information about *DM* in publicity materials; they have found it more effective to inform audiences that they are expected to dance only once they are at the venue, when the immersion tactics can best be deployed. Publicity materials for *DM* from 2009 to 2014 differ in what information was available to audiences prior to the event. Some materials explain to audiences that they will be in a dance marathon, that it will be a durational event, meaning longer than a typical performance of one or two hours, and that someone will emerge a winner. As a harbinger of the expectation of spectator engagement, almost all the materials advise wearing comfortable shoes for dancing.[12] Other materials simply state that *DM* is an interactive event.

In exchange for his or her ticket upon arrival, each audience member is given a numbered pinny to wear (Figure 5.4). After slipping the pinny over a participant's torso, the MC asks that audience member to identify two body parts: chest and feet. The MC explains that the number on the pinny corresponds with a numbered image of feet the participant will find taped to the floor when he or she enters the dance hall. This is a subtle tactic to focus the audience on their bodies and orient them in space, as they will need to return to their numbered feet as a kind of home base throughout the performance. The MC then instructs audience members—now contestants—to locate their feet on the dance floor.

Figure 5.4 Contestants wearing pinnies, with feet taped on the floor in front of them in bluemouth inc.'s *Dance Marathon*, Toronto, Canada, October 2009. Photograph by Nancy Palva, 2009.

On the dance floor, contestants find themselves facing a stranger; they are informed that this is their new dance partner for the evening. This tactic separates participants from those with whom they arrived at the performance and assigns them to new partners. As critic Martin Denton recounts, "You will be randomly assigned to dance with someone you don't know, and it will feel fine; gender is happily not taken into account—male/male and female/female couplings are as common as the traditional male/female ones; it's all about the body here" (2011). Cara Spooner, an embedded dancer in the first performances of *DM* in Toronto in 2009, relates how the pairing process serves the production's larger goals: "If you came with your partner or your date or whoever, you were split up from them so everyone was kind of equalized. Every single person in the room was now forced to be partners with a stranger. I think that kind of shared vulnerability was a huge aspect in that everyone sort of felt like they were in the same boat. There was this very real sense of awkwardness getting to know someone . . . but also the willingness to dive into that experience together" (interview with author 2014). Bluemouth inc.'s aim is to establish an environment in which individuals perceive themselves as being of equal status and thus accept the conditions of participation in *DM*, which require them to embrace the concept of working together through dance to manifest the performance.

Aware that dancing—let alone dancing with a stranger—could evoke vulnerability for audiences, bluemouth inc. initially offered "optional elimination" in the first versions of *DM*. Audience members could opt out of participation if they wished; or they could stay and watch as long as they relinquished their numbered pinny, to distinguish them from the contestants. As O'Connell explains, "The first couple times [we performed *DM*] we would lose a good portion of the audience who would sit down when we offered the elimination . . . They were just like, 'No, I'm not into it.' So we tried the free dance . . . then did the optional elimination after the free dance. And in the six years since we've been doing it, there have only been two people that have sat down [after the free dance]. We didn't really understand the power of the free dance until that just happened kind of by chance" (interview with author 2014).

The free dance is strategically situated before Reeves as the MC explains all the rules of the production. Lady Jane's voice and energy catalyzes the audience into motion as she recites lyrics from what the collective calls the "Free Dance Song" which are composed to verbally encourage the participants to "come on out and move it."[13] This swift transition into the free dance helps to mediate the potentially awkward moment of an audience member's meeting the stranger who will be his or her dancing partner by focusing the person on the task of dancing: "After the free dance, you see this really interesting physiological shift . . . Most people start all nervous, thinking about their anxieties, but as soon as they're given three minutes to shift into being in their bodies rather than their head, and the adrenaline kicks in, they move into a completely different emotional state" (O'Connell quoted in Friedman 2011).

The MC verbally presents five rules that guide participation in *DM*; the rules, similar to those of the early dance marathons, are intended to keep contestants in motion while controlling behavior. These rules are choreographic frameworks to help the MC steer toward crowning a pair of winners, which is the conclusion of the event. The rules are as follows:

Rule 1: Your feet must be moving at all times.

Rule 2: Knees may not touch the floor—floor may not touch the knees—any configuration that involves you on your knees on the floor and you are out.

Rule 3: Picking fights with other couples is strictly prohibited and will not be tolerated.

Rule 4: You will be given a five-minute rest period every hour. If you opt out of your rest period, you may not make it up at another time.

Rule 5: Sexually explicit behavior is strictly prohibited. (bluemouth inc. 2015a:5)[14]

As enforcer of the rules, the Ref functions as the antagonist of the audience-as-protagonist. In order to build a sense of community and camaraderie in the audience and to encourage their investment in dancing, the Ref functions as disciplinarian.

Pettrow, who originated the role of the Ref, careens around the dance hall on roller skates, making use of his height to appear more intimidating to the audiences. The Ref gives the impression of panopticism, circling the contestants incessantly, all the while surveying for infractions and barking out reminders to keep moving. Under constant surveillance, audience members develop a kind of solidarity, a herd united against a predator. Pettrow describes this role and how he understands audience perceptions: "I can move quicker than anybody on the floor. And if there's not a lot of noise, you can hear me coming. I knew early on that I wanted a mic, to be domineering at any moment. The whistle and the red flag are purely focus for audience members and a little theatricality. The physicality came out from being on the skates. I intentionally overexaggerate how I look at their feet. When I'm going around, people are looking at me, and I'll look at them in the eyes and then look back at their feet. So, it's like, 'Oh, he's really watching our feet' " (interview with author 2014). The Ref also offers praise. When Pettrow comes across individuals whom he perceives as particularly invested in their dancing, he encourages them as he skates past with "Looking good, Number 32, looking good!" or "You're my favorite couple tonight!" (15). Pettrow knows that the Ref is a paradoxical construct; he must adopt a "bad guy" approach to dominance for solidarity to develop in the audience. He carefully calibrates control with charm, however, so that while audiences are highly sensitive to his authoritative presence, they also notice his support of their dancing. His brutish tactics are deployed to enhance their pleasure during the event and, consciously or not, they are aware of this.

Audience participants who do not adhere to the rules, especially rules 1 and 2, risk elimination by the Ref. Bluemouth inc. incorporates several types of elimination contests, based on the early marathons. In particular, the company looked to Horace McCoy's 1935 novel *They Shoot Horses, Don't They?* and Sydney Pollack's 1969 film adaptation for inspiration and created their own version of the "derby" competition, a common elimination tactic, to winnow the crowd down to a pair of winners. As depicted in the novel and film, derbies require contestant pairs to walk as fast as possible around a track delineated in the space while in a tango-like embrace—one arm wrapped around the partner's waist and the other outstretched in front, with partners' hands clasped.[15] Bluemouth inc. transformed the derby from a foot race into a five-minute dance. The contestants' speed is controlled by a video that displays red, yellow, and green traffic lights. Prompted by the lights, partners must work together to stay within time restrictions and choreographic states of being; mobile, modulating motion, stillness. During red lights, partners lean into one another, shaping and counterbalancing their bodies to maintain their frozen positions. Yellow allows the most experimentation as couples work to match one another's tempo and range of motion while continuing to advance. There are winners and losers during every derby, with the finish line often drawn arbitrarily in space by the Ref. Adding to the chance of being eliminated, participants must provide correct answers in trivia quizzes presented as challenges throughout the event.

The different eliminations are "physical, artistic, knowledge-based or pure chance in nature—intended to promote a joint investment that encourages participants to playfully but thoroughly commit to their new partners as a means of protecting their own status in the event" (Barton 2009a:587). Barton suggests that participants work cooperatively with their partners for personal benefit, that is, to remain viable as competitors in the dance marathon. While this may indeed be true, I understand his phrase "joint investment" to be indicative of how partners engaged in collectively creating performance through dancing with one another, as well as with all participants of the event, including the core company members.

DM's sound design is a critical mechanism in setting the conditions for audience participation. Windeyer carefully curates the soundscape to both support the theatrical content and inspire the audience to dance. Windeyer describes the process of developing the soundscape: "Early on, it was clear that regardless of what the MC might be telling the audience or what other performers might be doing—that we needed to keep the energy up. So there's always . . . some kind of rhythm . . . something playing in the background. The first half of the show, there's a lot of classic disco . . . because it's really accessible. And then I kept pushing to get more contemporary and darker, more electro and techno. I think . . . there's a nicely curated collection of records because of the kind of history of dancing that it enables" (interview with author 2014). The soundscape at times motivates the audience to dance through familiar songs with cultural resonance. More contemporary songs allow the audience to improvise dance content by drawing upon their own skills and interpretations. With each new musical track, Windeyer's soundscape offers a different sonic pathway along which participants can experiment, without their movements being dictated.

In 2009, when bluemouth inc. was developing *DM* through a creative residency at Les Place des Arts in Montreal, they invited test groups of audience members to participate as contestants. The company quickly learned that audience members were not only ready for their tasked roles—but they were also willing to advocate on their own behalf to keep and even expand those roles. As O'Connell elaborates:

> We invited audiences at the end of each week of rehearsals to show what we worked on. They got pinnies, they got paired up with people. We started dancing around the audience and they were just standing there in their feet in their place, watching it. When we sat down and had a discussion with the audience, they were just like, "Wow. There was so much potential. We were so excited, and then basically you performed around us." The second week, we allowed them to engage more with their partners but we were still demanding their attention by screaming and doing these big dramatic gestures. Again, the audience said, "Wow. The conversation I was having with my dance partner was way interesting, but I couldn't talk, because you guys were forcing me to pay attention to something." That was the big aha moment—realizing that it was a task-based show, allowing them the agency to do what they wanted . . . that this particular show wasn't about us. (interview with author 2014)

The test audiences were pushing against entrenched notions of themselves as passive observers. In a similar example, Simic recounts a test audience member telling her, "Your theatrics got in the way of my authentic experience with my partner" (interview with author 2014). Discovering that their "desire to perform got in the way of allowing the audience to have an experience," bluemouth inc. reconceptualized the work, to actuate the audience during performances (interview with author 2014). Barton, who was present during the feedback sessions with audiences referenced by O'Connell, observed: "[The] participants spoke of their feeling that they and their partners had, in fact, been the most important 'characters' in the piece" (2009b:22). Again, Spooner offers her perspective: "I remember being very struck that it was different from anything else that I had done. It seemed like this really special show where the audience was activating it. And it was actually more about the audience than it was about the performers in a sense. That everyone was kind of the star of their own [*laughs*] mini-narrative within the events" (Spooner, interview with author 2014). The audiences are able to activate the show because bluemouth inc. has given them new status—that of protagonist—and actuated them in ways that invite them to contribute to making the performance happen through their actions, the most important of which is dancing (Figure 5.5).

Figure 5.5 Contestants in bluemouth inc.'s *Dance Marathon*, Vancouver, Canada, 2010. Photograph by Janet Baxter, 2010.

Actuating Audiences in *Dance Marathon*

DM is a complex production with many layers through which the audience participates in and experiences the performances. For the purposes of this chapter, I focus specifically on the situations where the audience is *actuated* to dance throughout the performance. I differentiate between the terms *engage* and *actuate*, because *actuate* best defines how audiences are impelled to dance in *DM*.

As described earlier, the initial free dance allows audiences to relinquish their inhibitions and concentrate on their bodies and the task of dancing. Audiences are further actuated in the first section when the singer Lady Jane teaches The Madison, an American social dance popularized in the late 1950s. Other dance lessons follow this one, as the Lady Jane's performance of a "History of Dance," a song that succinctly contextualizes dance historically, sociopolitically, and culturally while keeping contestants in motion. Accompanied by the Dance Marathon band, Lady Jane selects embedded dancers from the crowd to be her partners while singing and dancing the audience through dance forms from different continents and cultures, including the Argentinean tango, the waltz, and dances that emerged from the African diaspora such as the Lindy Hop.[16]

While *DM*'s first section aimed simply to get the participants dancing, the second section is designed to actuate audiences to invest more deeply in movement improvisation. The MC kicks off this section by asking the audience if anyone knows how to dance a "snowball."[17] When a contestant correctly describes a snowball as a dance that builds in size from a soloist to a group through a process of accumulation, the band starts up and the MC encourages that person to kick off the snowball. Each time the MC shouts, "Snowball!" more contestants are pulled in, and the energy of the crowd builds through spontaneous improvisation until all the contestants are dancing. The snowball ends when the MC invites Ramona to the stage to sing about her homeland of "Balkanistan." Ramona takes advantage of being onstage to demand a competition of male contestants. In her broken English, she states she wants "five mans" to compete against one another in an "Iggy Pop-Off" so she can choose the best to be her partner to win the marathon. She jumps off the stage and strides through the crowd, pointing to certain contestants and ordering them to stand in the center of the dance floor.[18] Windeyer cues the 1977 driving track "Lust for Life," and the contestants begin to dance improvisationally, prompted by the energy of the song and images of punk rock icon Iggy Pop dancing on the video monitor.

Back onstage, Ramona yells into a microphone, urging the contestants on while also demanding bigger and more spectacular movements. The contestants comply, enlarging and accelerating their dancing while performing variations of the dance styles of pogoing and moshing.[19] Together, this select group builds that evening's Iggy Pop-Off to a thrilling crescendo, at which point Little Stevie tears off his shirt and throws himself to the floor in a display of bravado solo slam dancing. Ramona chooses Little Stevie as her partner and they continue the performance as a couple. Ending the second section is the first derby, and while it results in the elimination of many contestants, their perceived immersion in the marathon prompts them to stay as spectators.

The intermission that follows comes midway in *DM*, each half approximately ninety minutes long. The tone and mood of the second half shifts as theatrical content—including more predetermined choreography by the core members and embedded dancers—is layered on top of the dancing competition with increasing frequency. At this point in the performance, the actuating of audiences becomes self-initiated as they exhibit more confidence and inventiveness in their generation of dance material. The third section commences and Lady Jane, Ramona, and the embedded dancers initiate a flash mob composed of predetermined choreography. Audience participants—who have been dancing for over two hours—quickly learn the choreography and take over the floor. I know from rehearsals that a pathway has been set; the flash mob is crafted to move diagonally from one side of the dance hall to another, with contestants following behind Lady Jane, Ramona, and the embedded dancers. Yet each evening, I observed that once audiences knew the flash mob choreography, they embellished it, incorporating other movements, changing the timing, and rerouting the pathways to perform in different spaces of the venue.

Following the flash mob is a spotlight moment for an embedded dancer who performs an improvised "Hipshake Dance" accompanied on drums by Windeyer. As the dancer finishes, Windeyer keeps up a pulsating rhythm on the drums while performing a text in a hypnotizing tone (see Appendix A). Through the text, he successfully draws all the contestants into an improvisation wherein they isolate their body parts to carve the space around them, continually expanding their range of motion and augmenting the size of their dancing. As Windeyer lets the text trail off and accelerates his drum solo, the final derby is announced, which the stage managers engineer so only six couples remain.

Ramona, who is eliminated in this derby, learns that Little Stevie wishes to stay with her rather than compete in the marathon, and they dance a romantic, slow waltz. The MC guides the remaining six couples—now semifinalists—to join them. Unexpectedly, the Ref ruptures the serenity of the waltz by gliding half naked through the remaining couples, wearing only his skates and a mini-Speedo swimsuit. He informs these couples they will need dance a "hula" so the crowd can choose the finalists who will compete for the grand prize. With humor and lightness, the Ref demonstrates a Westernized interpretation of a hula—swaying his hips and undulating his arms—and then turns it over to the couples as a structured improvisation, urging them to add their interpretations and variations. During this high-stakes moment, audiences are fully in control of actuating themselves, performing as inventively and expressively as they wish. The remaining six couples find themselves under the most scrutiny at this moment in the performance, and the Ref mirrors their vulnerability by exposing himself physically as well as divulging his fantasy of moving to Hawaii to live a life of ease. Adams, accompanying herself on the ukulele, sings the song "Easy," whose chorus is intended to put the couples at ease as they perform alone—no longer aided by the Ref—for the audience judging them:

> The things we can't control,
> Better to roll with it,
> Right now, all I know,
> Is that it's easy . . . it's so easy
> It's easy being with you.
> (bluemouth inc. 2015a:34)

The MC asks an eliminated contestant to choose two couples as winners of the hula competition and the Ref takes the winners backstage to prepare for the surprise final event. The rest of the eliminated audience members have a moment to rest while the MC performs a monologue, partnered with a solo by Ramona. As Reeves's monologue accelerates and builds in intensity, the band is simultaneously building to a crescendo and increasing in volume. Simic finishes her solo and dashes out of the space as the Ref ushers in the two couples. One member of each couple is blindfolded and trying to steer a little kiddie PlasmaCar through the space while pushed by the other (Figure 5.6).[20]

The PlasmaCar race is a spectacular finale that unfolds in cinematic slow motion. The lights, the sound of the band, and the video images of Reeves's face projected on multiple surfaces converge to induce disorientation, which is intensified by the cheers of audience members rooting for their favorite couple. With all eyes focused on the two couples, they have become the evening's penultimate performers. Lasting only forty-five seconds, the PlasmaCar race is compelling because of the concentrated, physical effort of the couples; there is no denying their sincere attempts to win as blindfolded partners are pushed around the track amid the screaming crowd. Often a couple will crash their car, and those moments are pure, unadulterated drama. When a couple crosses the finish line first and is crowned the winner, the ebullient, chaotic atmosphere becomes more subdued, with audience members embracing and congratulating one another for enduring to the very end. Dance disappears at this moment; only the sweat and exhaustion of each audience member remains as evidence of their dancing.

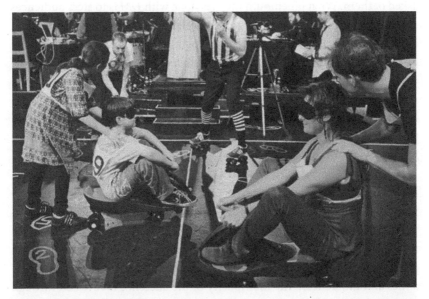

Figure 5.6 Contestants seated on PlasmaCars with their partners in bluemouth inc.'s *Dance Marathon*. Photograph by Janet Baxter, 2010.

Coauthorality in *Dance Marathon*

When Bella Fortune declared, "You made a team of two from strangers; we laughed, we tried and held on to each other," she was acknowledging the ways in which she was actuated to participate—physically, emotionally, relationally—in *DM* alongside bluemouth inc. core members, embedded dancers, and other audience members. Sociologist Rudi Laermans's concept of the "generic common" is central to why and how bluemouth inc. is able to set their audiences into motion so successfully. According to Laermans, the generic common is composed of characteristics that "co-define human-ness"—"assumed capacities [of] a generic nature: the ability to think, to com-municate, to feel or to imagine" (2012:96). In the case of *DM*, the creators assume—correctly, it seems—that people have in common some knowledge of how to organize their bodies in space and time together as a community. Through the use of dance as the primary strategy for immersing audiences, audiences are given the opportunity to apply and even augment their bodily knowledge throughout performances of *DM*.

Not only is the generic common an essential foundation that enables bluemouth inc. to actuate their audience, but it also is the way *DM* is struc-tured so that audiences have little cause to doubt their ability to do what is asked of them. What bluemouth inc. has done with *DM* is to steer audiences toward activating their participation by designing opportunities for them to apply agency during performances by dancing. Barton recounts that "in the first run of the production, audience members often strove to remain in the midst of the embedded dancers, no matter how difficult or demanding the movement sequences became. Understandably, participants were highly re-luctant to be denied their hard-won personal agency" (2009a:600). Through this agency, audiences can maximize the potentiality of their experience as full sensorial and corporeal entities.

Bluemouth inc. have depended upon the audience's generic common in previous productions, but never more so than in *DM*. The collective are interested in human potential and are cognizant that audiences are com-posed of individuals whose identities are multiple and diverse, with com-monalities but also differences. The audience's improvisational dances, partnered as they are with the curated sound score, reflect these common-alities and differences. The multiplicity of the audience is revealed through their dancing; as they perform, they make apparent their different movement histories, muscular memories, and individual personalities, all of which contribute to and shape each performance as a unique, danced event. In *DM*, bluemouth inc. has established audience participation and immersion in a shared aesthetic experience as the common cause, which, in turn, drives the generic common of dancing. Audiences, once actuated, become immersed and increasingly invested in their participation. Especially in the second half of the production, audience participants are determined to stay on the dance floor and work to learn the predetermined choreography as quickly as possible, to stay involved.

While bluemouth inc. core members, particularly O'Connell and Simic, performing as contestants, take primary responsibility of actuating audiences to dance, the number of audience participants precludes them from carrying responsibility alone. They are assisted by the local embedded dancers, who learn during their first rehearsal that they are responsible for encouraging the audience members with whom they are paired to dance.[21] As Spooner recounts, "Right from the very beginning, it was always in the back of my mind in terms of the role that I was learning . . . how we were to be partnered up with a member of the public . . . and how we were to . . . care for them in a way" (interview with author 2014). The embedded dancers act as intermediaries, existing in a place between the conditions set by bluemouth inc. and the participation of audiences. Their role is complex. On the one hand, they perform the predetermined choreography and are privy to many aspects of the production in advance, although many express surprise and delight at how all the elements—dramaturgy, dance, music, video, and sound—are integrated when the audience is present. As Katy Noakes, an embedded dancer in the Bristol performances, noted, "When it came to performing *Dance Marathon*, we [the embedded dancers] were watching for the first time as well. We hadn't seen all the choreography. We hadn't seen the art that happens *between* the audience and performers" (2015, emphasis in speech). On the other hand, the embedded dancers are an essential part of the production's infrastructure of "I can," (meaning to have the potential) as evident in their responsibility to assist in actuating audiences through dance during performance.

The embedded dancers use various strategies to actuate audiences to dance, trying to determine a partner's comfort level in order to make decisions as to how and when to engage. Frances Brown, a member of a local swing dance club in Halifax was an embedded dancer in *DM* at the 2014 Magnetic North Festival in that city: "I have a lot of energy and can be overwhelming, so to make the other person feel more comfortable, I tended to mirror what it was that they were doing . . . Later on, when they seemed to be more comfortable,

I'd back off and they would be comfortable to do their own thing" (interview with author 2014). In a reflection for *Dance Current* on her participation in *DM*, Spooner wrote:

> My focus isn't winning; it's the participants' experience. To intentionally integrate them into the complexity of the show and allow them to fully experience the *Dance Marathon*'s potential is my sole purpose. I play a supporting role (along with the other planted dancers and bluemouth inc. members), assisting the protagonists on their journey in the marathon. We blindfold them, we teach them dance steps, we play with their emotions, break out in spontaneous choreography. . . . We support the event; they live in it. (Spooner 2009)

Spooner's quote reflects the ways that the embedded dancers serve the goal of actuating audiences to dance by offering their dancing as an invitation to dance.

Raphael Martin, an audience member who attended *DM* in Halifax in 2014, remarked, "They [bluemouth inc.] do a very good job about contextualizing the atmosphere and making it feel very open and accessible. They were very good about leading you in, so already my body was very relaxed, I just relaxed into it. In *Dance Marathon*, the audience is the material and the journey is the performance" (Martin 2015:20). Ann-Marie Kerr, an audience member in *DM* at the 2014 Magnetic North Festival, shares her experience of being physically actuated to dance, saying, "There becomes some sort of agreement, a physical, nonspoken agreement of what's happening" (interview with author 2014). The accounts of audience members reveal how the structures of *DM*, along with the efforts of the core members and embedded dancers, support the goal of actuating audiences by triggering their potentiality. The embedded dancers support the production by assisting in the establishment of an environment that encourages and actuates the dancing of the audience. Actuating the audience in *DM* leads, in fact, to the development of a unique generic common that is shared by the contestants of each individual performance. In this generic common, audiences find possibilities to activate their "I can" by learning, doing, and dancing together.

Deepening Immersion through Coauthorality

So far, I have focused on how *DM* actuates its audience participants. And yet, while actuating is a strategy for immersing audiences, it also has another purpose: it is the means by which audiences come to be coauthorial. I propose that once they have been actuated, audiences shift into *states of being coauthorial*, for which I present the term *coauthorality*. I base my concept of coauthorality on Barthes's theory of the "death of the author," in which he relocates the authority of making meaning from a text from the author to the reader. I deploy Barthes's theory to explore how authority and authorship are playing out in new ways in immersive performance as coauthorality. In the case of *DM*, audiences not only perform the dances they learn; they also generate dance content alongside bluemouth inc. core members and embedded dancers. I consider the possibilities of coauthorality to explain the agency applied by audiences within structures meant to immerse them. The dance content generated by audiences constitutes the performance; and at the same time, it is also the mechanism through which they make meaning of the experience. Thus, coauthorality functions in two ways, as an outcome of actuation that deepens immersion and as a tool for meaning-making.

Performance studies scholar Melanie Bennett participated as an audience member in one of the first performances of *DM* in Toronto in 2009 and observed the following: "As the night wore on, I began to feel more confident about my longevity and dance moves and found myself performing for the judges and those already eliminated" (2010:98). Bennett's statement suggests that her confidence grew through her involvement in dancing and emboldened her to invest more in her performance as a contestant. As a contestant (meaning protagonist), she understood that she had the ability ("I can") to dance, as well as the authority to revise and invent while performing for the judges and other audience members. At the risk of reading too much into Bennett's statement, I suggest that as she became more confident in her movement, she became more invested in the performance, which in turn, enabled her to make meaning from it. Coauthorality, in the case of *DM*, encompasses both the generating of dance content *and* the process of making meaning from dancing. As Bennett's quote suggests, audiences become increasingly invested in generating movement as the performance progresses, taking over the floor and dancing with their own interpretations and expressions. Although the audience is not "rewriting" the production, their bodily involvement operates as textual material, which can be interpreted as their re-reading of the performance as they work out their understanding of it through dancing. It is through their corporeal effort—their sweat, their muscle fatigue, and their dancing—that they are actively contributing to the performance and making it meaningful.

An anecdote from Simic from a performance in the town of Norwich, England, suggests how meaning created by audience members emerges through dancing:

> When we were in Norwich, I was dancing with a man, maybe a little bit older than me, maybe my age . . . and he was a little bit reserved in the beginning. . . . At first he was like, "Oh, I think I need a drink. I think I need another drink. I think . . ." You know? He told me, "I won tickets through the radio. . . . I didn't know I would be dancing. I thought I'd be watching other people dance, which I love to do, but I'm a little bit—." And then he started noticing the "YMCA" video—and he's was sort of like, "Oh, OK." And he became more and more open. Later he told me, "I didn't know what to expect. This has been an incredible evening for me. . . . My feet are hurting right now—I'm wearing my father's shoes, and it's the first time I've worn them since my father passed away. My father's dancing with me right now . . . and my father loved dancing." It was so beautiful to me—you never know what's going on in someone's life and how they can attach their history. (interview with author 2014)

This is a moment of coauthorality; the audience member became more comfortable when actuated to dance, felt his confidence in dancing evolve, and shared a story with Simic, thus creating a unique moment of performance for both her and himself. Simic has performed *DM* over fifty times with over seven thousand audience members, yet this man's voice and story is inscribed in her memory, retaining significance as an example of how audiences contribute to performances.

Sarah Murray, a producer who first attended *DM* in Edinburgh in 2011 and subsequently booked the production for additional performances, remarked:

> *Dance Marathon* has a different demand of audiences, and it is a shared experience, even as you are having an individual experience. You catch on quickly to the setup, but it does mean that you observe more carefully the people in the space and what your relationship to them might or

could be. What is elegant about this show is that it does allow you to build relationships within and amongst the audience and think about your response to them. *Dance Marathon* seems much more about the collective experience. (interview with author 2014)

Machon suggests that expertise in deploying immersive practices can be assessed when "the artist or the company [has] an authoritative grasp of the artistic potential and creative constraints of the form . . . in order to enable the participant in the event to have a full, undeniable immersive experience" (2013:100). Through bluemouth inc.'s "authoritative grasp" of collective creation, they succeeded in creating *DM*—judging from the statements of critics, scholars, audiences, and core members themselves—as an immersive experience that offers opportunities for audiences to engage in coauthorality.

I am not suggesting that coauthorality is the same thing—or provides the same outcomes—as the collaborative processes of collective creation. Through collective creation, artists such as bluemouth inc. members establish the context and content of the productions they offer audiences. When I queried bluemouth inc. core members about coauthorality, I received some push back from them about the role of the audience. Windeyer, for example, observed, "The *DM* audience . . . do not have the ability to revise/change the larger structures and sequences of the event in response to their individual or collective experiencing of it. To my mind, if they are not permitted to revise/create the event's materials, sequences, structures, then they cannot be considered co-authors" (email correspondence with author 2016). Indisputably, bluemouth inc. are the authors of *DM* as a production, and indeed, audiences are not coauthors as the collective might understand it in the sense that they did not design its structures and cannot fundamentally change them during performance. However, these structures designed by bluemouth inc. are precisely the kinds of mechanisms that can enable coauthorality.

As exchanges with bluemouth inc. core members indicate, audiences' views of immersive performance do not always align with the intentions or perceptions of artistic directors and dancers/performers. While that is true of any production, immersive performance gives us an opportunity to approach this incongruity differently because of the explicit roles given to audiences. In fact, some of my interviews with bluemouth inc. core members reveal that they were surprised by how much the audience wanted the opportunity to engage.[22] It is important to acknowledge productions and performances as spaces in which multiple things can and do occur; and this is particularly so in immersive productions, where indeterminacy is magnified through audience participation and action. A production can be tightly choreographed *and* afford the audience agency, or at least perceptions of agency. Such perceptions reflect the desires of audiences, and while they may in fact be experiencing a fantasy of agency, this is indeed what seems to compel audiences to participate in immersive performance.

In their fictional dance marathon, bluemouth inc. situate competition in an environment intended to foster and support collective contribution and egalitarianism. That said, bluemouth inc. also plays with the tension between egalitarianism and collectivism in order for *DM* to be perceived by audiences as an experience that is playful while emotionally, choreographically, and dramaturgically complex. Bluemouth inc.'s aim is not competition; it is to actuate the audience to dance, to keep them moving, discovering, and creating in relation to one another. The home page of bluemouth inc. asks, "What level of experience are you committed to having?" They seem to be posing this question to themselves as much as to their audiences, particularly in *DM*. Perhaps another question is worth posing here: what about their intentions for *DM* and what they actually enable for audience during performances? On one hand, the company's members could contest the existence of *DM* coauthorality because audiences cannot revise the inherent structures of the production. On the other hand, statements from audiences suggest they perceive themselves as having agency, having been cast as contestants and encouraged to participate in a situation where there is "no 'us and them' divide," to realize the performance.[23] According to Bennett, "*Dance Marathon*'s achievement is entirely contingent on the spectators' response and contribution to the narrative" (2010:98). While bluemouth inc. does have the authority to revise or restructure the production, they cannot revise or re-create all the dance content of any singular performance. If we think of *DM* as a palimpsest, the production is a layered surface that, even as it retains its original form, bears the traces of the thousands of audience members who have performed it.

6

Speculative Futures

This book has argued that not only are audiences physically present in works described and promoted as immersive theater, or more broadly, immersive performance; but they are also situated to participate as *subjects of choreography*, accountable to and shaped by the choreographic imperatives of the worlds designed and constructed by practitioners. Choreography, operating as a technology within immersive performance, goes beyond its direct attachment to dance as an art form that is expected to be presented under certain conditions in specific places as a tool to organize the movements of the dancing body. Following the assertions that choreography functions as an apparatus of capture, it is possible to understand how choreography captures every movement that goes beyond dance and, at the same time, relocates dance from its established traditional notions and places it in new realms, as it is in immersive performance. My role here has been to orient the discourse back to the fact that at the core of this phenomenon known as immersive performance there is choreography, an artistic practice that is about the presence of bodies and flesh in a space. And critical to this choreographic practice has been the turning toward the audience in order to design structures that impel these audiences to embrace their physical capacities and fleshiness as contributors to and participants in the experience of art-making and meaning-making.

For the artists making works that are intended to immerse audiences, it is specifically because of how they have conceptualized those audiences and designed choreography for their participation that audiences are able to enter into and perform these productions. In the preceding chapters, I have considered how dance is expanding as a discipline in the twenty-first century and, in particular, how choreography is contributing to new forms of performance that challenge ideas about audience engagement. The use of choreography to create forms of participatory performance, whether productions are labeled as immersive or otherwise, through the inclusion of audiences as subjects of choreography, contributes to the fields of dance and theater by complicating expectations of what choreography is, what it can be, and who

Tandem Dances. Julia M. Ritter, Oxford University Press (2021). © Oxford University Press.
DOI: 10.1093/oso/9780190051303.001.0001.

performs it. What is possible through choreography in the future depends only on the imagination and speculation of those who adopt and adapt it as a technology for creation.

Immersion, in so much as it is perceived as an outcome of performance, is only possible because of choreography. This technology requires the kind of intellectual and physical attention to the flesh, to the bodily capacities of audiences and performers, in order to craft works that can effectively elicit affective response. In order to have audiences engage in the *doing of performance*, there must be rigor in the designing and testing of what can be done through the body in space and in time. The potential for immersion to manifest happens through the countless hours of time practitioners devote to choreographic thinking and choreographic practices. It is this real and difficult work of conceptualizing, generating, selecting, and crafting choreography, as well as the revising, adjusting, and refining of that choreography, that is required to make worlds that elicit participation and evoke a broad spectrum of physical, emotional, and cognitive responses. Choreography is the craft, the technology for mapping out immersive worlds, whether they are epic or modest in scale, and for choreographing the participation of the inhabitants of those environs, including spectators and performers. The practitioners making these participatory performance worlds that are intended to immerse audiences—including Punchdrunk, Third Rail Projects, and bluemouth inc., among countless others—understand that the gap between audience and performer cannot be fully closed, since, following Gerald Siegmund, the split is always present within theatrical contexts. Indeed, choreography allows practitioners to set the conditions for and organize the potential participation of the future spectator in ways that inconspicuously, invisibly, covertly acknowledge the gap. Audiences then can take the singular initiative to enter and participate within imperative parameters of the choreography, and potentially experience whatever affective outcomes that may result—immersion being only one of many potential outcomes.

While Punchdrunk, Third Rail, and bluemouth inc. do not publicize *Sleep No More* (*SNM*), *Then She Fell* (*TSF*), and *Dance Marathon* (*DM*) specifically as dance, it is the central role of dance in each that sets these productions apart as works of immersive performance. Dance is not just one discipline among many used to create *SNM, TSF,* and *DM*; rather, its choreographic principles are integral to the design of these productions. Choreography is critical to the productions' infrastructure and deployed as a key strategy for immersing audiences during performances. *SNM* and *TSF* can be considered, and are often cited as, pioneering examples of what is known as immersive theater, and thus far, hold the singular status of the two immersive productions of the twenty-first century to achieve sustained critical and commercial success. Punchdrunk, Third Rail Projects, and bluemouth inc. have all used essential concepts, frameworks, and techniques from dance and prioritized choreography in ways that augment the experiences of live performance for audiences. Therefore, as I have argued, dance and choreography have significantly contributed to and irrevocably shaped both the practices for making this type of work and the perceptions of immersive performance as a new form of contemporary art.[1] Choreography is most productively understood as a technology with origins in dance that now serves as a nexus of several different forms of live performance, especially those involving audience participation. These diverse forms, including what is referred to as immersive theater, draw upon choreography's application as fundamentally intentional, portable, and ubiquitous when creating multiple kinds of productions in myriad contexts.

Of course, the discipline of dance does not have a monopoly on movement, nor on embodiment; and indeed, as discussed earlier in this book, choreography has expanded beyond the boundaries of dance. And yet to reveal the embeddedness of choreography in immersive performance through discussion of distinct histories, theories, and practices that have originated from dance is to acknowledge that such distinctions are valid and meaningful. I have argued throughout this book that practitioners rely heavily on dance for performance material and for mechanisms and structures that can function to immerse audiences, not the least of which is their transformation into subjects of choreography whose participation becomes performance. Simply put, those making immersive performance are drawing upon dance as a discipline and a field of knowledge; they are able to create such participatory and potentially immersive works because they have adopted and apply choreography. It is only because of the labor of those dedicated to dance as a discipline, specifically the choreographers and dancers who continually explore the practical, philosophical, and theoretical possibilities of the form, that choreography has been able to be harnessed as a technology for immersive performance.

The interdependency of theater and dance within a form like immersive performance is easily understood, as per Elswit, and when analyzing the proliferation of participatory performances forms, including those labeled as immersive, it is necessary to demand that dance neither be excluded from nor made subalternate to other disciplines. Throughout history, dance has advanced live performance, sometimes by leading innovation and at other times by working alongside other disciplines in interdependent and inter-disciplinary ways to forge new forms. In the case of immersive performance, I assert that dance has not only contributed to but led innovation to indel-ibly influence fundamental aspects of the form. Given this fact, there must be recognition of dance, and even more so, an acknowledgment of the ways dance builds and contributes knowledge within social and cultural domains as well as within institutions of learning. My efforts to bring attention to choreography's invisibilization within the discourses surrounding immer-sive theater is inextricably tied to the necessity for advocacy of dance, partic-ularly the relocation of dance from the peripheral margins to a role of central prominence within the curricula of Western institutions of secondary and post-secondary education. At best, dance has historically existed as tangen-tial to education, and at worst, it has been neglected entirely within curricula. As much as dance is a professional practice, it is equally a realm of historical and theoretical investigation, and it is a lack of dance literacy even with the performing arts, let alone disciplines farther afield such as the natural sci-ences, that contributes to its marginalization. Understanding dance's many dimensions as a field of study that builds knowledge through its professional practices as well as through its historical, philosophical, and theoretical foundations augments the critical thinking already present in the discourses surrounding immersive performance and allows for more comprehensive analyses. And importantly, because the participation of spectators in immer-sive performance is mediated by choreography, they have the opportunity to experience their bodies as tools for gaining knowledge, enacting agency, and generating transformation, whether or not they are cognizant of the opera-tional function or impact of choreography itself.

This is a critical moment from which we can move beyond dance's mar-ginalization as feminine to break down institutional misogynies around the form, a moment when we can utilize dance to surge forward and grasp opportunities to demonstrate its capacity to facilitate integrative approaches. The power of dance lies particularly in choreographic thinking and in its ca-pacity as a technology for organizing participatory arts practices. In terms of range and scope, the pedagogical applications of dance are untapped— and as such, it can be resourced to establish collaboration across multiple fields, both within and beyond the arts, to forge transdisciplinary research and establish integrative approaches. These innovations are crucial since

solutions to critical challenges found through dance will inherently prioritize the sensorial, kinesthetic human as central. Performing artists emerging
from institutions of higher learning are already drawn to working within the
realms of immersive and interactive performance for multiple reasons, including its potential economic viability and popular prominence, yet also
due to what are perceived as the possibilities for building community and
doing good through social inclusion via participation such as fandom activity. How can these artists gain knowledge, experience, and further literacy
of dance when it is significantly disadvantaged compared to other arts disciplines in higher education, under-resourced both in terms of personnel and
fiscal resources? And, on the other hand, it may be necessary to advocate for
immersive performance within the realms of dance scholarship, and to push
for dialogues that encourage discussion around how dance scholars are regarding the form.

Given that, thus far, only a handful of writings have emerged from dance
scholars about immersive performance, does this lack of attention reflect a lack of interest, or might some dance scholars hold rigid perceptual
frameworks about what dance and choreography are, which then contributes
to their disregard of the form? How might perceptions of immersive performance as "more entertainment than art" factor into the attention this form
receives from dance scholars? Are there questions as to what value immersive
performance has to dance, including discernment of increased economic viability, or lack thereof? How might turning towards immersive performance
allow dance scholarship to dive more deeply into studies of audience and
spectatorship, which in turn could provide data for better understanding
how dance is imbricated in the wide range and scope of concerns around
immersive works and participation in dance spectatorship more broadly?
Approaching immersive performance from multiple vantage points allows
for a more thorough understanding and comprehensive analysis of what the
form is contributing to cultural fabrics of international communities and
affords possibilities for new inquiries to be initiated.

Opening this book was a description of a gathering of international immersive practitioners in 2017, wherein I noted the absence of choreography
and choreographic practices from their collective discussion. Several years
later, while use of the term *immersive* has spread pervasively, one could argue
that choreography remains quietly hidden, surreptitiously invisible as ever.
Throughout the preceding chapters, I have made reference to the reasons
why choreography may be obscured and the methods used to accomplish its

implementation through a kind of camouflage. Because choreography is such an efficacious method for capturing movement, it must work subliminally during immersive performance so as not to disrupt the audience perception of agency and mobility. The diffusion of "immersive" as a term, concept, and label for practices is important to address. It appears to have risen to the top of the semantic heap of possible descriptors for this work because, I argue, there is an implicit understanding that audiences prefer to hear that they will be (or to conceive of themselves as being) *immersed* in worlds, rather than *choreographed* in them.

The prevalence of "immersive" as a term was particularly evident at the second annual Immersive Design Summit (IDS) held in 2019 in San Francisco. This event, promoted as "the premiere gathering of immersive creators worldwide," attracted more than two hundred attendees from four continents.[2] The international profile and programming of the summit evidenced that a wide range of projects and initiatives, both small- and large-scale, are being created and promoted under the rubric of immersive design. IDS organizers dedicated a full day of programming to discussion around the potential of developing immersive works as a "catalyst of change" and for social impact.[3] Yet, efforts to both make and monetize immersive art as viable business ventures leads to a tension between art and economics. For example, during her presentation at IDS 2019, Fri Forjindam, Co-Founder and Senior Creative Director of Mycotoo, a California-based entertainment production company, identified what she refers to as a "battle" between practitioners and those from the commercial business sector who have become conscious of the excitement around and the impact of new forms of innovative storytelling (Forjindam 2019). Interestingly, Forjindam describes this conflict using a dance metaphor, framing it as an "awkward tango" that will require artists and business executives to alternate between leading and following—improvisationally, as another form of tandem dancing—to engender the kind of cooperative synchronization that can afford future sustainability (2019).

On the second day of the Immersive Design Summit, the organizers unveiled what they described as "the first ever immersive industry annual report," claiming that the term *immersive* and its related practices now constitute an independent industry of which live performance, nested under the label "entertainment," is just one part, alongside retail, education, and activism (Brigante 2019:2). Prepared specifically for attendees of the 2019 summit, the IDS report focuses primarily on what its writers describe as the "Immersive Entertainment Industry."[4] Identifying a dozen or so different sub-industries beyond immersive theater, such as themed entertainment, escape rooms, and haunted attractions, as well as virtual reality and augmented reality, among others, the report claims that "never before has there been more attention fixated on entertainment that surrounds and envelopes its audiences, while giving them agency to become *fully embodied* in experiences" (4, emphasis added). Asserting that in 2018, more than seven hundred immersive productions were presented in North America alone, the writers suggest the economic value of the evolving immersive entertainment industry at more than $4.5 billion, which they note is a figure that is "not even factoring in the $45.2 billion theme park industry" (2).[5] The report comments on the fact that large entertainment conglomerates have adopted immersive approaches in their expansion, particularly The Walt Disney Company.[6]

In addition to citing the economic growth of immersive theater as an independent industry, the IDS report notes "a gradual yet noticeable shift in design methodologies" that offers audiences "*a more embodied role* in the entertainment" (14, emphasis added). Perhaps unsurprisingly, albeit disappointingly, choreography is never mentioned in the report, let alone identified as constituting one of these design methodologies. Indeed, the term "embodied" is referenced repeatedly in the document; in addition, the author of the report surveyed one hundred international practitioners and lists "embodied" as one of the most popular descriptors, ranking just below "intimate," "experiential," "storytelling," "participatory," and "agency," and above "environmental" and "transformative" (8). As humans, we are always already embodied, so why the dependency on this term to describe what is going on in immersive performance? What are the implications of the term "embodied" being applied to what is now being discussed as an immersive industry? If embodied experience is central to immersive entertainment, as well as its sub-disciplines, such as immersive theater, then it is precisely the *application of choreography* that makes these kinds of embodied experiences possible. It is choreography that, when used effectively, sets the conditions for potential audience immersion. Notably, the report cites both *SNM* and *TSF* as examples of successful models of immersive performance; in this book, these two productions as well as *DM* have all proven to be illustrative as productions where the overt and intentional use of choreography and dance are seen as a means for both communicating content and designing possibilities for different kinds of audience experiences, including immersion.

While my theorizing focuses on these theater productions, it also points to the need for deeper analyses and consideration of choreography in all immersive performance. My attention to this claim of a larger immersive entertainment industry is an attempt to consider what its growth and potential expansion might mean for choreography. In the realm of the theme park industry, for example, choreography and choreographic thinking have been integral since at least the 1950s, when Walt Disney conceptualized the upgrade of amusement parks from episodic experiences of thrilling rides and games to cohesive, singular experiences of miniature worlds. Theme parks were reimagined as self-contained worlds conceptualized around specific themes and designed for audiences to enter and explore along with its inhabitants, all of whom are performers playing recognizable characters from the company's influential film franchises. The parallels between theme parks and immersive productions have led theme park industry leaders to turn to the latter as inspiration, with immersive theater now named as "one of the biggest upcoming trends throughout hundreds of theme parks worldwide" (Brigante 2019:22). What this trend will mean for choreography, choreographers, and choreographic thinkers in the coming decades remains an open question.

While choreography may have to be obscured within immersive performances themselves in order to facilitate audience immersion, such invisibility must be actively resisted with the *discourses* surrounding immersive theater. Once we recognize the critical role of choreography within immersive performance and events, we see that the growth of the immersive entertainment industry raises several pressing questions with regard to the training of artists skilled to create and perform such works, engage across disciplines, and navigate their careers as a new sort of artist-entrepreneur. Questions requiring further exploration include the following: How might training programs be improved to better prepare practitioners and performers to create compelling immersive works that prove economically viable? And, critically, how might such programs prepare them to be choreographic thinkers in ways that lead to safe and effective immersive design for the roles that professionals and audiences perform? Beyond the theory and practice of arts disciplines, what other trainings might be necessary so that artists who wish to work this way can best promote their skills, and attain compensation for their labor? Moreover, given the expansion of immersive performance as an industry and its potential impact within multiple domains of society, how might artists be better prepared for the inevitable crossing-over to work within and across such domains, including the non-profit, commercial, and community sectors of society? What kinds of trainings need to be developed for artists to be artistically enterprising and innovative, as well as adopting advocacy approaches to their sustainability as practitioners? How can artists who have knowledge and skills as choreographers and as choreographic thinkers develop business acumen in order to monetize their expertise? What are some best practices for choreographing and designing immersive works that could potentially serve the greater social good with their impact?

In addition to the questions raised about practitioners and their training, the arguments of this book also raise questions about audience members themselves. How might audiences be more fully developed into active participants in creating experiences, beyond their roles as subjects of choreography? Are there certain kinds of sensibilities and behaviors desirable in audiences, and can they be guided to develop them in order to productively engage in such experiences? Is there a way for audience participation in immersive performance participation to be harnessed beyond its entertainment value, toward other forms of cultural and social engagement? These questions, too, invite further study and exploration.

This book's foregrounding of choreography as a design technology for audience participation has revealed immersive performance to be fundamentally about *the presence of bodies, bodies that are in motion and attend to motion.* The preceding chapters have shown how, through the activation of kinesthesia and the actuation of movement, audiences can experience action and interactions that may lead to immersion as a possible affective outcome. Immersion is not something the practitioners can give to spectators; rather, it is a possible affective response that may be generated through experience. Perhaps immersion is best understood as a perceptual framework: it is what practitioners hope to make happen for the spectator, through the elicitation of audience participation. The technology that is used to design, elicit, and facilitate that audience participation is choreography.

Lyrics for bluemouth inc.'s *Dance Marathon*

Lyrics for "The History of Dance"

In ancient times with dance sublime,
We prayed to god, to buy more time,
and celebrate in sacred shrines, our lives.
Egyptian kings, pharaohs dancing with the street
Walk like an Egyptian.
By the Renaissance the courts caught on,
And European monarchs flung
their partners round the banquet hall with ease.
The minuet, allemande, mazurka and waltz.
Bow to your partner and give them your hand.
Step in step out and face the back wall.
Step touch, step touch,
Step hop, step hop, step hop walking back around.
Let's try that again everyone
Bow to your partner and give them your hand.
Step in step out and turn to the stage.
Step touch, step touch,
Step hop, step hop, step hop walking back around.
The less sophisticated folks,
Used Country Dance to get them close,
handed down through centuries
this folkdance is still popular today,
1, 2, 3, 4
Clogging, Maypole, Irish dance,
Do the Polka, come on prance,
Round and round your partner go,
Ball de bastons, square dance, slow.
Morris, sword and country dance,
Swing your partner, come on prance,
Once more round your partner go,

That's enough of going slow.

1, 2, 3, 4

Clogging, Maypole, Irish dance,

Do the Polka, come on prance,

Round and round your partner go,

Ball de bastons, square dance, slow.

Morris, sword and country dance,

Swing your partner, come on prance,

Once more round your partner go,

That's enough theirs [*sic*] more to know.

Somewhere round the 1910's,

A little dance from Argentinian

Society, would change the world.

May I?

First in Paris, then, it spread to London,

Soon New York, Tangoed in abundance,

Valentino helped popularize it,

Rudolph dancing cheek to cheek

Argentina's Tango change the world,

Spread by sailor's, courting local girls,

Mistenguett had couple's dancing slowly,

At Waldorf they Tangoed during tea.

By 1920, life had changed,

A war had made things all seems strange,

Folks seeked opportunities for fun,

Any excuse to put down that old gun!

Then came, the one, most fun, the Charleston,

[*Lady Jane starts basic Charleston for audience*]

Oh, it proved, we could move, just by,

Kicking our out legs out. [*she adds the high kick*]

Used to, shed the blues, mock the "drys"

Had us Running Wild,

The Charleston, swung us,

In to Lindy hop dancing.

—From *Dance Marathon* by bluemouth inc. Written and
    performed by Ciara Adams. Copyright bluemouth inc., 2009.
    bluemouth inc. 2015a:12

Lyrics for "Hipshake Solo"

It's wonderful when a girl shakes her hips like that.

Because you know it's not about her hips.

No.

It has nothing to do with her hips.

What you have to look at is the space around her.

Me, I believe that when you see someone, you should look at the space
    around them.

Don't watch what their body is doing.

Don't look at the way they're moving.

What you should be focusing on is the space that is sculpted by their body.

I'm serious.

Look at it.

You should really see people as a sculpture.

No, you should see people as a sculptor.

As someone who sculpts space with their body.

What you need to do is imagine the air is clay.

Everything is clay.

And the person you're watching is a sculpting instrument.

Like they're a sculpting tool.

Like they're a cutting knife.

—From *Dance Marathon* by bluemouth inc. Written and performed by
    Richard Windeyer. Copyright bluemouth inc., 2009, bluemouth inc.
    2015a, 22

Word Cloud for *Dance Marathon*

Word cloud generated by the author from the verbal responses of audience participants collected as they exited a performance of *Dance Marathon* during Mayfest Bristol. Mayfest Bristol, United Kingdom, May 19, 2015.

Exhilarating

I learned some different dances

No "us and them" divide   lovely participatory experience

I loved every minute of it   Thought-provoking

Very beautiful Learned the Madison

Absolutely amazing   Beautiful

Much more than I thought it would be   Exhilarating

Well-planned   Very entertained   Terrific night

snapshots of life   Fun and inclusive   silly

Thoroughly enjoyed   Energy

I am pooped right now   Eye-opening   Danced a lot

I loved it   Great evening

Powerful   Brilliant   so much dancing

Lovely way into the world of dance marathons   Surprising

Incredible   Professionals and locals

Awe-inspiring   Really cool   The most exercise I have ever done

Really great fun   Interesting   Just brilliant   Triumphant

Sweaty   Energizing   Good time

Absolutely

Unexpected   Team-bonding

Fantastic musicians   Really enjoyed it

Met some really great people   Poignant moments

Dance for three hours   Quite surprised   Best thing we've done all year

If exercise was like that every day then I would do it

Not necessarily a sequence of narratives

Participatory theater done brilliantly

Amazing

Notes

Introduction

1. See https://futureofstorytelling.org/fest.
2. Hector Harkness, "All the World Is a Stage," panel presentation, The Future of Storytelling Festival, October 8, 2017, Snug Harbor Cultural Center, Staten Island, New York. Harkness is Associate director of UK-based Punchdrunk.
3. Justin Bolognino, "All the World Is a Stage," panel presentation, The Future of Storytelling Festival, Moderator Jacob Marshall, October 8, 2017, Snug Harbor Cultural Center, Staten Island, New York. Bolognino's company, META, promotes "The Art of Being There," and creates festivals and events for Beyoncé and other mega-entertainment artists (https://meta.is/).
4. The Windmill Factory, founded by artistic director Jon Morris and producer Ana Constantino, is a creative collective based in Brooklyn, New York, that is dedicated to "manufacturing the sublime." See http://thewindmillfactory.com/?portfolio=we-create-art.
5. Bolognino, in particular, clarified that choreography was critical to devising *Right of Passage* as a prelude event to the festival. The twelve-minute performance involved twenty dancers moving walls in choreographed patterns that shaped the safe entry of up to 250 spectators at a time into the venue (interview with author 2017).
6. Foster has previously addressed the ways in which choreography is often overlooked, suggesting it is referenced in some contexts but "ignored or suppressed in others," specifically citing the popular TV shows *So You Think You Can Dance* and *Dancing with the Stars* (2009:98). She points out that in these particular representations of dance in popular culture the focus is on performance while choreography is neglected as a process for devising the dances that are performed.
7. For comprehensive discussion of the long lineage and broad range of historical precedents for immersive theater as part of participatory performance, see discussions by the following: Machon (2013:28–40), Kattwinkel (2003:ix–xvii), White (2013:14–20), Alston (2016:5–11), and Schechner's *Environmental Theater* (1994).
8. The term *immersive* appears in LeNoir (2003:125).
9. See also Joshua Abrams's essay on work of Germany choreographer Felix Ruckert in Kattwinkel's anthology (Abrams 2003).
10. Art historian Claire Bishop describes "people as privileged materials" within the live performance process in reference to writer/filmmaker Guy DeBord's construction of situations in which "the audience function disappear[s] altogether in the new category of *viveur* (one who lives)." It is this idea of the spectator as "one who lives" alongside the cast members in the worlds created by immersive practitioners that I wish to

study, particularly how spectators understand and advance the agency of their *mo-bility* and their *movement potential* to live in such worlds (2006:13).

11. Frieze suggests, these claims can be seen as "rhetoric that promotes as much as it frames the practice it purports to describe" (2016:12). Helen Freshwater also calls for critical assessment of the notion that audiences are empowered via the opportunities they are afforded to participate in immersive theater (2009:71).

12. Readers particularly interested in the relationship between immersive theater and video-gaming will find Biggin's text to be a valuable resource.

13. Productions involving only one performer and one audience member are known as "one-to-one" performances in the United Kingdom; in the United States, they are typically referred to as "one-on-one" or even 1:1, common shorthand within immersive fandoms in the United States for such encounters.

14. While dance may be under-theorized in relation to immersive performance, many of the concepts crucial to the genre—such as phenomenology, corporeality, embodiment, kinesthesia, and intersubjectivity—have been thoroughly examined in dance scholarship. Comprehensive examination of any, let alone all, of these aforementioned concepts would be impossible within the scope of this book; I address them when appropriate throughout to reinforce theory building and when drawing parallels between the workings of dance and those of immersive performance.

15. Foster also includes a statement by an unknown critic, who described Monk's 1971 production of *Vessel* as "a major work in an art form for which there is no proper name" (1986:225).

16. Mike Pearson's book, *Site-Specific Performance* (Palgrave 2010), presents the topic of site-specific performance through his perspectives as a theater artist and scholar.

17. Druckler explains that on the day of the performance, one individual came to do his laundry; he was asked by production staff if he could wait until the show was over and he said no. Thus, the man became part of the performance, doing "his laundry in the middle of the show" alongside the dancers performing choreography (Pavlik 2013:87).

18. http://www.heididuckler.org/portfolio-posts/most-wanted-1997/.

19. Katalin Trencsényi and Bernadette Cochrane, building on the work of Van Kerkhoven, propose a three-part paradigm of new dramaturgies in which they include the following concepts: post-mimetic, interculturalism, and process-conscious (2014:xii).

20. Profeta suggests Gilpin was the first to "rightfully tie the advent of the dance dramaturg to a larger shift toward postdramatic theater aesthetics," although she notes Gilpin did not use the term *dance dramaturgy* (2015:10).

21. Profeta notes a contemporary preference for the term *dramaturgical* rather than *dramaturg*, since there may be no one individual designated as dramaturg in a contemporary theater and movement-based production, which is also the case of the immersive productions featured in this book. Especially in contemporary forms of movement performance, including dance and theater, choreographers, directors, dramaturgs, and designers may perform multiple roles, and/or collaboratively share

dramaturgical responsibility across the various duties of researching, composing, and implementing content.

22. Code-switching, a linguistic phenomenon, refers to the process of alternating between the use of two or more languages by bilingual and/or multilingual speakers. The term has been utilized within the study of cultural adaptation to describe the process of an individual shifting between the behavioral norms of different races, ethnicities, and/or cultures order to adhere to the perceived expectations of particular situations in society.

23. Synne K. Behrndt, drawing upon the work of dance critic and journalist Jean-Marc Adolphe, suggests that dramaturgical thinking can be understood "as something that can be facilitated in a number of different ways and by different collaborators" (2010:191). This would seemingly include audiences.

24. See Ritter 2015, 2016, and 2017.

25. The practice of supplying spectators with instructional scores or instructional pieces as a means of participation has a long history, most notably in the United States and Europe through the work of postmodernist dance artists as well as that of artists creating visual and performance art such as Allan Kaprow, Yoko Ono, and Marina Abramović.

26. This does not preclude, however, the possibility of different kinds of thinking in movement; Sheets-Johnstone suggests that thinking in movement within infants, for instance, may have "practical, self-instructional or exploitive ends," although this would represent an intentionality distinct from the aesthetic aims of improvisational dance (1999:484).

27. While this text prioritizes analysis of productions created by Anglo-American practitioners in the United Kingdom, Canada, and the United States, it is my hope that the arguments around the relationship between choreography and immersive performance as presented here will serve as starting points for much-needed further research around works created by practitioners from diverse backgrounds whose approaches are informed by and reflect multiple aesthetic perspectives and artistic practices.

28. One spectator I interviewed, Jay Bushman, an Emmy-winning writer and producer of interactive media and transmedia storytelling, who actively seeks out opportunities to experience immersive productions, suggested *Sleep No More* represents a kind of "conversion moment" and thus, "will probably always be at the top of the pantheon" (interview with author 2019).

29. I have not had the opportunity at the time of writing to experience the work of the UK-based SHUNT collective, considered a pioneer of the form, yet my discussions with Gemma Brockis, co-founder, have revealed richly rewarding insights into their approach to audiences and choreography.

30. See Lepecki (2012:15).

31. See Risner (2007:968).

Chapter 1

1. Performance studies scholar André Lepecki suggests *orchésographie*, coined in 1589, was the first version of the word choreography (2006:7).
2. In French, the title reads as *Orchésographie. Et traicte en forme de dialogve, par leqvel tovtes personnes pevvent facilement apprendre & practiquer l'honneste exercice des dances.* For the English version of the title, I use the translation by Mary Stewart Evans; *Orchesography. And treatise in the form of dialogue, whereby all may easily learn & practice the honourable exercise of dancing.*
3. For Capriol, knowledge of dance translates into access and agency; as the treatise concludes, it is clear he understands that his newly acquired skills will enable him to finesse future journeys into aristocratic realms.
4. Lepecki references Arbeau when arguing that choreography emerged as a political tool from the social activity of dance, stating, "at a certain point in the history of Western subjectivity, a certain social (and socializing) activity called dance fell prey to a Stately (and theological) apparatus of capture called choreography" (2007:122).
5. See Foster 2011, Chapter 2, for an expansive, historical theorization of the relationship of choreography and cartography. Theater scholar Rachel Fensham, commenting on Foster's research, notes that "we became choreographic the more we could abstract the movement of bodies into symbolic representations of place" (2014:101).
6. *Zork* was created by Tim Anderson, Bruce Daniels, Dave Lebling, and Marc Blank, who met as students at MIT's Laboratory for Computer Science. https://www.technologyreview.com/s/608670/the-enduring-legacy-of-zork/.
7. Command and response can be understood as dialogic, yet perhaps it can also be understood as imperative, with the command representing an imperative aspect of communication and the response representing the dialogic aspect.
8. Music scholar Kiri Miller suggests the term "avatar relations" for the implied relations between players and game characters in her book *Playable Bodies: Dance Games and Intimate Media* (2017). However, Miller's research focuses specifically on the relationality between players and dance video games designed to teach choreographic content that they enact within real world contexts. As Miller states, "*these games evaluate players on the basis of their actions in the actual world, not the virtual world,*" which is to say, "the player's performance in [their] living room" (2017:16, emphasis original). As she argues, "in this version of 'avatar relations,' the player who faithfully performs the kinesthetic repertoire of an on-screen character is representing that character in the actual world in much the same way that traditional game avatars represent human players in virtual worlds" (16). Given that the example of *Zork* differs from Miller's examples, how might we consider the player's embodiment as both sitting in a chair and also inhabiting the virtual world of the "Great Underground Empire"?
9. I emphasize the textual evidence of choreography in dance manuals from the Renaissance and in computer games on digital platforms not to assert that proof of choreography is only to be found in written form but rather to establish the presence of choreography outside of "dance" with full acknowledgment of the ways in which choreography exists as a phenomenon that is non-written and non-notated, and in

fact, resists being written. Significant debates exist in the field of dance as per the notion of dance as text and dance as writing; see Franko (2011).

10. Connections between video gaming and immersive performance have been made by Biggin (2017).

11. Immersive theater was cited by Ben Brantley, theater critic for *The New York Times*, as one of "33 Ways to Remember the 2010s." https://www.nytimes.com/interactive/2019/11/24/arts/2010s-decade-end.html.

12. Kobayashi's production has been publicized and reviewed as a one-woman show, although the fact that the audience is required to manifest this production makes that label debatable; thus, I have placed the distinction in quotes. See https://www.vogue.com/article/say-something-bunny-alison-kobayashi and the *Say Something Bunny!* website, https://saysomethingbunny.com/.

13. The term *storyworld* was coined by David Herman, professor of engaged humanities, as per his theorizing of narratology. The concept of a storyworld can be understood in relation to immersive performance as the contexts or environments constructed by practitioners to ground narratives in ways that audiences will experience them implicitly and explicitly through the elements they encounter during performances including text, choreography, action, scenography, etc. As Herman explains, "storyworlds are mentally and emotionally projected environments in which interpreters are called upon to live out complex blends of cognitive and imaginative response" (Herman 2005:570).

14. See https://en.oxforddictionaries.com/definition/choreography.

15. My use of the term *intentionality* in this context is not be confused with its function as a principle theme in phenomenology, beginning with Aristotle, reframed by Franz Bretano, developed in the work of Edmund Husserl, and expanded further by Maurice Merleau-Ponty.

16. See McFee 2011, Chapter 5, for discussion of how the concept of *intentionalism*, as well as the theory of *intentional fallacy* relate to dance.

17. Sedgman forewarns us to "beware the idea that deliberately participatory events are more productive or democratic than 'traditional' theatrical forms" (2018: 291).

18. As McFee notes, "one cannot [always] *find out* what the author intended. But one may still understand his/her works" (2011:122, emphasis original).

19. McFee draws upon Danto's concept of transfiguration when discussing the "transformation of 'ordinary' movements into dance" (2011:33).

20. For further distinction between artworks and "mere real things," see Danto's argument for the "confusable counterpart" (1981:138).

21. As McFee argues "dancers do not *cause* the dance: rather they *are* the dance—their movements instantiate it" (in Pakes et al. 2013:28).

22. It is also possible that spectators "make things happen" by *not participating* in the choreographic structures offered—questions related to issues of complicity and compliance are addressed in Chapters 3, 4, and 5.

23. In focusing on Western theatrical context or discourse, I differentiate that I am addressing choreography created as theatrical performance, acknowledging that cultures throughout Western societies have social, recreational forms as well as folk

and cultural forms that are composed of choreography. Some dancing masters were teachers as well as choreographers, and created dances for public participation rather than for the stage or public presentation. There were also dancing masters who traveled regionally and widely to teach others to compete; some social dances were highly prized choreographies rather than improvised dances and thus, were the intellectual property of an individual dancing master.

24. The *invention* of choreography is attributed by Foster to Pierre Beauchamps, who was the dancing master of Louis XIV, the King of France. Beauchamps never completed the assignment given to him by the King, which was to notate the dances he had created; it was completed instead by Feuillet (2009:100).

25. Dancing masters were incentivized to promote dancing among the citizenry because they profited from the sale of treatises, which augmented the incomes they received from their aristocratic patrons.

26. McGowan observes that "the context for dance was, of course, the court, where the dominant atmosphere was one of rivalry: competition for place, for being noticed, for outdoing one's peers in performance" (18).

27. Andrew Hewitt makes this clear with his theorizing of social choreography, noting the "disappearance from the ballroom of masculine self-representation" as men pursued other forms of power within society when governments formed, and they retreated to their cabinet offices to do their work out of sight of others (2005:32).

28. Foster associates the return of choreography as a term to events of 1927, specifically the fact that "all three major newspapers in New York City hired dance critics, and they implemented the term in all their reviews of dance concerts" (Connor 1997:1, in Foster 2009:105).

29. See also Machon, White, and Elswit for other perspectives on historical antecedents of immersive performance.

30. What I am researching is different from the social practice or participatory arts described by Bishop as embodied in works that emphasize "collaboration and the collective dimension of social experience" (2006:10). In the United Kingdom, participatory art is understood as a social practice with political intentions; Bishop discusses the practices of artists working in this realm as "striving to collapse the distinction between performer and audience, professional and amateur, production and reception" (10).

31. Sánchez-Colberg points out that Artaud's "theatre of cruelty" has been subjected to "common literal misunderstanding" as "a gratuitous engagement in violent acts" when in fact his intention was to bring these two terms together to promote his philosophy that theatrical forms should advance through the introduction of organized anarchy that would instigate new forms of wakefulness among audiences (1996:43).

32. See Matthew Isaac Cohen (2010:142).

33. Kaprow's *Yard* (1961) was presented in the garden of the Martha Jackson Gallery in New York City. See Jeff Kelley's *Childsplay: the Art of Allan Kaprow* (2004:58–62).

34. *Promenade theater* is the term for another form that requires audiences to move during a performance that came to prominence in the mid-twentieth century alongside Schechner's environmental theater. While environmental theater is designed

to include the audience participation beyond observation, promenade theater may or may not be designed as such. In both forms, spectators may stand or be seated, be guided through the action or follow the action of the performance. *Fefu and Her Friends* (1977, New York City), a work by acclaimed Cuban American playwright María Irene Fornés, is noted for its theatrical staging requiring audiences to move throughout the performance venue and is described as an early example of ground-breaking promenade theater in the United States. See García-Romero (2016) and Cummings (2013).

35. Tobin Nellhaus, general editor of *Theatre Histories: An Introduction*, defines *immersive theater* in the volume's glossary as "a recent expansion of environmental theatre" (2016:599).

36. Artists in the early twentieth century experimenting with chance operations include Marcel Duchamp, whose 1913 composition *Musical Erratum* was created by selecting musical notes at random by drawing them from a hat. This work is known to have influenced Cage's later work.

37. Halprin's presentation *Parades and Changes* in New York City in 1967 drew attention due to the nudity of participants while undressing, and authorities issued a summon for her arrest. The work was last performed in 2013 in Berkley, California. See www.annahalprin.org.

38. Murphy reminds us that "while Judson resides in the cultural memory as a *group* of innovators, they did not set out to function, nor end up functioning, as a unified artistic unit" (133, emphasis original). Instead, she cites the actual performance space of the Judson Church itself as that which served as the "unifying element" (133).

39. I understand experimental devices within dance to be the use of chance operations alongside the development of scores, games, exercises, instructional improvisational structures, tasks, and tools used in various processes to generate and select movement.

40. See Sánchez-Colberg (1996), Murray and John Keefe (2007), and Murphy (2015).

41. Sánchez-Colberg has noted that the terms "physical theatre" and "dance-theatre" were "at times used interchangeably" when the former first emerged as a distinct form (48). In addition, she asserts that one motivation for physical theater was a reaction against what was seen as the emphasis on abstraction in "New Dance," a term sometimes used to describe an aesthetic vision of "movement-for-movement's sake" prevalent from the late 1960s through the 1970s (48). She claims that the focus of physical theater was "not in an exploration of formal concepts within the dance medium, but an exploration of aspects of humanity via the theatrical medium" (49).

42. See Elswit (2018) and George-Graves (2015) for further discussion about theater's place of privilege in relation to the perception of dance's more "subaltern" position, a descriptor drawn from Lepecki.

43. Bausch's version of *tanztheatre* has been specifically associated with the development of *physical theater*, by scholars Murray and Keefe. They assert that, "dance theatre is almost as difficult to circumscribe and delineate as [physical theatres]," underscoring the challenge of naming and defining performance projects that cross boundaries and

function as sites of interdependency, following Elswit, rather than representing distinct disciplinary foundations and perspectives (Murray and Keefe 2007:75).

44. The Canadian performance collective bluemouth, as well as Maxine Doyle, associate artistic director and choreographer for Punchdrunk, have cited the work of Bausch as inspiration for their immersive approaches to choreography and performance. For more detailed analysis, see Lucy Weir's *Pina Bausch's Dance Theatre* (2018), and *The Pina Bausch Sourcebook: The Making of Tanztheater* (2012), edited by Royd Climenhaga.

45. Forsythe also uses the phrase choreographic objects to describe the installations, sculptures, and films he has created since the 1990s. https://www.icaboston.org/exhibitions/william-forsythe-choreographic-objects.

46. See Spier (2011). *White Bouncy Castle* (originally titled *Tight Roaring Circle*) was commissioned in 1993 by Artangel, a UK-based company that produces temporary site-specific works.

47. Other scholars have made note of structural similarities between Punchdrunk's *Sleep No More* production and video games; see Biggin (2017) and Thiel (2017). Punchrunk founder Felix Barrett has made specific reference to *BioShock,* a first-person shooter game published in 2007. https://www.vice.com/en_us/article/d7xkqv/delicious-brainwashing-why-you-absolutely-must-go-see-isleep-no-morei.

48. In discussion of spatial navigation as a property of digital design, Murray states, "the navigational space of the computer allows us to express a sequence of thoughts as a kind of dance" ([1997] 2017:100).

49. In her discussion of forms of live participation, including immersive theater and role-playing games, Murray labels such events as "holodeck experiences without the machinery" ([1997] 2017:50). Murray describes Punchdrunk productions as "a kind of holodeck experience in real space" (75).

50. James Paul Gee, writing about embodiment in video-gaming, proposes the term "projection stance" to describe a "type of embodied thinking characteristic of many (but not all) video games, as well as a form of thinking that is also, but more subtly, pervasive in everyday life and social interaction as well" (253). As a corollary, in his article "Thinking with the Body," cognitive scientist David Kirsh explores what he calls "physical thinking" in the work of dancers who use a rehearsal technique called "marking" to visualize movement, that is, imagine themselves performing as a means of preparing for future physical performances (2864). The propositions of both Gee and Kirsh could be related to the conceptualization of choreographic thinking as put forth by Forsythe, and subsequently expanded upon by Manning.

51. Gemma Brockis, a co-founder of the UK-based SHUNT collective, readily acknowledges that from the beginning she and her colleagues understood that "how the audience moves through the space is a masterful part of choreographing" an immersive production (interview with author 2019).

Chapter 2

1. Quote from page ix of Templeton's book and on marketing materials (DVD and website). The premiere of *YOU-The City* in New York City was a sold-out run that occurred between May 18 and June 5, 1988, with performances offered between 3 p.m. and approximately 8:30 p.m. five days per week. Templeton reproduced the work in London in 1989; Adrian Dannatt, writing for the *Sunday Times* exclaimed, "*YOU-The City* is so unique in idea, execution and audience, that it beggars the most technical of descriptions" (July 2, 1989). Subsequent productions were staged in The Hague, as well as in Ljubljana and Zurich in 1990, and in Munich, Germany, in 1991.

2. In addition to Templeton, other artists were experimenting with choreographing the audience in the 1980s. As referenced in the notes for Chapter 1, *Fefu and Her Friends* (1977, New York City) by Cuban American playwright María Irene Fornés is an early example choreographing of audiences via the convention of promenade theater. When summarizing developments in environmental theater in the 1980s, theater scholar Steve Nelson makes specific reference to what he calls the "actor/audience choreography" of *Tamara*, a production directed by Richard Rose that premiered in 1989 at the Seventh Avenue Armory in New York City (now known as the Park Avenue Armory). *Tamara* can be understood as an incunabulum of immersive performance alongside *YOU-The City* (Nelson 1989:77). Nelson describes the choreographic structure of *Tamara* as shaped by a passport of rules, titled "The Ten Commandments," and that these, along with the directive to follow one performer, enabled the creators to enforce a "tight but relatively unobtrusive means of crowd control" (77). *Tamara* is important for understanding antecedents to contemporary immersive theater, yet I do not analyze the production in depth here; the reader is encouraged to see Nelson (1989).

3. The scenario that opens this chapter is based on my interpretations of a DVD of the production provided by Templeton.

4. Templeton confirmed she conceives of both the Client Flow and Performer Shuttles as choreography, stating the former "came from using complex diagrams for performer movement even in non 'dance' works. Choreography is a term I've used, but also architecture" (email correspondence with the author 2019).

5. Templeton shared that "scoring is a word I didn't use then but I use it all the time now" (interview with author 2019).

6. Templeton clarifies the *unintendable* further stating, "in any performance work there is at some level the unintendable, even in the very precision-based work of mine from the 1970s. It's the human-ness of live work. [In] many of my works there is a kind of gap or lacuna at the center. In *YOU-The City* it's in particular the moment where the two clients are left with each other for a moment at the crossover" (email correspondence with author 2019).

7. Templeton explicitly acknowledges the importance of choreography in her work, stating that she conceptualizes movement from the outset of creation as its own language. However, she also intentionally crafted the script of *YOU-The City* so that "the text is not instructions, per se, but reveals, tacitly, scores for action" (interview with author 2019). In this way, the text itself is a form of choreographic score that serves

as another structure for guiding the movement of clients, in that addition to the two previously mentioned—the Client Flow and Performer Shuttles.

8. The fact that Templeton offers the reader the opportunity to "eavesdrop on moments from after-performance conversations between clients, performers and production people" further underscores her mindful prioritization of audiences and their reception in the development and design of her work (1990:vii). Templeton frames these post-performance reflections as *unintendable*, noting that such comments provide insight into the intersections between her intentional, aesthetic design choices and how they were perceived via processes of audience reception. She states, "reception is also an intention: what I meant [as director] depended on what you thought I meant, and this was what I meant" (vii).

9. Excerpted from "An Introduction to Design Thinking Process Guide" (2010), published by The Hasso Plattner Institute of Design at Stanford University in the United States, also known as the d.school, which centralizes the study of design thinking in its curriculum.

10. Norman's notion of cultural constraints is analogous with what sociologist Erving Goffman has called "frames" (129). For further discussion of Goffman's theories in relation to immersive performance, see Gareth White (2013).

11. Forsythe's *Improvisation Technologies* project was created in cooperation with The ZKM/Center for Art and Media in Karlsruhe, Germany.

12. In art, it is not always true that such technologies, for example, choreography, are invisibilized. The point of Weiser's essay was to assert the ubiquity of technology; he coined the term *ubiquitous computing*, by which he means computer technologies that are all pervasive and embodied in our daily life practices.

13. My sense of audiences becoming *proformers* within immersive performance is also informed by the ways in which some repeat their attendance, particularly in regard to Punchdrunk's works, with the goal of learning the inner workings and structures of a production so they can "perform" more proficiently during each subsequent performance they attend. My thanks to Darrah Carr for the suggestion of the term *proformer* in this context.

14. Jenkins coined the phrase participatory culture in 1992 yet historically, the practices of such a culture, as he defines it, pre-date the internet; individuals have been generating and sharing content within communities for centuries. Certainly, dance and other arts constitute examples of the kinds of practices that have developed through collective, communal energies and intelligences of multiple members of global societies.

15. WolfBrown focused on what they frame as "active arts participation" with their study drawing upon data from more than one hundred organizations across the United States, United Kingdom, and Australia (2). The researchers do not identify a specific timeframe; instead they place "participatory practice in the context of the larger cultural ecology, with consideration of the role of the Internet in fostering interactivity" (3). With this in mind, it appears the timeframe they analyze is between 2004 (a year associated with an explosion of interactive possibilities via the initiation of Web 2.0) and 2010.

16. The framework in *Getting In on the Act* was adapted from the Creative Community Index, developed by arts researchers John Kreidler and Philip Trounstine in 2005. Kriedler and Trounstine define cultural literacy as "fluency in traditions, esthetics, manners, customs, language and the arts, and the ability to apply critical thinking and creativity to these elements" (Brown and Novak-Leonard 2011:43).

17. My understanding of *sensorium* is informed by the writings of Marshall McLuhan, philosopher of communication theory.

18. Felix Barrett, founder and artistic director of the UK-based Punchdrunk company, identifies the changing of the "status" of audience members as "key to audience immersion" (Machon 2013:161). In her Table 1, titled "Traditional Theatre vs. Immersive Theatre," Machon claims that during an immersive theater experience audiences are, "aware that you have taken on a character, you are playing out a role" (2013:54–55). Machon also asserts that audiences in immersive theater shift roles between "that of witness, an associate, a client, a guest, a co-producer and a protagonist" (2013:73). The co-directors of Third Rail Projects—Zach Morris, Tom Pearson, and Jennine Willett—while not employing the term *status* specifically, acknowledge casting audiences as protagonists in roles and responsibilities, and identify them as "scene partners" (Pearson 2014:34).

19. Franko, in analyzing Duncan's use of expression, notes that, "Duncan staged herself as a subject of expression, not an expressive subject" (1995:11).

20. See also Reason and Reynolds (2010) for further critique of Martin.

21. McConachie frames empathy as an imaginative process of "stepping into an actor/ character's shoes" in order to distinguish it from his notion of sympathy as that which involves "projecting her or his own beliefs and feelings onto the stage figure" (2008:99). Fensham positions embodied spectatorship as a distinct methodology for considering what she calls "the viscerality of theatre images" that have been brought about through what Lehmann has identified as postdramatic theater, that is, the move from text-based works to performances emphasizing corporeality (2016:40). Garner's discussion of kinesthesia is focused upon theater presentations in more traditional presentation formats, although immersive is referenced briefly in *Kinesthetic Spectatorship: Phenomenology, Cognition, Movement* (2018). See also Fensham's discussion of embodied spectatorship and affective spectatorship in, respectively, *To Watch Theatre: Essays on Genre and Corporeality* (2009), and in *Unfolding Spectatorship: Shifting Political, Ethical and Intermedial Positions*, by Stalpaert, et al. (2019).

22. Referencing the courts of the fifteenth and sixteenth centuries, Foster suggest how the body's "empathic connection to others" was "actualized in the sovereign hierarchies of nobility and order stipulated by the court" (2011:175).

23. Foster, building on Martin, states that "not only events but also objects elicit this kinesthetic responsiveness" (2008:48).

24. The *Watching Dance: Kinesthetic Empathy* project partners include Manchester University, Glasgow University, and York St. John University as well as Imperial College, London.

25. McConachie's writings on mirror neurons and the impact of cognition in spectating provide further insight into such analysis, particularly around the ideas of imitation and mimesis. McConachie suggests that contrary to "conventional mimetic theory," wherein the actors are imitating life, it is the spectators who "mirror the actions of those watch on stage; cognitive imitation is a crucial part of spectating" (2008:72).

26. In this way, Reynolds echoes the concerns of Foster and Franko regarding Martin's early theorizing of kinesthetic empathy.

27. As Reynolds makes clear, "subjectivity is embodied and [this] embodiment grounds our experiences of the world and each other. It follows, therefore, that changes in embodied experience have the capacity to transform both subjective consciousness and relationships between subjects" (2012:88).

28. The theory of suture from film studies is of interest here, when considering the ways in which audience participants "stitch" themselves into the fabric of a production, taking on the perspectives (often male, and exemplifying the male gaze, as per film theorist Laura Mulvey) to identify with certain characters.

Chapter 3

1. On July 5, 2019, Third Rail celebrated the 4,000th performance of *Then She Fell*. https://www.theatermania.com/off-broadway/news/then-she-fell-4000th-performance_89191.html?fbclid=IwAR2RfgswTUJLQXI4npjUweAs19xWh8zajF8WUqVfmTyEPij4IoYn_cE1Hz0.

2. Third Rail received a 2012–2013 New York Dance and Performance Bessie Award for Outstanding Production for *Then She Fell*, which was also named a New York Times Critic's Pick/Top Ten for 2013 by theater critic Ben Brantley.

3. The idea presented here, specifically that the physical enactment of an action may produce lasting emotional and/or cognitive affects, is drawn from the research of Sheets-Johnstone (see interview with Nancy Eichhorn 2016). Also of note is current research on active learning, which theorizes that retention of information is positively impacted through multi-modal engagement in structures that support a range of activities that include doing, thinking, and reflecting.

4. To clarify, I believe that spectators can indeed experience both kinesthetic and verbal responses in more conventional theatrical settings; in such contexts, the former (kinesthetic responses) may be understood as more internal rather that external, physicalized expressions while verbal responses would likely reflect whatever standards are appropriate for the circumstances of that particular performance.

5. From an announcement for a workshop conducted by Martin Nachbar and Jeroen Peeters, titled "Physical Dramaturgy: Backtracking," posted at http://sarma.be/pages/Physical_dramaturgy_-_Backtracking, 2011.

6. While I am familiar with these particular productions, I have not had the opportunity to experience them so understand them only through Boenisch's analyses.

7. Gardner's research prioritizes those with exceptional physical skills; dancers, as well as swimmers, have served as key research subjects during his investigation of "the ability to use one's body in highly differentiated and skilled ways, for expressive as well as goal-oriented purposes" (1983:218).

8. The English translation of Lehmann's *Postdramatic Theatre* became available in 2006, almost a decade after its original publication. In addition to describing the discourse surrounding this type of theater, Lehmann's term *postdramatic* is also used to describe types of productions themselves.

9. As Lehmann states, "[t]he adjective 'postdramatic' denotes a theatre that feels bound to operate beyond drama, at a time 'after' the authority of the dramatic paradigm in theatre" (2006:27).

10. Theater scholars Marvin Carlson, Rachel Fensham, and Bruce McConachie have each cited immersive performance as an example of Lehmann's theory of postdramatic theater. However, they do not specifically address the new kinds of dramaturgical thinking this new form of contemporary art has initiated. See Carlson 2015, Fensham 2012, and Underiner 2016.

11. While narrative shapes the form, the practitioners I have interviewed uniformly state that performers are not directed to act or emote; instead, they are directed to inhabit the world of the production as fully as possible via the precision performance of their character's choreography. They utilize the qualitative dynamics of the choreography and the idiosyncratic movements of their character so that at all times narrative is communicated through choreography; emotion manifests through the dance, and any perceptions of emotion should arise through the interpretations of spectators rather than be demonstrated by the performer.

12. I first proposed the idea of a "tandem dance" between spectators and dancers in regards to Punchdrunk's *Sleep No More* (Ritter 2015). Definition of *tandem*, as per the Merriam Webster Dictionary online: http://www.merriam-webster.com/dictionary/tandem.

13. Interviews with practitioners and performers of several companies revealed the term "loop" is commonly used to identify any track that is performed repeatedly over the course of one performance, thus reflecting the difference in its spatio-temporal function.

14. To explain this notion further, Willett refers to a choreographed fight sequence between the Hatter and the White Rabbit involving the long and narrow table used later for the tea-party; both characters approach and use the table as a prop and a surface for dancing in keeping with their individual, idiosyncratic, task-based movement vocabularies. She clarifies that "the way that the [White Rabbit] happens to get from here to there is that he flips over the table, because that is just how he does it, not because he is suddenly launching into choreography" (interview with author 2014). In other words, during the parry with the Hatter, the Rabbit's flips and jumps are intended to be read as necessary countermoves and not as virtuosic choreographic displays that could cause spectators to distance themselves from the action unfolding in front of them. These statements underscore some of the choreographic tensions between abstraction and narrative representation in immersive works.

15. Pearson explained that when training new dancers to perform roles in *TSF*, he informs them that, "every audience member that comes in is your new scene partner" (2014:34). Spectator status in *TSF* has a threefold conceptualization: spectators are understood by the artistic directors and the performers as (1) protagonists, (2) scene partners, and (3) medical interns within the hospital that is the fictional setting for the production.

16. Murray suggests that when teaching interaction design, "if the interactor does not know what to do then there is something wrong with your design. The ideal you are going for is *transparency* (sometimes confusingly called "intuitive" design) where the interactor can draw upon known experiences to immediately understand what is possible, and so they are not distracted by thinking about the interface, and can focus on what they want to happen in the interactive environment" (interview with author 2019, emphasis in speech).

17. The degree to which spectators can improvise to generate content that contributes to a performance varies from production to production; questions regarding the freedom to improvise and invent are central to ongoing debates within immersive performance, particularly in the discourses surrounding interactivity.

Chapter 4

1. The second version of *SNM* at American Repertory Theater (ART) in Boston won the Elliot Norton Award for Outstanding Theatrical Experience in 2010. http://punchdrunk.com/past-shows/column/10.

2. Collaborating with SMG Live, the live performance arm of Shanghai Media Group, one of the largest media and cultural organizations in China, Punchdrunk converted a former factory in the Jing'an district into the McKinnon Hotel, the sister hotel of the McKittrick. I experienced three performances of the Shanghai version of *SNM* in May 2017.

3. Doyle cites "locating the audience at the epicenter of experience" as central to Barrett's aims as a theater practitioner (Doyle et al. 2012:3).

4. Another long running production is Third Rail Project's *Then She Fell*, featured in Chapter 3, which premiered in 2012 and is presently still in production.

5. Barrett describes going back to visit *SNM* a year after it opened in New York and deciding to "test the choreography . . . I put myself into the scene and the choreography was exactly the same" (interview with author 2015a). He praises the *SNM* team, which includes Doyle, for "applying the rigidity that is needed so [the performance] feels slightly out of control" yet is consistent night after night in terms of action and structure (Barrett 2015b).

6. The vignette that opens this chapter, as well as those offered throughout, represent reconstructions of my experiences and observations as an audience participant during *SNM* performances. In sharing them, I acknowledge the problematic possibility of attributing motivation and intention to spectators whom I have observed but not interviewed. My aim is not to generalize audience experience nor to promote

assumptions about the impact of immersion as an affective experience. Rather, I offer the vignettes to illustrate my research methods, namely, choreographic analysis and spectator-participation-as-research, or SPaR. As discussed in Chapter 2, Heddon et al., followed by Babbage, have theorized that the boundaries around practice-as-research (PaR), a research method typically associated with processes of making performance, can be expanded to encompass spectating. I am cognizant, as this chapter reveals, that I may not be the only one engaging in SPaR in these contexts; just as I am spectating others, they may be spectating me as well.

7. See Michael Billingham's review of Punchdrunk's *It Felt Like a Kiss* (Guardian 2009) as well as *The Guardian Observer* profile of Barrett written by Liz Hoggard (Guardian 2013). https://www.theguardian.com/culture/2009/jul/03/manchester-international-festival; https://www.theguardian.com/theobserver/2013/jul/14/felix- barrett- punchdrunk-theatre-stage.

8. Punchdrunk works during this time include: *The Firebird Ball* (2005), a collision of *Romeo & Juliet* and Stravinsky's *The Firebird* in the abandoned Offley Works factory in South London; and their *Faust* (2006/07), in which Goethe's masterwork plays out within the vast 150,000-square-foot former warehouse in East London, reconfigured as a small American town in the 1950s; as well as *The Masque of the Red Death* (2007/08), which situated Edgar Allan Poe's classic tales within the confines of the former Battersea Old Town Hall, built in 1893.

9. Lecoq, a teacher of multiple methods of physical theater, founded the École Internationale de Théâtre Jacques Lecoq in Paris in 1956. The school continues to enroll students at the time of this writing.

10. When deciding to restage *SNM* in 2009, Barrett and Doyle expanded upon knowledge gained from productions created since the 2003 version and collaborated with American Repertory Theater in Boston for a limited run in the Old Lincoln School, the site of another defunct school for boys. Following the success of the Boston version, Punchdrunk premiered the New York version in 2011, partnering with the New York–based Emursive Productions to reinvent a series of former Chelsea warehouses into the fictional hotel known as the McKittrick, referencing Hitchcock's *Vertigo*. The venue is located at 530 West 27th Street in New York City and was previously the site of several notable nightclubs, including Sound Factory (1989–1995), Twilo (1995–2001), and B.E.D. (2004–2007). Jonathan Hochwald, Arthur Karpati, and Randy Weiner founded Emursive in 2010 to produce immersive theater in extraordinary places; *SNM* was Emursive's first production.

11. Erik Piepenberg's article in the *New York Times* online includes an audio commentary by Punchdrunk's artistic directors, Felix Barrett and Maxine Doyle, who describe the scenographic realms of the production (2011).

12. The principles of contact improvisation include the democratization of gender roles, no leaders, and interchangeable partners; contact improvisation understood as a form in and of itself, requiring nothing more to exist as art; the orientation of the body can be challenged so there is no "front"; pathways are not predetermined and allowed to unfold over time and space; spatial exploration is encouraged; movement

and movement ideas flow through space and others; situations are created through action and response (adapted from Novack 1990:114–49).

13. Doyle uses the term *site-sensitivity* rather than *site-specificity* to describe the dramaturgical and choreographic design processes involved in creating the extensive and intricate scenography of Punchdrunk's work, including *SNM*. The space of the McKittrick was constructed (rather than adapted, as site-specific works often are) with the intention of involving spectators in worlds that provoke reaction to objects and actions while leaving them generally free to improvise their movement paths. Included within this site-sensitive design are multitudes of surfaces that offer both performers and audiences opportunities to climb and sit and otherwise make contact within the space.

14. Machon defines a "contract for participation" as "either explicitly or implicitly shared in order to allow full immersion in the world" (2013:278). The immersive practitioners she has interviewed speak of a "contract that is entered into between audience-participant and performer to ensure a safe (even if it *feels* dangerous) journey through the work" (2013:150, emphasis in original).

15. Murray coins the term *threshold object* and relates it to immersive events such as amusement park rides and video gaming. An amusement park ride is a threshold object that "carries you into the immersive world—and then back out again" while within video-gaming, it is typically a computer mouse or a game console joystick serving as the threshold object that "takes you in and leads you out of the experience" (1997:108; 2017:134).

16. The concept of *kinesphere*, developed by dance artist and theorist Rudolf Laban in *Choreutics*, is "the sphere around the body whose periphery can be reached by easily extending the limbs without stepping away from that place which is the point of support" (Laban and Ullman 1966:10). Laban acknowledges that "the kinesphere of . . . one will at times overlap with that of the other" (39). Peggy Hackney describes kinesphere as "the space that is mine" and "the space [the mover] effects" implying social and emotional notions of personal space (2004:243).

17. *Breath timing* can be described as non-verbal, sensed rhythms that are used by and between dancers to instigate and arrest movement.

18. Notable examples of immersive productions that productively expand the aesthetic boundaries of the form through representation of marginalized groups include the work of Lauren Ludwig and Monica Miklas, founders of the Los Angeles–based company Capital W; *K-POP* (2017, New York City), produced by Ars Nova, in association with Woodshed Collective and Ma-Yi Theater company; and *The Jungle*, a play by Joe Murphy and Joe Robertson depicting the stories of residents of the Calais refugee camp in France, based on their experiences running an interactive arts center in the encampment between 2015 and 2016.

19. Alston extends Zaiontz's argument for the ways in which audiences adopt a kind of presumptive intimacy by suggesting the term "presumptive entitlement" (Alston 2019).

20. Like the original version of *SNM*, the plot of the Shanghai production is a mashup of Shakespeare's *Macbeth* with Hitchcock's films, namely *Rebecca* and *Vertigo*, yet dramaturgically and choreographically adapted to include the Chinese folktale "The Legend of the White Snake," also known as "Madame White Snake."

21. See the following: "Immersive Theater catches on in China," ChinaDaily.com.cn, April 16, 2019, https://www.chinadaily.com.cn/a/201904/16/WS5cb548fea3104842260 b6761.html, as well as Rachel Cheung's reporting in the *South China Morning Post* (September 8, 2018), https://www.scmp.com/lifestyle/arts-culture/article/2163193/ chinese-audiences-novel-approach-immersive-theatre-mob. See Hannah Lund's interview with Zhang Chunyang, a Chinese producer whose immersive production of *Mythic Stories of Fanling Township* was presented in the city of Shenyang, located in Liaoning province, Northeast China, published in *Sixth Tone: Fresh Voices from Today's China* (December 11, 2019), https://www.sixthtone.com/news/1004943/enter-ghost-chinas-growing-obsession-with-immersive-plays. See Christopher House's review of the immersive production *Moulin Dream*, a bilingual immersive production integrating the storylines of *Moulin Rouge*, the classic Chinese novel *Dream of the Red Chamber* with fictionalized renderings of 1920s Shanghai, http://www.timeoutshanghai.com/ features/Blog-Stage/70928/Get-a-taste-of-1920s-Shanghai-at-this-new-immersive-theatre-show.html. For additional insight into the perspectives of several fans dedicated to the Shanghai production see Jin Qian, "The Sleep No More Superfan, Explained," in SmartShanghai.com (August 20, 2018), http://www.smartshanghai.com/articles/arts/ the-sleep-no-more-superfan-explained.

22. The fan comics of Toronto-based artist Melanie Hider (Hider and McCuskey 2013) are additional evidence of such extended audiencing creativity, as are the blog posts dedicated to *SNM* by best-selling novelist Erin Morgenstern.

23. See also Nield (2008) and Freshwater (2009), for further discussion of the ways in which some audiences react less than enthusiastically to such participatory experiences, including resisting and rejecting the parameters established to engage and potentially immerse them.

24. Biggin draws upon Matthew Reason's research into dual perception in young audiences when deconstructing the "theoretical binary between critical distance and immersion" (2017:102). In addition, Frieze has also theorized the relationship between immersion and critical distance, offering the term *resistant immersion*, by which he means an audience response that "acknowledges the dichotomous nature of maintaining the critical distance needed to make sense of a new and disorienting experience whilst surrendering to intimate engagement" (2016:5).

25. I was informed by the *SNM* company manager that information about the percentage of return visits by spectators could not be shared. However, I was told by members of the fandom that there is an "unofficial estimate" that approximately 25% of spectators return.

26. Information regarding fan experience was gathered from various blogs and interviews with spectators who posted on blogs and websites.

27. For a different yet related perspective of spectator investigation within theatrical events, including in immersive theater, see Frieze's proposal of "forensic aesthetics" (2019).

28. In my research, I have been able to locate some Tumblrs devoted to other immersive productions, including the productions by Third Rail Projects, but the fandoms that have formed around *SNM* are by far the largest and now function as an internationally linked community. More than one hundred thousand posts referencing the *SNM* production can be located on Instagram with the hashtags, #sleepnomore, #sleepnomorenyc, and #sleepnomoreshanghai.

29. Interestingly, the blogs also serve as evidence that the *SNM* fandom has become increasingly devoted to dance more broadly; fans create posts reflecting their attendance at dance performances other than *SNM*, as they support dancers currently in the production and those who have left the cast to dance with other companies and projects. In addition, fans have been generous contributors to online crowdfunding campaigns that current and former dancers have established in order to support independent performance and/or choreographic projects. Thus, it is possible to see how spectators are expanding their audiencing of dance beyond *SNM* as they attend other productions featuring dance.

Chapter 5

1. Theatre Bristol is a collective of producers that, as an Arts Council England National Portfolio Organization, works together with artists and producers to both commission and produce new work and to develop national and international exchange opportunities in the United Kingdom and elsewhere (see Theatre Bristol 2015).

2. Bluemouth inc. is now based both in Toronto and in Brooklyn, New York. Adams, Simic, and Windeyer are Canadian, while O'Connell, Reeves, and Pettrow are American. Adams, Reeves, and Windeyer live in Canada, while Simic, O'Connell, and Pettrow are based in New York.

3. Bluemouth inc.'s *Dance Marathon* performance history: multiple venues in Canada including the Harbourfront Centre, Toronto (2009); at the Cultural Olympia, part of the 2010 Winter Olympics in Vancouver; at the Harbourfront Performing Arts' World Stage Festival (2012); and in Halifax as part of the Magnetic North Festival (2014). In England, *DM* has been presented in London at part of the BITE and Dance Umbrella Festival (2011), at the Norfolk & Norwich Festival (2013), and at Mayfest in Bristol (2015). Other international venues that have presented *DM* include the MidSummer Festival of the Senses 2009 (Cork, Ireland), Traverse @ Lyceum Rehearsal Room, Edinburgh Fringe Festival 2011 (Scotland), the Dance Massive Festival 2011 in Melbourne and the Ten Days on the Island Festival 2011 in Tasmania (Australia), the Incubator Arts Project's Other Forces Festival 2011 (New York City), and Tanztage Fabrik Festival 2015 (Potsdam, Germany).

4. O'Connell and Simic served as co-artistic directors of Radix Theatre for many years and Windeyer was a collaborating artist on several productions.

5. *The Canadian Encyclopedia* defines *collective creation* as "the technique of devising a play as a group, with or without the aid of playwright or dramaturge" (Filewod 2006).

6. Definitions are from *Oxford Dictionaries: English* (http://www.oxforddictionaries.com/definition/english/actuate; http://www.oxforddictionaries.com/definition/english-thesaurus/actuate).

7. In advance of every performance of *DM*, bluemouth inc. contacts members of the local dance community in which the production will be presented in order to recruit fifteen to twenty volunteers to perform as embedded dancers. The embedded dancers serve in various functions during performances, which will be detailed in this chapter.

8. Martin reproduces a quote attributed to dance marathon promoter Leo Seltzer from 1934: "The contestant is exalted to the position of combination gladiator and night-club entertainer" (40).

9. Martin describes types of elimination contests that were implemented as races; one such elimination consisted of blindfolding contestants and forcing them to run in dimly lit spaces, while another consisted of taping two contestants together and having them sprint through the dance hall (55).

10. Two other groups perform in *DM*; there are "guest" artists, among them local break-dancers, recruited for a surprise interlude two-thirds of the way through the performance, as well as local celebrities or regional artists who wish to publicize their own productions through exposure in *DM*. Bluemouth inc.'s inclusion of guests echo how promoters of the 1920s and 1930s would schedule guest artists to draw crowds to the marathon, some of which lasted as long as ninety days. When *DM* is presented at festivals, artists hoping to promote their own productions are eager to make cameo appearances. These individuals enhance the choreographic and theatrical content of the performance. The other group of performers are professional musicians hired by Windeyer and Adams to be the Dance Marathon band in each city where *DM* is presented, contributing to the sonic environment that supports the dancing. Such efforts by bluemouth inc. reveal the extent to which they engage in community outreach.

11. For a thorough discussion of deception and betrayal in *DM*, see Barton 2009a.

12. Regarding access for individuals using assistive devices, Adams adds that they've had audience members participate while using a wheelchair, adding, "[o]ften the venue is more of a hindrance than the show itself. For the most part, they are able to participate without any challenges" (email correspondence with author 2016).

13. See Appendix A for lyrics to songs composed by bluemouth inc.'s *DM*.

14. Rules 3 and 5 are particularly important for maintaining a safe space for all audiences to participate in *DM*, including children under eighteen, who are welcome to participate when in the presence of a parent or guardian.

15. Audience members are still partnered with the stranger when the first derby occurs in *DM*.

16. For more on the styles of dance the audience explores, and the complete lyrics of "The History of Dance," see Appendix A.

17. A snowball is a swing dance variation that accumulates dancers through a structure of call and response. Starting with a circle of people, one designated dancer begins

to dance improvisationally at the center. When the bandleader calls "snowball," the dancer in the center responds by pulling in a partner from the circle. In the next round, the two dancers now in the center pull in two more, and the process continues everyone is dancing.

18. During two *DM* performances I experienced, I witnessed Simic perform Ramona with a high level of awareness of gender variance in the audience when selecting individuals to be part of the group of "five mans" who would perform the "Iggy Pop-Off." Such inclusion supports bluemouth inc.'s mission of respecting and representing different voices during the creation and performance of its work.

19. The pogo is a dance style that originated in the hard-core punk music scene of the United States in the late 1970s. Moshing and slam dancing developed in the punk scene in the early 1980s.

20. The PlasmaCar is a trademarked product of PlaSmart, a Canadian-based distributor of educational toys for children.

21. Claire Bishop's theory of "delegated performance" might hold that the embedded dancers, and possibly the audiences of *DM*, are a form of outsourced labor. Bishop defines *delegated performance* as "the act of hiring nonprofessionals or specialists in other fields to undertake the job of being present and performing at a particular time and a particular place on behalf of the artist, and following his or her instructions" (2012:91). These terms have political and economic implications for labor and representation that are not the focus of this chapter. In addition, I note that the Berlin-based artist collective Gob Squad uses what codirector Nina Tecklenburg describes as "remote-acting" technique—audiences, wearing headphones, are instructed how to perform actions during performances and thus "become the performers' messengers, prosthesis-like extensions of ourselves and our improvisations. . . . The participants become so preoccupied that they have no time to fully consider the meaning and style of their actions and words. As a result, their actions look astonishingly authentic" (Tecklenburg and Carter 2012:29). I focus on my concept of *actuating*, which I understand as different from these two terms, as I feel it suggests a kind of empowerment of audiences and represents an altogether different example of how artists such as bluemouth inc. are further complicating notions of participation in live performance.

22. As Stephen O'Connell recounts: "I remember a moment during *Dance Marathon* in Cork, Ireland, when a contact improv dancer unknowingly decided to test the democracy of the show by taking the floor during the 'Rain' section. I remember thinking at the time—I am not really enjoying what he is doing—and wanted to shut him down, but realized there was little I could do because we had invited the audience to insert themselves into the piece. We obviously determined the structure of the show and curated the content, but it was the transparency and malleability of what we had constructed that allowed for moments like that to occur. I bring up that moment because I believe it illustrates how the degree of co-authorship in *DM* is greater than most of our other shows. In *Dance Marathon*, the audience often surprises us with wonderful, unexpected moments, like a little girl singing a song during one of the spotlight moments and we feel like we designed it that way. However, other times someone does something that we don't want, like a young woman dancing around

Little Stevie with a silk scarf during the 'Yellow Bike' scene and we can't control it" (email correspondence with author 2016).

23. After participating as a registered contestant in the May 19 performance of *DM* presented during Mayfest Bristol 2015, I left the venue immediately after the winners were announced and waited outside in the courtyard, where I knew audience members would be exiting. As they arrived in the courtyard, I asked if they were willing to share their thoughts about participating in the production. I explained to each person whom I approached that his or her contributions were anonymous and that responses would be recorded via voice memo and incorporated into a word cloud in my dissertation. Each person was asked to give me a sound bite of 140 characters, or more, if the person wished. Given the nature of the event, I anticipated it would not be possible to conduct a proper interview with consent forms and other permissions, because of my limited time with the individuals exiting the venue. After their three hours participating in *DM*, I also assumed that audience members were interested in getting on with their evening, whether that meant moving on to a pub to extend their participation through conversations or going directly home to rest. However, I found that many were excited about what they had just experienced and very willing to share their perceptions. No one refused my request, and, in fact, several spoke at length, sharing their experiences in detail. One of the audience participants specifically used the phrase "no 'us and them' divide" and further clarified this by identifying the audience as the "us" and the bluemouth inc. performers as the "them." This tactic of gathering off-the-cuff reactions proved successful in the ways I had hoped, which was to capture the immediate reflections of participants. I transcribed the recordings verbatim into a document and put the document through an online word cloud generator, which produced a representation of responses (see Appendix B).

Chapter 6

1. Some practitioners, including Maxine Doyle and Felix Barrett, among others, have pushed against the term *immersive theater* being applied to their work. Doyle has stated outright her belief that there is neither "immersive theater" nor "immersive dance" but rather just productions that involve, "performers who are brave, strong, mature, professional, skilled, sensitive, mindful, and talented" (Doyle 2018). The frustration felt by artists is understandable; the concept of immersion has been co-opted as a marketing language; as much as the term now serves as a "floating signifier" as per Alston, it is also a label that resonates with a certain kind of influential power used strategically to generate revenue when applied to a huge range of products, experiences, and events (Alston 2019).

2. In January 2018, three organizations—Adventure Design Group, Epic Immersive, and No Proscenium—described as "the leading voices in California's burgeoning immersive community" co-produced what they identified as the first Immersive Design Summit (IDS) in San Francisco, California. In promoting this first summit, these entities proclaimed immersive as "a discipline" as well as "a transformative approach

to storytelling" that "connects with audiences at a visceral level." According to the website, the aim of the Immersive Design Summit is to bring together "the most innovative creators and thinkers in the emerging experiential and immersive fields" in a discussion about "the state of the immersive art, and the future of this rapidly growing industry." See https://immersivedesignsummit.com/2018.html and https://immersivedesignsummit.com.

3. Program Schedule, San Francisco Immersive Design Summit 2019.

4. The report is authored by Ricky Brigante, founder and former editor of *Inside the Magic*, a news source for the themed entertainment industry and edited by Noah Nelson, founder of No Proscenium: The Guide to Everything Immersive, an online publication and podcast about the immersive arts and entertainment industry. The report states that the Immersive Entertainment Industry "is defined by the sum of its commercial and artistic successes, technological advancements, and social and cultural impacts" (22).

5. See Brigante 2019 and Nelson 2018.

6. It is important to note that some of the data and statistical evidence that comprise this report are drawn from online sources as well as speculation by the writer and editor, which makes verification of facts difficult. Some of the links included in the bibliography were defunct at the time of this writing.

References

Abercrombie, Nicholas, and Brian Longhurst. 1998. *Audiences: A Sociological Theory of Performance and Imagination*. Los Angeles: Sage.

"About Contact Improvisation (CI)." 2009. *Contact Quarterly: Dance and Improvisation Journal*. http://www.contactquarterly.com/contact-improvisation/about/index.php.

Abrams, Joshua. 2003. "Ethics of the Witness: The Participatory Dances of Cie Felix Ruckert." In *Audience Participation: Essays on Inclusion in Performance*, edited by Susan Kattwinkel, 1–14. Westport, CT: Praeger.

Adams, Ciara. 2014. Interview by Julia M. Ritter, June 27.

Adventure Design Group. http://www.adventuredesigngroup.com.

Allsopp, Ric, and André Lepecki. 2008. "Editorial: On Choreography." *Performance Research: A Journal of the Performing Arts* 13 (1): 1–6.

Alston, Adam. 2013. "Audience Participation and Neoliberal Value: Risk, Agency and Responsibility in Immersive Theatre." *Performance Research: A Journal of the Performing Arts* 18 (2): 128–138.

Alston, Adam. 2016. *Beyond Immersive Theatre: Aesthetics, Politics and Productive Participation*. London: Palgrave Macmillan.

Alston, Adam. 2019. "Safety, Risk and Speculation in the Immersive Industry." *Contemporary Theatre Review* 29 (3).

Anderson, Dee Anne. 2017. Interview with author. New York, January 11.

Anderson, Jack. 1986. *Ballet & Modern Dance: A Concise History*. Princeton, NJ: Princeton Book Company.

Arfman. 2016. Skype interview with author, June 14.

Artaud, Antonin. 2014. "Theater and Cruelty." In *The Twentieth-Century Performance Reader*, 3rd ed., edited by Teresa Brayshaw and Noel Witts, 31–34. London: Routledge.

Babbage, F. H. 2016. "Active Audiences: Spectatorship as Research Practice." *Studies in Theatre and Performance* 36 (1): 48–51.

Balzer, David. 2015. *Curationism: How Curating Took Over the Art World and Everything Else*. London: Pluto Press.

Barba, Eugenio. 2010. *On Directing and Dramaturgy: Burning the house*. Translated by Judy Barba. London and New York: Routledge.

Barrett, Felix. 2015a. Telephone interview with author, September 7.

Barrett, Felix. 2015b. "Felix Barrett on Sleep No More." Interview at AOL Headquarters in New York City for AOL Build Series. YouTube. Published July 28, 2015. Accessed November 11, 2017. https://www.youtube.com/watch?v=CKxtDQl5hfQ&list=PLYki5 QKfxW8eDZrryc4umX2aAgKm4xne9&index=7&t=0s.

Barthes, Roland. 1978. *Image-Music-Text*. New York: Macmillan.

Barton, Bruce. 2009a. "Paradox as Process: Intermedial Anxiety and the Betrayals of Intimacy." *Theatre Journal* 61 (4): 575–601. http://www.jstor.org/stable/40660553.

Barton, Bruce. 2009b. "Stop Looking at Your Feet." *Performance Research* 14 (3): 13–25.

Bastian, H.C. 1897. "The Muscle Sense: Its Nature and Cortical localisation." *Brain* 10: 1–137.

behindawhitemask. 2012. "The Big List of *Sleep No More* Links & Blogs." *Behind a White Mask* (blog). Accessed September 19, 2014. https://behindawhitemask.tumblr.com/.

Bennett, Melanie. 2010. "So They Think I Can Dance: A Reflection on Bluemouth Inc.'s *Dance Marathon.*" *Canadian Theatre Review* 141: 96–99.

Bennett, Susan. 1997. *Theatre Audiences: A Theory of Production and Reception.* 2nd ed. London: Routledge.

Behrndt, Synne K. 2010. "Dance, Dramaturgy and Dramaturgical Thinking." *Contemporary Theatre Review* 20 (2): 185–196.

The Bessies. 2013. "Winners of the New York Dance and Performance Awards—the Bessies." *Dance Enthusiast*, October 8. http://www.dance-enthusiast.com/features/view/Winners-of-the-New-York-Dance-And-Performance-Awards-The-Bessies-2013-10-08.

Biggin, Rose. 2017. *Immersive Theatre and Audience Experience: Space, Game and Story in the Work of Punchdrunk.* London: Palgrave Macmillan.

Billingham, Michael. 2009. "It Felt Like a Kiss." Review in theguardian.com. Culture, July 2. https://www.theguardian.com/culture/2009/jul/03/manchester-international-festival.

Bishop, Claire. 2006. "Introduction." In *Participation: Documents of Contemporary Art*, edited by Claire Bishop, 10–17. Whitechapel: Documents of Contemporary Art. Cambridge, MA: MIT Press.

Bishop, Claire. 2012. "Delegated Performance: Outsourcing Authenticity." *October* 140 (Spring): 91–112.

bluemouth inc. 2009. "Production Notes and Overview." In *Worldstage @ Harbourfront Centre*, 3. http://old.harbourfrontcentre.com/worldstagemedia/pdf/Press%20Kit%20-%20bluemouth%20inc%20-%20dance%20marathon_revised.pdf.

bluemouth inc. 2015a. "*Dance Marathon* Script." Collection of the author.

bluemouth inc. 2015b. "Mission/Mandate." Accessed March 5. http://www.bluemouthinc.com/about/missionmandate.

bluemouth inc. 2016. Email correspondence. Ciara Adams, Stephen O'Connell, Sabrina Reeves, Lucy Simic, and Richard Windeyer with author Julia M. Ritter, April 7–22. Transcript.

Boenisch, Peter. 2014. "Acts of Spectating: The Dramaturgy of Audience's Experience in Contemporary Theatre." In *New Dramaturgy: International Perspectives on Theory and Practice*, edited by Katalin Trencsényi and Bernadette Cochrane, 225–241. London: Bloomsbury.

Bolognino, Justin. "All the World is a Stage." Panel presentation, Future of Storytelling Festival, October 8, 2017, Snug Harbor Cultural Center, Staten Island, New York.

Bolognino, Justin. 2017. Interview with Julia M. Ritter, October 18. Transcript.

Bowditch, Rachel, Jeff Casazza, and Annette Thornton. 2018. *Physical Dramaturgy: Perspectives from the Field.* London: Routledge.

Brantley, Ben. 2012. "Lewis Carroll Is in a Hospital." *New York Times*, November 30. http://www.nytimes.com/2012/12/01/theater/reviews/then-she-fell-at-greenpoint-hospital-in-brooklyn.html?_r=1.

Breitwieser, Sabine. 2016. "Choreography." In *In Terms of Performance*, edited by Shannon Jackson and Paula Marincola. Brooklyn Academy of Music, Brooklyn, New York. Produced by The Pew Center for Arts & Heritage, Philadelphia, PA and the Arts Research Center, University of California, Berkeley. http://intermsofperformance.site/keywords/choreography/sabine-breitwieser.

Brigante, Ricky. 2019. "Interactive, Intimate, Experiential: The Impact of Immersive Design." Editor Noah Nelson, with additional contributions by Kathryn Yu and Rachel Stoll. San Francisco: Immersive Design Summit.

Brockis, Gemma. 2019. Interview with Julia M. Ritter, May 21. Transcript.

Brown, Alan S., and Jennifer L. Novak-Leonard. In partnership with Shelley Gilbride. 2011. *Getting In on the Act: How Arts Groups Are Creating Opportunities for Active Participation*. Commissioned by the James Irvine Foundation, conducted by WolfBrown, October.

Brown, Frances. 2014. Interview with Julia M. Ritter, July 2. Transcript.

Bushman, Jay. 2019. Interview with Julia M. Ritter, July 11. Transcript.

Carena, Elizabeth. 2014. "Passing the Hat." Elizabeth Carena, December 19. http://elizabethcarena.tumblr.com/search/Passing+the+hat.

Carlson, Marvin. 2015. "Postdramatic Theatre and Postdramatic Performance." *Revista Brasileira de Estudos da Presença: Brazilian Journal on Presence Studies* 5 (3): 577–595. http://www.seer.ufrgs.br/presenca.

Carr, Cynthia. 1993. *On Edge: Performance at the End of the Twentieth Century*. Hanover, New Hampshire: Wesleyan University Press.

Charmaz, Kathy. 2006. *Constructing Grounded Theory: A Practical Guide through Qualitative Analysis*. Thousand Oaks, CA: Sage.

Cohen, Matthew Issac. 2010. *Performing Otherness: Java and Bali on International Stages 1905-1952*. Basingstoke, UK: Palgrave Macmillan.

Cohen, Selma Jeanne. 1974. *Dance as a Theatre Art: Source Readings in Dance History from 1581 to the Present*. Princeton, NJ: Princeton Book Company.

Conroy, Colette. 2010. *Theater & The Body*. London: Palgrave Macmillan.

Couldry, Nick. 2005. "The Extended Audience: Scanning the Horizon." In *Media Audiences*, edited by Marie Gillespie, 183–222. Maidenhead: Open University Press.

Cousin, Glynnis. 2010. "Neither Teacher-Centered nor Student-Centered: Threshold Concepts and Research Partnerships." *Journal of Learning Development in Higher Education* 2: 1–9.

Cummings, Scott T. 2013. *María Irene Fornés: Routledge Modern and Contemporary Dramatists*. Oxon, UK: Routledge.

Dannatt, Adrian. 1989. "YOU-The City." Review in the *Sunday Times*. July 2.

Danto, Arthur C. 1981. *The Transfiguration of the Commonplace: A Philosophy of Art*. Cambridge, Massachusetts: Harvard University Press.

Denton, Martin. 2011. "Dance Marathon." Review in nytheatre.com. Indie Theatre Now, January 6. http://www.nytheatre.com/Review/martin-denton-2011-1-6-dance-marathon.

Doyle, Maxine. 2013. Interview with Julia M. Ritter, October 10. Transcript.

Doyle, Maxine. 2017. Interview with Julia M. Ritter, September 29. Transcript.

Doyle, Maxine. 2018. Winter Intensive for BFA Dance majors. Dance Department, Mason Gross School of the Arts at Rutgers, The State University of New Jersey. January 8–19.

Doyle, Maxine, Conor Doyle, Tony Bordonaro, and Tori Sparks. 2012. "Rutgers University *Sleep No More* Presentation." Rutgers University, New Brunswick, NJ, March 7. Transcript.

Edwards, Micah. 2014. Interview with Julia M. Ritter, May 20. Transcript.

Eichhorn, Nancy. 2016. "The Psychopathology of Disembodiment and Reconnection through Enactment: A Conversation with Maxine Sheets-Johnstone, PhD." *Somatic Psychotherapy Today* 6 (1): 98–101.

Ellis, Sarah Taylor, 2013. "Off-Broadway Theater Review: THEN SHE FELL (Third Rail Projects at St. John's in Brooklyn)." Stage and Cinema, March 26. http://www.stageandcinema.com/2013/03/26/then-she-fell/#sthash.5jtosxQw.dpuf.

Elswit, Kate. 2018. *Theater & Dance*. London: Palgrave Macmillan.

Epic Immersive. https://www.epicimmersive.com/home.html.

Fensham, Rachel. 2009. *To Watch Theatre: Essays on Corporeality*. Brussels, Belgium: P.I.E. Peter Lang.

Fensham, Rachel. 2012. "Postdramatic Spectatorship: Participate or Else." In *Critical Stages/Scènes Critiques, IATC webjournal/Revue web de i'AICT*, no 7. http://www.critical-stages.org/7/postdramatic-spectatorship-participate-or-else/.

Fensham, Rachel. 2014. "DRJ Review Essay–*Choreographing Empathy: Kinesthesia in Performance and Kinesthetic Empathy in Creative and Cultural Practices*." *Dance Research Journal* 46 (2): 97–104.

Fensham, Rachel. 2016. "Affective Spectatorship: Watching Theatre and the Study of Affect." In *Unfolding Spectatorship: Shifting Political, Ethical and Intermedial Positions*, edited by Christel Stalpaert, Katharina Pewny, Jeroen Coppens and Pieter Vermeulen, 39–60. Gent: Academia Press.

Filewod, Alan. 2006. "Collective Creation." *The Canadian Encyclopedia*, February 7. Last edited April 3, 2015. http://www.thecanadianencyclopedia.ca/en/article/collective-creation/.

Fisher, Eran. 2015. "'You Media': Audiencing as Marketing in Social Media." *Media, Culture & Society* 37 (1): 50–67. Accessed June 28, 2016. http://journals.sagepub.com/doi/10.1177/0163443714549088.

Fiske, John. 1992. "Audiencing: A Cultural Studies Approach to Watching Television." *Poetics* 21 (4): 345–359.

Forjindam, Fri. 2019. "Disruptive Alchemy for an Immersive Future." Presentation at the 2019 Immersive Design Summit, San Francisco, California. February 22, 2019. Available at https://www.youtube.com/watch?v=Gimorufn6NQ&list=PLYki5QKfxW8feOTthAkWrGfBYNWVnPeR2&index=3&t=737s.

Forsythe, William, and Gerald Siegmund. 2001. "La pensée chorégraphique. Un entretien de William Forsythe réalisé par Gerald Sigmund." In *Ballett International/Tanz Aktuell*, numéro annuel 2001, Berlin, Friedrich Verlag.

Fortune, Bella. 2015. "Mayfest: *Dance Marathon* by bluemouth inc." Review. *Writing in Residence* (blog), May 20. http://www.theatrebristolwriters.net/Mayfest-Dance-Marathon-by-Bluemouth-inc.

Foster, Susan Leigh. 1986. *Reading Dancing: Bodies and Subjects in Contemporary American Dance*. Los Angeles: University of California Press.

Foster, Susan Leigh. 2003. "Taken by Surprise: Improvisation in Body and Mind." In *Taken by Surprise: A Dance Improvisation Reader*, edited by Ann Cooper Albright and David Gere, 3–10. Middletown, CT: Wesleyan University Press.

Foster, Susan Leigh. 2008. "Movement's Contagion: The Kinesthetic Impact of Performance." *The Cambridge Companion to Performance Studies*, edited by Tracy C. Davis, 46–59. Cambridge, UK: Cambridge University Press.

Foster, Susan Leigh. 2009. "Choreographies and Choreographers." In *Worlding Dance*, edited by Susan Leigh Foster, 98–118. London: Palgrave Macmillan.

Foster, Susan Leigh. 2011. *Choreographing Empathy: Kinesthesia in Performance*. London: Routledge.

Foster, Susan Leigh. 2016. "Choreography." In *In Terms of Performance*, edited by Shannon Jackson and Paula Marincola. Brooklyn Academy of Music, Brooklyn, New York. Produced by The Pew Center for Arts & Heritage, Philadelphia, PA and the Arts Research Center, University of California, Berkeley. http://intermsofperformance. site/keywords/choreography/susan-leigh-foster.

Franko, Mark. 1995. *Dancing Modernism/Performing Politics*. Bloomington: Indiana University Press.

Franko, Mark. 2000. "The Readymade as Movement: Cunningham, Duchamp, and Nam June Paik's Two Merces." *Anthropology and Aesthetics* 38: 211–219.

Franko, Mark. 2002. *The Work of Dance: Labor, Movement and Identity in the 1930s*. Middletown, CT: Wesleyan University Press.

Franko, Mark. 2011. "Writing for the Body: Notation, Reconstruction, and Reinvention in Dance." *Common Knowledge* 17 (2): 321–334.

Freshwater, Helen. 2009. *Theatre & Audience*. London: Palgrave Macmillan.

Friedman, Sam. 2011. "Target: Audience." *Fest*, July 27. https://www.festmag.co.uk/archive/2011/100123-target_audience.

Frieze, James. 2016. "Reframing Immersive Performance: The Politics and Pragmatics of Participatory Performance." In *Reframing Immersive Performance: The Politics and Pragmatics of Participatory Performance*, edited by James Frieze, 1–26. London: Palgrave Macmillan.

Frieze, James. 2019. *Theatrical Performance and the Forensic Turn*. London: Routledge.

Fujishima, Kenji. 2019. "Then She Fell to Celebrate 4000th Performance on July 5." *TheaterMania.com. Theater News*. Off Broadway Section. July 1, 2019. https://www. theatermania.com/off-broadway/news/then-she-fell-4000th-performance_89191. html?fbclid=IwAR2RfgswTUJLQXI4npjUweAs19xWh8zajF8WUqVfmTyEPij4IoYn_cE1Hz0.

García-Romero, Anne. 2016. *The Fornes Frame: Contemporary Latina Playwrights and the Legacy of Maria Irene Fornes*. Tuscon: University of Arizona Press.

Gardner, Howard. 1983. *Frames of Mind: The Theory of Multiple Intelligences*. Updated ed. New York: Perseus Books. First published 2011.

Garner, Stanton B., Jr. 2002. "Urban Landscapes, Theatrical Encounters: Staging the City." In *Land/Scape/Theater*, edited by Elinor Fuchs and Una Chaudhuri, 94–118. Ann Arbor: University of Michigan Press.

Garner, Stanton B., Jr. 2018. *Kinesthetic Spectatorship in the Theatre: Phenomenology, Cognition, Movement*. Cognitive Studies in Literature and Performance. Cham, Switzerland: Palgrave Macmillan.

Gee, James Paul. 2008. "Video Games and Embodiment." *Games and Culture* 3 (3–4): 253–263.

George-Graves, Nadine. 2015. "Magnetic Fields: Too Dance for Theater, Too Theater for Dance." In *The Oxford Handbook of Dance and Theater*, edited by Nadine George-Graves, 1–18. New York, London: Oxford University Press.

Gilbride, Shelley. 2011. "Getting In on the Act: Activating in the Arts." Dancers Group, December 1. http://dancersgroup.org/2011/12/getting-in-on-the-act-activating-the-arts/.

Gilpin, Heidi. 1997. "Shaping Critical Spaces: Issues in the Dramaturgy of Movement Performance." In *Dramaturgy in American Theater: A Source Book*, edited by Susan Jonas, Geoff Proehl, and Michael Lupu, 83–87. Orlando, FL: Harcourt Brace College.

Groys, Boris. 2008. "A Genealogy of Participatory Art." In *The Art of Participation: 1950 to Now*, edited by Rudolf Frieling, 18–31. New York: Thames & Hudson.

Hackney, Peggy. 2004. *Making Connections: Total Body Integration through Bartenieff Fundamentals*. London: Routledge.

Harkness, Hector. "All the World is a Stage." Panel presentation, Future of Storytelling Festival, October 8, 2017, Snug Harbor Cultural Center, Staten Island, New York.

Harvie, Jen. 2013. *Fair Play—Art, Performance and Neoliberalism*. Houndmills: Palgrave Macmillan.

Hayes, Gina Marie. 2014. Interview with Julia M. Ritter, July 1. Transcript.

Heck, Tim. 2014. Interview with Julia M. Ritter, June 30. Transcript.

Heddon, Deirdre, Helen Iball, and Rachel Zerihan. 2012. "Come Closer: Confessions of Intimate Spectators in One to One Performance." *Contemporary Theatre Review* 22 (1): 120–133.

Herman, David. 2005. "Storyworld." *Routledge Encyclopedia of Narrative Theory*, edited by David Herman, Manfred Jahn, and Marie-Laure Ryan, 569–570. Oxfordshire: Routledge.

Hewitt, Andrew. 2005. *Social Choreography: Ideology as Performance in Dance and Everyday Movement*. Durham, NC: Duke University Press.

Hider, Melanie. 2015. Interview with Julia M. Ritter, August 21. Transcript.

Hoggard, Liz. 2013. "Felix Barrett: the visionary who reinvented theatre." The Observer Profile in theguardian.com, July 13. https://www.theguardian.com/theobserver/2013/jul/14/felix-barrett-punchdrunk-theatre-stage.

Immersive Design Summit. 2018. https://immersivedesignsummit.com/2018.html.

Immersive Design Summit. 2019. https://immersivedesignsummit.com/.

ICA Magazine. Fall 2018. "William Forsythe: Choreographic Objects." Institute of Contemporary Art. Boston: Massachusetts, 6–7. https://www.icaboston.org/exhibitions/william-forsythe-choreographic-objects.

Jamieson, Amber. 2018. "Performers and Staffers at 'Sleep No More' Say Audience Members Have Sexually Assaulted Them." *Buzzfeed News*. February 6. Accessed April 5, 2018. https://www.buzzfeednews.com/article/amberjamieson/sleep-no-more.

Jenkins, Henry. 2006. *Convergence Culture: Where New and Old Media Collide*. New York: New York University Press.

Jenkins, Henry. 2009. "Confronting the Challenges of Participatory Culture: Media Education for the 21st Century." With Ravi Purushotma, Margaret Weigel, Katie Clinton and Alice J. Robison. The John D. and Catherine T. MacArthur Foundation Reports on Digital Media and Learning. Cambridge, MA: The MIT Press.

Jenkins, Henry. 2011. "Acafandom and Beyond: Week One, Part One (Anne Kustritz, Louisa Stein, and Sam Ford)." *Confessions of an Acafan*. Blog. June 13. http://henryjenkins.org/blog/2011/06/acafandom_and_beyond_week_one.html.

Jones, Amelia. 2012. "Foreword." *Kinesthetic Empathy in Creative and Cultural Practices*, edited by Dee Reynolds and Matthew Reason, 11–15. Bristol, United Kingdom: Intellect Books.

Kaprow, Allan. 1991. "On Reinventions of *Yard*." Allan Kaprow. http://allankaprow.com/about_reinvetion.html.

Kaprow, Allan, and Jeff Kelley. 2003. *Essays on the Blurring of Art and Life*. Exp. ed. Berkley: University of California Press.

Kattwinkel, Susan. 2003. *Audience Participation: Essays on Inclusion in Performance*. Westport, CT: Praeger.

Kelley, Jeff. 2004. *Childsplay: The Art of Allan Kaprow*. Berkeley: University of California Press.

Kerr, Ann-Marie. 2014. Interview with Julia M. Ritter, July 24. Transcript.

Kirsh, David. 2010. "Thinking with the Body." In *Proceedings of the 32nd Annual Conference of the Cognitive Science Society August*, edited by Stellan Ohlsson and Richard Catrambone, 2864–2869. Austin TX: Cognitive Science Society.

Kolesch, Doris. 2019. "Immersion and Spectatorship at the Interface of Theatre, Media Tech and Daily Life: An Introduction." In *Staging Spectators in Immersive Performances: Commit Yourself!*, edited by Doris Kolesch, Theresa Schutz and Sophie Nikoleit, 1–18. London: Routledge.

Korish, David. 2002. "The Mud and the Wind: An Inquiry into Dramaturgy." *New Theatre Quarterly: NTQ* 18 (71): 284–289.

Kourlas, Gia. 2011. "Sleep No More but Move Nonstop." *The New York Times*. Dance Section. September 6, 2011. https://www.nytimes.com/2011/09/07/arts/dance/sleep-no-more-is-theater-embedded-with-dancers.html.

Laban/Bartenieff Institute of Movement Studies (LIMS). 2009. "About LIMS|Irmgard Bartenieff." limsonline.org. Accessed December 20, 2016. www.limsonline.org/about-lims-irmgard-bartenieff.

Laban, Rudolf, and Lisa Ullmann, eds. 1966. *Choreutics*. London: MacDonald and Evans.

Laermans, Rudi. 2012. "Being in Common: Theorizing Artistic Collaboration." *Performance Research: A Journal of the Performing Arts* 17 (6): 94–102.

Lam, Tina. 2016. Skype interview with author, June 10.

Laura. 2014. Blog post. *drinkthehalo*, September 29. Accessed October 15, 2016. http://drinkthehalo.tumblr.com/post/98658350173/last-night-at-the-late-show-i-did-the-usual.

Laura. 2015a. Blog post. *drinkthehalo*, March 13. Accessed October 27, 2016. http://drinkthehalo.tumblr.com/post/113512384718/the-late-show-tonight-will-be-my-100th-visit-to.

Laura. 2015b. Blog post. *drinkthehalo*, November 23. Accessed November 7, 2016. http://drinkthehalo.tumblr.com/post/133792463838/boy-witch-is-a-difficult-character-to-get-right.

Laura. 2016. Blog post. *drinkthehalo*, September 1. Accessed November 7, 2016. http://drinkthehalo.tumblr.com/post/149790211388/i-havent-been-writing-about-the-show-as-much.

Laura. 2017. Interview with author. New York, January 11.

Lecoq, Jacques. (1987) 2006. *Theatre of Movement and Gesture*. First published in French as *Le Théâtre du Geste*. Paris: Bordas, 1987. English edition, London: Routledge.

Leder, Drew. 1990. *The Absent Body*. Chicago and London: University of Chicago Press.

Lehmann, Hans-Thies. 2006. *Postdramatic Theatre*. Translated by Karen Jürs-Munby. Oxon, UK: Routledge.

LeNoir, Nina. 2003. "The Audience in Cyberspace: Audience-Performer Interactivity in Online Performances." In *Audience Participation: Essays on Inclusion in Performance*, edited by Susan Kattwinkel, 115–132. Westport, CT: Praeger.

Lepecki, André. 2006. *Exhausting Dance: Performance and the Politics of Movement*. New York: Routledge.

Lepecki, André. 2007. "Choreography as Apparatus of Capture." *TDR/The Drama Review* 51 (2): 119–123.

Lepecki, André. 2012. "Introduction: Dance as a Practice of Contemporaneity." In *Dance*, edited by André Lepecki, 14–23. Cambridge, MA: The MIT Press.

Lepecki, André. 2016. *Singularities: Dance in the Age of Performance*. Oxon, UK: Routledge.

Lindsey. 2017. Interview with Julia M. Ritter, May 20. Transcript.

Lu, Zhihao. 2017. Interview with Julia M. Ritter, October 9. Transcript.

Machon, Josephine. 2009. *(Syn)aesthetics: Redefining Visceral Performance*. London: Palgrave Macmillan.

Machon, Josephine. 2013. *Immersive Theatres: Intimacy and Immediacy in Contemporary Performance*. London: Palgrave Macmillan.

Machon, Josephine. 2016. "On Being Immersed: The Pleasure of Being: Washing, Feeding, Holding." In *Reframing Immersive Performance: The Politics and Pragmatics of Participatory Performance*, edited by James Frieze, 29–42. London: Palgrave Macmillan.

Manning, Erin. 2012. *Always More Than One: Individuation's Dance*. Durham and London: Duke University Press.

Marinetti, Filippo Tommaso. 2006. *Critical Writings: New Edition*. Translated by Doug Thompson. Edited by Gunter Berghaus. New York: Farrar, Straus and Giroux.

Martin, Carol J. 1994. *Dance Marathons: Performing American Culture of the 1920s and 1930s*. Jackson: University Press of Mississippi.

Martin, John. 1933. *The Modern Dance*. New York: A. S. Barnes.

Martin, John. 1936. *America Dancing*. New York: Dodge.

Martin, John. 1939. *Introduction to the Dance*. New York: W. W. Norton.

Martin, John. 1946. *The Dance: The Story of the Dance Told in Pictures and Text*. New York: Tudor.

Martin, Raphael. 2015. Interview with Julia M. Ritter February 20. Transcript.

Massumi, Brian. 2015a. "Preface." In *The Politics of Affect*. Cambridge, UK: Polity Press. vii–xvi.

Massumi, Brian. 2015b. "Ideology and Escape: Interview by Yubraj Aryal." In *The Politics of Affect*. Cambridge, UK: Polity Press. 83–111.

Mcauley, Gay. 2008. "Not Magic but Work: Rehearsal and the Production of Meaning." *Theatre Research International* 33: 276–288. doi:10.1017/S0307883308003970.

McConachie, Bruce. 2008. *Engaging Audiences: A Cognitive Approach to Spectating in the Theatre*. New York: Palgrave Macmillan.

McConachie, Bruce, Tobin Nellhaus, Carol Fisher Sonrgenfrei, and Tamara Underiner. 2016. *Theatre Histories: An Introduction*. 3rd ed. Tobin Nellhaus, gen. ed. New York: Routledge.

McCoy, Horace. 1935. *They Shoot Horses, Don't They?* London: Arthur Barker.

McFee, Graham. 2011. *The Philosophical Aesthetics of Dance: Identity, Performance and Understanding*. Hampshire: Dance Books, Ltd.

McFee, Graham. 2013. "'Admirable legs'; or, the dancer's importance for the dance." In *Thinking Through Dance: The Philosophy of Dance Performance and Practices*, edited by Anna Pakes. Jenny Bunker, and Bonnie Rowell, 22–45. Hampshire: Dance Books, Ltd.

McGowan, Margaret M. 2008. *Dance in the Renaissance: European Fashion, French Obsession*. New Haven, CT: Yale University Press.

McKinney, Joslin. 2012. "Empathy and Exchange: Audience Experiences of Scenography." In *Kinesthetic Empathy in Creative and Cultural Practices*, edited by Dee Reynolds and Matthew Reason, 219–236. Bristol, United Kingdom: Intellect Books.

Merwin, Ted. 1998. "Loïe Fuller's Influence on F. T. Marinetti's Futurist Dance." *Dance Chronicle* 21 (1): 73–92.

Meyer, Jan, and Ray Land. 2010. "Threshold Concepts and Troublesome Knowledge: Linkages to Ways of thinking and Practising within the Disciplines." *Enhancing Teaching-Learning Environments Project* 4: 1–12.

Miller, Kiri. 2017. *Playable Bodies: Dance Games and Intimate Media*. New York, London: Oxford University Press.

Mitra, Royona. 2016. "Decolonizing Immersion." *Performance Research: A Journal of the Performing Arts* 21 (5): 89–100.

Morgenstern, Erin. 2009. Blog. October 14. Accessed June 12, 2013. http://erinmorgenstern.com/tag/sleep-no-more/.

Morin, Rebekah. 2014. Interview with Julia M. Ritter, June 16. Transcript.

Morris, Jon. 2017. Interview with Julia M. Ritter, October 18. Transcript.

Morris, Zach. 2014. Interview with Julia M. Ritter, May 9. Transcript.

Mulvey, Laura. 1975. "Visual Pleasure and Narrative Cinema." *Screen* 16 (3): 6–18.

Murphy, Maiya. 2015. "Fleshing Out: Physical Theater, Postmodern Dance and Som[e] agency." In *The Oxford Handbook of Dance and Theater*, edited by Nadine George-Graves, 125–147. Oxford: Oxford University Press.

Murray, Janet H. (1997) 2017. *Hamlet on the Holodeck: The Future of Narrative in Cyberspace*. Updated edition, Cambridge and London: The MIT Press.

Murray, Janet H. 2019. Interview with Julia M. Ritter. March 8. Transcript.

Murray, Sarah J. 2014. Interview with Julia M. Ritter, October 30. Transcript.

Murray, Simon and John Keefe. 2007. *Physical Theatres: A Critical Introduction*. London, New York: Routledge.

Nachbar, Martin, and Jeroen Peeters. 2011. "Physical Dramaturgy-Backtracking." *Sarma: Laboratory for Discursive Practices and Expanded Publication* (blog), http://sarma.be/pages/Physical_dramaturgy_-_Backtracking.

Nelson, Noah. 2018. "Everything Immersive This Year—2018." *No Proscenium* (blog). https://noproscenium.com/everything-immersive-this-year-2018-659acccb736b.

Nelson, Noah. 2019. "Those That Play: Notes on Building the Immersive Audience. Finding a New Paradigm on Old Paths." *No Proscenium* (blog). September 16. Accessed September 18, 2019. https://noproscenium.com/those-who-play-notes-on-building-the-immersive-audience-53d973b959f5.

Nelson, Steve. 1989. "Redecorating the Fourth Wall: Environmental Theatre Today." *TDR/ The Drama Review* 33 (3): 72–94.

Nield, Sophie. 2008. "The Rise of the Character Named Spectator." *Contemporary Theatre Review* 18 (4): 531–544.

Nielsen-Pincus, Marissa. 2014. Interview with Julia M. Ritter, June 16. Transcript.

Noakes, Katy. 2015. Interview with Julia M. Ritter June 5. Transcript.

Noland, Carrie. 2009. *Agency & Embodiment: Performing Gestures/Producing Culture*. Cambridge and London: Harvard University Press.

No Proscenium. https://noproscenium.com/about.

Norman, Don. 2013. *The Design of Everyday Things*. Rev. and exp. ed. New York: Basic Books.

Novack, Cynthia Jean. 1990. *Sharing the Dance: Contact Improvisation and American Culture*. Madison: University of Wisconsin Press.

O'Connell, Stephen. 2014. Interview with Julia M. Ritter, July 31. Transcript.

Pavlik, Carolyn. 2009. "An Interview with Heidi Druckler." In *Site Dance: Choreographers and Lure of Alternative Spaces*, edited by Melanie Kloetzel and Carolyn Pavlik, 84–93. Gainesville: University Florida Press.

Pearson, Tom. 2014. Interview with Julia M. Ritter, May 12. Transcript.

Pettrow, Daniel. 2014. Interview with Julia M. Ritter, July 27. Transcript.

Piepenberg, Eric. 2011. "Punchdrunk Transforms Chelsea Warehouses for *Sleep No More*." *The New York Times*, March 16. Accessed January 29, 2012.

Pine, B. Joseph, and James H. Gilmore. 1999. *The Experience Economy: Work is Theater & Every Business a Stage*. Boston: Harvard Business School Press.

Profeta, Katherine. 2015. *Dramaturgy in Motion: At Work on Dance and Movement Performance*. Madison: The University of Wisconsin Press.

Reason, Matthew, and Dee Reynolds. 2010. "Kinesthesia, Empathy, and Related Pleasures: An Inquiry into Audience Experiences of Watching Dance." *Dance Research Journal* 42 (2): 49–75.

Reilly, Megan. 2014. "Learning from the Gamification of Theater." HowlRound, June 18. http://howlround.com/learning-from-the-gamification-of-theater.

Reynolds, Dee. 2012. "Kinesthetic Empathy and the Dance's Body: From Emotion to Affect." In *Kinesthetic Empathy in Creative and Cultural Practices*, edited by Dee Reynolds and Matthew Reason, 121–138. Bristol, United Kingdom: Intellect Books.

Reynolds, Dee. 2013. "Empathy, Contagion and Affect: The Role of Kinesthesia in Watching Dance." In *Touching and Being Touched: Kinesthesia and Empathy in Dance and Movement*, edited by Gabriele Brandstetter, Gerko Egert, and Sabine Zubarik, 211–231. Berlin, Germany: De Gruyter.

Ridout, Nicholas. 2009. *Theatre & Ethics*. London: Palgrave Macmillan.

Risner, Doug. 2007. "Critical Social Issues in Dance Education Research." In *International Handbook of Research in Arts Education*, edited by Liora Bresler, 965–982. Dordrecht, The Netherlands: Springer.

Ritter, Julia M. 2012. "Voice Journal: Audience Participant of *Sleep No More* in New York City." Transcript.

Ritter, Julia M. 2015. "Danse en tandem: Étude du mouvement des spectateurs et des performeurs dans *Sleep No More* de Punchdrunk." In *Engagement du spectateur et théâtre contemporain*, edited by Hervé Guay and Catherine Bouko. Special issue, *La Revue Tangence: Revue d'Études Littéraires*, no. 108 (Autumn 2015): 51–76. www.revuetangence.com.

Ritter, Julia M. 2016. "The Body of the Beholder: Insider Dynamics Transform Dance Spectatorship in *Sleep No More*." In *Reframing Immersive Theatre: The Politics and Pragmatics of Participatory Performance*, edited by James Frieze, 43–62. London: Palgrave Macmillan.

Ritter, Julia M. 2017. "Fandom and Punchdrunk's *Sleep No More*: Audience Ethnography of Immersive Dance." *TDR/The Drama Review* 61 (4): 59–77.

Sánchez-Colberg, Ana. 1996. "Altered States and Subliminal Places: Charting the Road towards a Physical Theatre." *Performance Research* 1 (2): 40–56.

Savarese, Nicola, and Richard Fowler. 2001. "1931: Antonin Artaud Sees Balinese Theatre at the Paris Colonial Exposition." *TDR/The Drama Review* 45 (3): 51–77.

Scarfo, Gunny. 2014. Interview with Julia M. Ritter, August 19. Transcript.

Schechner, Richard. 2000. *Environmental Theatre*. Montclair, NJ: Applause Theatre & Cinema Books.

Sedgman, Kirsty. 2018. "Training . . . immersion and participation: What can Audience Research Tell Us about the Immersive Theatre Experience?" *Theatre, Dance and Performance Training*, 9:2, 291–293.

Shearing, David. 2018. "Training . . . immersion and participation: On Immersion." *Theatre, Dance and Performance Training*, 9:2, 291–293.

Sheets-Johnstone, Maxine. (1966) 2015. *The Phenomenology of Dance*. Fiftieth Anniversary Edition. Reprint, Philadelphia: Temple University Press.

Sheets-Johnstone, Maxine. 1981. "Thinking in Movement." *The Journal of Aesthetics and Art Criticism* 39 (4): 399–407.

Sheets-Johnstone, Maxine. 1990. *The Roots of Thinking*. Philadelphia, PA: Temple University Press.

Sheets-Johnstone, Maxine. 1999. *The Primacy of Movement*. Amsterdam, Philadelphia: John Benjamins.

Sheets-Johnstone, Maxine. 2009. "Thinking in Movement." In *The Corporeal Turn: An Interdisciplinary Reader*, 28–63. Charlottesville, VA: Imprint Academic.

Sheets-Johnstone, Maxine. 2018. "Why Kinesthesia, Tactility and Affectivity Matter: Critical and Constructive Perspectives." *Body & Society* 24 (4): 3–31.

Siegmund, Gerald. 2005. "The Desiring Body in Dance." In *Space and Composition*, edited by Miriam Frandsen and Jesper Schou-Knudsen, 24–37. Copenhagen: NordScen and the Danish National School of Theatre, Continuing Education.

Simic, Lucy. 2014. Interview with Julia M. Ritter, June 27. Transcript.

Simic, Lucy. 2015. Facebook post, May 23. https://www.facebook.com/lucy.simic.5/posts/10155626933315578.

Spångberg, Mårten. 2012. "Choreography as Expanded Practice, Barcelona 29–31 March 2012." *Choreography as Expanded Practice* (blog), February 25. https://choreographyasexpandedpractice.wordpress.com/tag/marten-spangberg/.

Sparks, Tori. 2014. Interview with Julia M. Ritter, June 6. Transcript.

Spooner, Cara. 2009. "Participatory Performance: Looking On from Inside." *Dance Current: Canada's Dance Magazine*, June 22. http://www.thedancecurrent.com/feature/participatory-performance.

Spooner, Cara. 2014. Interview with Julia M. Ritter, August 18. Transcript.

Sullivan, Graeme. 2009. "Making Space: The Purpose and Place of Practice-led Research." In *Practice-led Research, Research-led Practice in the Creative Arts*, edited by Hazel Smith and Roger T. Dean, 41–65. Edinburgh: Edinburgh University Press.

Symonds, Alexandria. 2011. "Art Not without Ambition: Sleep No More's Maxine Doyle." *Interview Magazine*, May 25, 2011. http://www.interviewmagazine.com/culture/sleep-no-more-maxine-doyle#page2.

Taussig, Michael. 1992. *Mimesis & Alterity: A Particular History of the Senses*. London: Routledge.

Tecklenburg, Nina, and Benjamin Carter. 2012. "Reality Enchanted, Contact Mediated: A Story of Gob Squad." *TDR/The Drama Review* 56 (2): 8–33.

Templeton, Fiona. 1990. *YOU-The City*. New York: Roof Books.

Theatre Bristol. 2015. Home page. *Writing in Residence* (blog). Accessed May 30. http://www.theatrebristolwriters.net/THEATRE-BRISTOL.

"*Then She Fell*." 2013. "The Theatre: Now Playing." *The New Yorker*, April 1. http://www.newyorker.com/goings-on-about-town/theatre/then-she-fell-3.

Thiel, Sara. 2017. "Game/Play: The Five Conceptual Planes of Punchdrunk's Sleep No More." In *Immersive Theatre: Engaging the Audience*, edited by Josh Machamer, 55–64. Champaign: University of Illinois.

Third Rail Projects. 2012. "*Then She Fell*: About." Accessed October 31. http://www.thenshefell.com/about/.

Third Rail Projects. 2015a. "*Looking Glass*: Project Description." Accessed August 4. www.thirdrailprojects.com/lookingglass.

Third Rail Projects. 2015b. "One New York Plaza—Third Rail Projects Creative Residency (2011–2012)." Accessed August 4. http://thirdrailprojects.com/one-new-york-plaza/.

Third Rail Projects. 2015c. "*Vanishing Point*: Project Description." Accessed July 28. http://thirdrailprojects.com/vanishingpoint.

Third Rail Projects. 2016. Facebook page, April 2. https://www.facebook.com/ThirdRailProjects/?fref=nf.

Underiner, Tamara. 2016. "Theatre in Networked Culture, 1990 to the Present." In *Theatre Histories: An Introduction*, 3rd ed., edited by Tobin Nellhaus, 549–582. New York: Routledge.

Van Kerkhoven, Marianne. 1994a. "On Dramaturgy: Introduction." In *Theaterscrift (On Dramaturgy)* no. 5–6, 8–32.

Van Kerkhoven, Marianne. 1994b. "Looking without Pencil in the Hand." In *Theaterscrift*, no. 5–6, 140–149.

Watching Dance: Kinesthetic Empathy. 2014. "About Us." Accessed July 14. http://www.watchingdance.org/about_us/contact/index.php.

Weisner, Mark. 1991. "The Computer for the 21st Century." *Scientific American* 265 (3): 94–105.

White, Gareth. 2009. "Odd Anonymized Needs: Punchdrunk's Masked Spectator." In *Modes of Spectating*, 219–230. Bristol and Chicago: Intellect Books.

White, Gareth. 2012. "On Immersive Theatre." *Theatre Research International* 37 (3): 221–235.

White, Gareth. 2013. *Audience Participation in Theatre: Aesthetics of the Invitation*. London: Palgrave Macmillan.

Willett, Jennine. 2014. Interview with Julia M. Ritter, May 9. Transcript.

Windeyer, Richard. 2014. Interview with Julia M. Ritter, July 29. Transcript.

Windmill Factory. 2017. "Right Passage." WindmillFactory.com. Accessed October 25. http://thewindmillfactory.com/?portfolio=right-passage.

Worthen, William B. 2012. "The Written Troubles of the Brain: *Sleep No More* and the Space of Character." *Theatre Journal* 64 (1): 79–97.

Young, Alan. 1981. *Dada and After: Extremist Modernism and English Literature*. Manchester: Manchester University Press.

Zaiontz, Keren. 2014. "Narcissistic Spectatorship in Immersive and One-on-One Performance." *Theatre Journal* 66 (3): 405–425.

Zivkovich, Paul. 2014. Interview with Julia M. Ritter, August 18. Transcript.

Index